# mini atlas

Bartholomew

Edinburgh

Printed and Published in Great Britain by
John Bartholomew & Son Ltd. MCMLXXXI

Reprinted MCMLXXXII

ISBN 0 7028 0456 8
9335X

## Contents

**Contents**

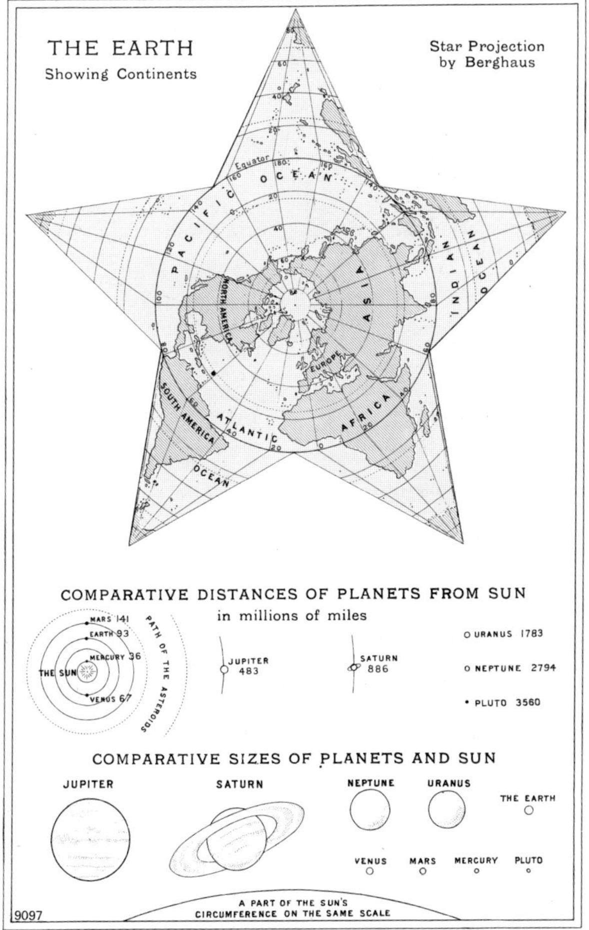
THE EARTH
Showing Continents
Star Projection
by Berghaus
PACIFIC OCEAN
INDIAN OCEAN
ATLANTIC OCEAN
NORTH AMERICA
SOUTH AMERICA
EUROPE
ASIA
AFRICA
Equator
COMPARATIVE DISTANCES OF PLANETS FROM SUN
in millions of miles
MARS 141
EARTH 93
MERCURY 36
THE SUN
VENUS 67
PATH OF THE ASTEROIDS
JUPITER 483
SATURN 886
URANUS 1783
NEPTUNE 2794
PLUTO 3560
COMPARATIVE SIZES OF PLANETS AND SUN
JUPITER
SATURN
NEPTUNE
URANUS
THE EARTH
VENUS
MARS
MERCURY
PLUTO
A PART OF THE SUN'S
CIRCUMFERENCE ON THE SAME SCALE
9097

WESTERN HEMISPHERE
North Pole
Arctic Ocean
Greenland
Iceland
Baffin B.
Davis Str.
C. Farewell
Bering Str.
Bering Sea
Aleutian Is
Alaska
Arctic Circle
Hudson Bay
Labrador
Newfoundland
Canada
Vancouver I.
L. Superior
Ottawa
Halifax
New York
Washington
C. Mendocino
San Francisco
California
NORTH AMERICA
United States
NORTH ATLANTIC OCEAN
Azores
Bermuda
Los Angeles
New Orleans
Florida
The Bahamas
Tropic of Cancer
NORTH PACIFIC OCEAN
Hawaii
Gulf of Mexico
Mexico
West Indies
C. Verde Is
Marshall Is
Caribbean Sea
Central America
Venezuela
Orinoco R.
Georgetown
Gilbert Is
Colombia
Guiana
Cayenne
Panama
Quito
Equator
Kiribati
Galapagos Is
Ecuador
R. Amazon
Marquesas Is
Tuvalu
Solomon Is
SOUTH AMERICA
Lima
Peru
Brazil
Vanuatu
Society Is
Tahiti
Tuamotu Arch.
Fiji Is
Bolivia
Brasilia
Tonga Is
Tropic of Capricorn
New Caledonia
OCEANIA
Juan Fernandez
Rio de Janeiro
Chile
Argentina
Uruguay
Montevideo
R. La Plata
Buenos Aires
SOUTH PACIFIC OCEAN
Valparaiso
New Zealand
Wellington
Chatham I.
Dunedin
Cape Horn
Falkland Is
Antarctic Circle
South Shetlands
Sth Georgia
South Victoria Land
Palmer Ld
ANTARCTICA
South Pole
Equatorial Sc

EASTERN HEMISPHERE
North Pole
Arctic Ocean
Spitsbergen
Iceland
Norway
Sweden
British Is.
Leningrad
Moscow
Berlin
Paris
France
EUROPE
Vienna
Spain
Portugal
Union of Soviet Soc. Rep.
Siberia
L. Baikal
R. Amur
Sea of Okhotsk
Sakhalin
Japan
Sea of Japan
Tokyo
Peking
ASIA
Aral Sea
Caspian Sea
Black S.
Turkey
Mediterranean Sea
Algiers
Algeria
Morocco
Canary Is.
Tripoli
Cairo
Syria
Iran
Kabul
Tehran
Pakistan
Himalaya Mts
Lahore
Delhi
Lucknow
Karachi
Ganges
Calcutta
India
Bombay
Bay of Bengal
Madras
Sri Lanka
Burma
Chungking
Nanking
China
Canton
Yellow Sea
Tropic of Cancer
NORTH PACIFIC OCEAN
Philippines
Indo China
Thailand
China Sea
Mindanao
Halmahera
Borneo
Sulawesi
Indonesia
Java
Sumatera
New Guinea
Sahara
Egypt
Saudi Arabia
Red Sea
Aden
Arabian Sea
Socotra
C. Guardafui
Timbuktu
Dakar
R. Niger
Nigeria
Lagos
G. of Guinea
Sudan
L. Chad
R. Nile
Ethiopia
AFRICA
Mogadiscio
L. Albert
L. Victoria
Zaire
R. Congo
L. Tanganyika
Zanzibar
Seychelles
Chagos Is.
INDIAN OCEAN
Ascension
Loanda
Angola
Lobito
St. Helena
C. Frio
R. Zambezi
Mozambique Chan.
Madagascar
Mauritius
Réunion I.
C. S. Marie
Tropic of Capricorn
SOUTH ATLANTIC OCEAN
South Africa
Natal
Port Elizabeth
Cape Town
Cape of Good Hope
Amsterdam
St. Paul
Kerguelen I.
AUSTRALIA
Northern Territory
Western Australia
South Australia
Queensland
New S. Wales
Victoria
Perth
Adelaide
Brisbane
Sydney
Canberra
Melbourne
Tasmania
Antarctic Circle
Wilkes Ld.
ANTARCTICA
South Pole
Arctic Circle
New Siberian Is.
Novaya Zemlya
Kara Sea
NORTH ATLANTIC OCEAN
0
20
40
60
80
100
120
140
30000000

# RELIEF

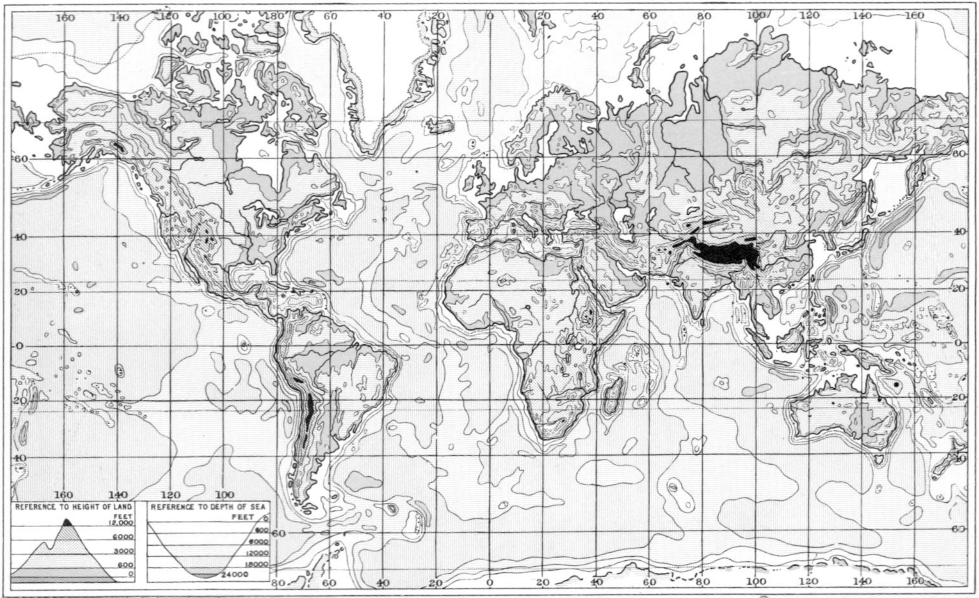

REFERENCE TO HEIGHT OF LAND
FEET
12,000
6000
3000
600
0
REFERENCE TO DEPTH OF SEA
FEET
0
600
6000
12000
18000
24000

ARCTIC OCEAN

New Siberian Is

Tundras

Spitsbergen

Greenland

Baffin Bay

Hudson Bay

Alaska

NORTH AMERICA

Vancouver I.

Newfoundland

Arctic Circle

Iceland

British Isles

Scandinavia

EUROPE

ASIA

Caspian Sea

Mediterranean Sea

Gobi

China

Sea of Okhotsk

Bering Sea

Sahara

Arabia

India

AFRICA

Philippine Is

Caroline Is

Borneo

New Guinea

Sumatra

Madagascar

OCEANIA

AUSTRALIA

New Zealand

West Wind Drift

California Current

North Equatorial Current

Gulf Stream

Gulf Stream Drift

Labrador Current

E. Greenland Current

Limit of Floating Ice

ATLANTIC OCEAN

West Indies

PACIFIC OCEAN

Galapagos Is

South Equatorial Current

Peru Current

Tropic of Capricorn

SOUTH AMERICA

Humboldt Current

Cape Horn Current

Brazil Current

Guinea Current

Ascension

St Helena

Tristan da Cunha

Benguela Current

Mozambique Current

S.W. & N.E. Monsoon Drift

Equator

INDIAN OCEAN

South Equatorial Current

W. Australian Current

E. Australian Current

Kerguelen

Kuro Siwo

Tropic of Cancer

| | |
|---|---|
| Tundra and Alpine | Tropical Forest |
| Coniferous Forest | Semi-Arid Cultivation |
| Mixed Cultivation and Forest | Desert |

Cold Currents

Warm Currents

Limit of Floating Ice

# TEMPERATURE—JANUARY

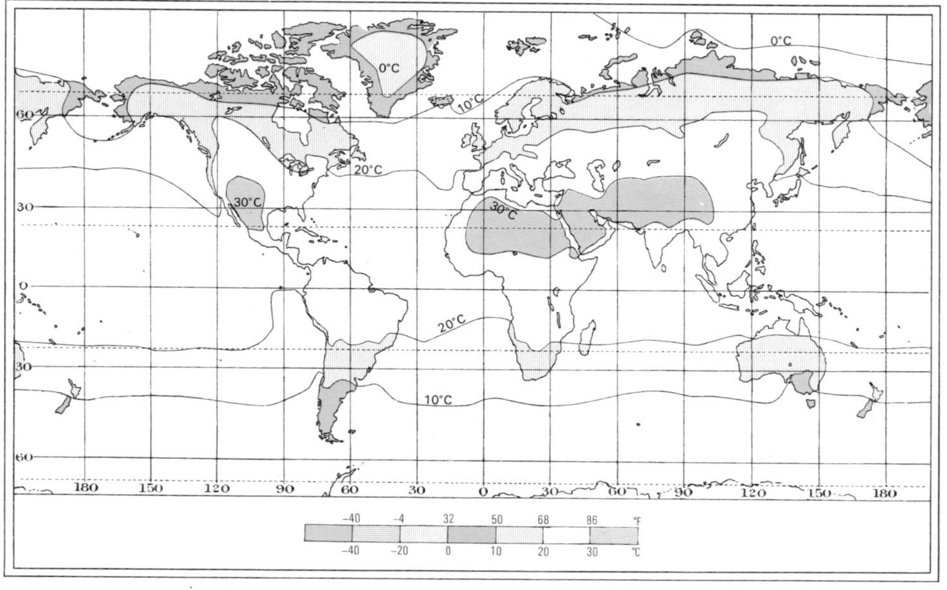
0°C
0°C
10°C
20°C
30°C
30°C
20°C
10°C
60
30
0
30
60
180
150
120
90
60
30
0
30
60
90
120
150
180
-40
-4
32
50
68
86
°F
-40
-20
0
10
20
30
°C

# COMMUNICATIONS

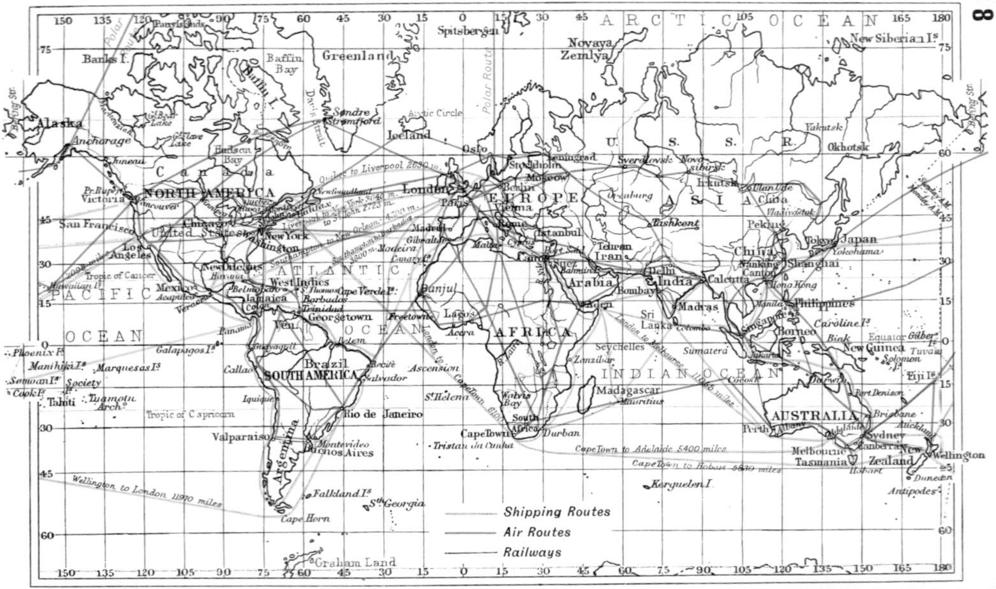

ARCTIC OCEAN
Spitsbergen
Novaya Zemlya
New Siberian Is
Banks I.
Baffin Bay
Baffin I.
Greenland
Davis Strait
Sondre Stromfjord
Arctic Circle
Iceland
Polar Route
Alaska
Anchorage
Juneau
Hudson Bay
Canada
NORTH AMERICA
Pr. Rupert
Victoria
Vancouver
San Francisco
Los Angeles
United States
Chicago
New York
Washington
New Orleans
Havana
Mexico
Acapulco
Veracruz
Tropic of Cancer
Hawaiian Is
PACIFIC OCEAN
Oslo
London
Paris
Leningrad
Stockholm
Moscow
Berlin
EUROPE
Vienna
Rome
Madrid
Gibraltar
Malta
Cyprus
Istanbul
Cairo
Tehran
Iran
Arabia
Bahrain
Aden
U. S. S. R.
Sverdlovsk
Novosibirsk
Irkutsk
Orenburg
Tashkent
ASIA
Ulan Ude
China
Vladivostok
Peking
Yakutsk
Okhotsk
Tokyo
Japan
Yokohama
Shanghai
Nanking
Canton
Hong Kong
Manila
Philippines
Delhi
India
Calcutta
Bombay
Madras
Sri Lanka
Colombo
Quebec to Liverpool 2630 m.
Newfoundland
Liverpool to New York 3040 m.
to St John 2723 m.
Southampton to New Orleans 4700 m.
Southampton to Barbados 3600 m.
Madeira
Canary Is
ATLANTIC OCEAN
West Indies
St Thomas
Cape Verde Is
Jamaica
Barbados
Trinidad
Colon
Panama
Georgetown
Ven.
Belem
Banjul
Freetown
Lagos
Accra
AFRICA
Galapagos Is
Phoenix Is
Manihiki Is
Marquesas Is
Samoan Is
Society Is
Cook Is
Tahiti
Tuamotu Arch.
Tropic of Capricorn
Callao
Brazil
SOUTH AMERICA
Recife
Salvador
Iquique
Rio de Janeiro
Valparaiso
Montevideo
Buenos Aires
Argentina
Falkland Is
St Georgia
Cape Horn
Graham Land
Wellington to London 11970 miles
Ascension
St Helena
London to Cape Town 6100
Walvis Bay
South Africa
Cape Town
Durban
Tristan da Cunha
Zanzibar
Seychelles
Madagascar
Mauritius
INDIAN OCEAN
London to Melbourne 11065 miles
Sumatera
Cocos
Cape Town to Adelaide 5400 miles
Kerguelen I.
Singapore
Borneo
Jakarta
Caroline Is
Biak
Equator
New Guinea
Solomon Is
Fiji Is
Darwin
Port Denison
AUSTRALIA
Perth
Albany
Adelaide
Brisbane
Sydney
Canberra
Melbourne
Tasmania
Hobart
Auckland
New Zealand
Wellington
Dunedin
Antipodes

Shipping Routes
Air Routes
Railways

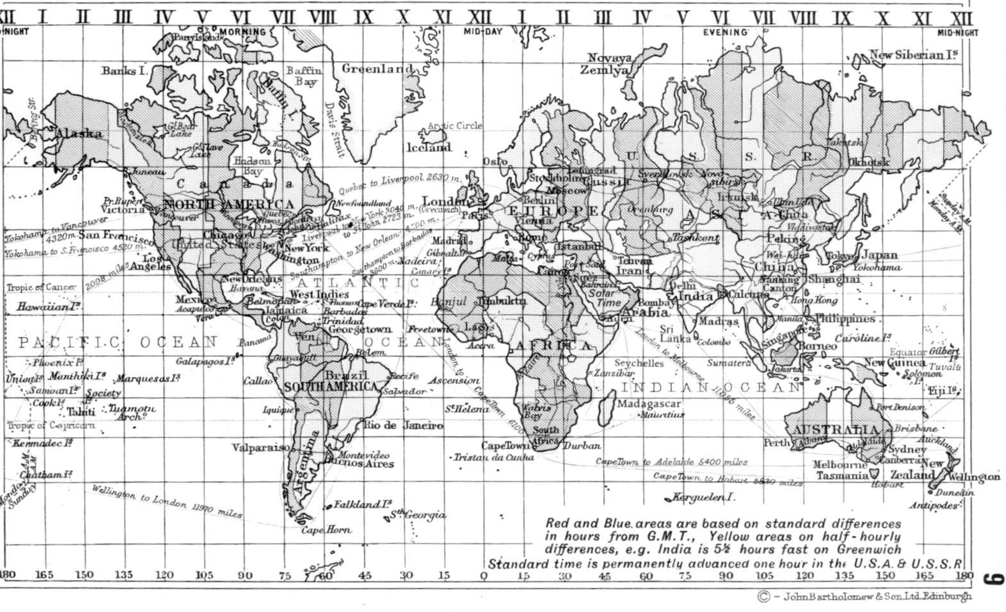
XII I II III IV V VI VII VIII IX X XI XII I II III IV V VI VII VIII IX X XI XII
MID-NIGHT
MORNING
MID-DAY
EVENING
MID-NIGHT
Banks I.
Baffin Bay
Baffin I.
Greenland
Davis Strait
Arctic Circle
Iceland
Alaska
Hudson Bay
Canada
NORTH AMERICA
Pr. Rupert
Victoria
Vancouver
Juneau
San Francisco
Los Angeles
Chicago
United States
New York
Washington
New Orleans
Mexico
Acapulco
Havana
West Indies
Jamaica
Colon
Panama
Trinidad
Barbados
Georgetown
Belem
Recife
Salvador
Brazil
SOUTH AMERICA
Callao
Iquique
Valparaiso
Argentina
Montevideo
Buenos Aires
Rio de Janeiro
Falkland Is
Cape Horn
Sth Georgia
Galapagos Is
Quebec to Liverpool 2630 m.
Newfoundland
Halifax
Liverpool to New York 3040 m.
to St John 2723 m.
to New Orleans 4500 m.
Southampton
Southampton to Barbados 3600 m.
Yokohama to Vancouver 4320 m.
Yokohama to S. Francisco 4520 m.
2098 miles
Wellington to London 11970 miles
London to Cape Town 6100
London to Melbourne 11056 miles
CapeTown to Adelaide 5400 miles
CapeTown to Hobart 5830 miles
London
(Greenwich)
Paris
Oslo
Stockholm
Leningrad
Moscow
Russia
Berlin
EUROPE
Vienna
Rome
Madrid
Gibraltar
Madeira
Canary Is
Malta
Cyprus
Istanbul
Port Said
Cairo
Suez
Bahrain
Solar Time
Aden
Arabia
Tehran
Iran
AFRICA
Timbuktu
Banjul
Freetown
Lagos
Accra
Cape Verde Is
Ascension
St Helena
Walvis Bay
South Africa
Cape Town
Durban
Tristan da Cunha
Zanzibar
Seychelles
Madagascar
Mauritius
U. S. S. R.
Sverdlovsk
Novosibirsk
Irkutsk
Orenburg
Tashkent
ASIA
Chita
Vladivostok
Peking
China
Nanking
Canton
Shanghai
Hong Kong
Tokyo
Japan
Yokohama
Delhi
India
Calcutta
Bombay
Madras
Sri Lanka
Colombo
Yakutsk
Okhotsk
Novaya Zemlya
New Siberian Is
Philippines
Manila
Caroline Is
Borneo
Singapore
Sumatera
Jakarta
New Guinea
Solomon Is
Equator
Gilbert Is
Tuvalu
Fiji Is
INDIAN OCEAN
ATLANTIC OCEAN
PACIFIC OCEAN
Tropic of Cancer
Tropic of Capricorn
Hawaiian Is
Phoenix Is
Union Is
Manihiki Is
Marquesas Is
Samoan Is
Society Is
Cook Is
Tahiti
Tuamotu Arch.
Kermadec Is
Chatham Is
Bering Str.
Sunday A.M.
Monday A.M.
AUSTRALIA
Perth
Port Denison
Brisbane
Sydney
Canberra
Melbourne
Tasmania
Hobart
New Zealand
Auckland
Wellington
Dunedin
Antipodes
Kerguelen I.
Red and Blue areas are based on standard differences in hours from G.M.T., Yellow areas on half-hourly differences, e.g. India is 5½ hours fast on Greenwich
Standard time is permanently advanced one hour in the U.S.A. & U.S.S.R.
180 165 150 135 120 105 90 75 60 45 30 15 0 15 30 45 60 75 90 105 120 135 150 165 180

# NORTH AMERICA

ARCTIC OCEAN
BEAUFORT SEA
GREENLAND
Baffin Bay
Davis Strait
Hudson Strait
HUDSON BAY
Labrador Peninsula
NEWFOUNDLAND
CANADA
NORTHWEST TERRITORIES
MANITOBA
SASKATCHEWAN
ALBERTA
BRITISH COLUMBIA
YUKON TERRY.
ALASKA
UNITED STATES
ASIA
BERING SEA
Gulf of Alaska
PACIFIC
Iceland
Spitsbergen
Queen Elizabeth Is.
Banks I.
Victoria I.
Baffin Island
Vancouver I.
Queen Charlotte Is.
Mackenzie River
Great Slave Lake
Gt. Bear Lake
Lake Winnipeg
Quebec
Montreal
Halifax
Regina
Winnipeg
Anchorage
Fairbanks
Juneau

UNITED STATES
MEXICO
CENTRAL AMERICA
SOUTH AMERICA
WEST INDIES
GULF OF MEXICO
CARIBBEAN SEA
OCEAN
The Bahamas
Bermuda
CUBA
JAMAICA
HAITI
DOMINICAN REP.
Puerto Rico
Florida
Tropic of Cancer
Lower California
Gulf of California
Sierra Madre
Sierra Nevada
Rio Grande
Panama Canal
San Francisco
Los Angeles
San Diego
Carson City
Salt Lake City
Great Salt Lake
Denver
Santa Fe
Albuquerque
Phoenix
El Paso
Chihuahua
Monterrey
Zacatecas
Guadalajara
Leon
Guanajuato
MEXICO
Popocatepetl
Orizaba
Veracruz
Acapulco
Mazatlan
C. S. Lucas
C. Corrientes
Socorro I.
Guadalupe
Pierre
Omaha
Kansas C.
St. Louis
Chicago
Milwaukee
Detroit
Indianapolis
Cincinnati
Louisville
Pittsburgh
WASHINGTON
New York
Philadelphia
New Haven
Providence
Richmond
Raleigh
Wilmington
C. Hatteras
Charleston
Savannah
Jacksonville
Atlanta
Memphis
Little Rock
Dallas
Austin
San Antonio
Galveston
New Orleans
Mobile
Vicksburg
Brownsville
Tampico
Gulf of Campeche
C. Catoche
Yucatan
Havana
C. Sable
Florida Strait
San Salvador (Watling I.)
Kingston
Port au Prince
St. Domingo
Belmopan
BELIZE
GUATEMALA
Guatemala
SALVADOR
S. Salvador
HONDURAS
Tegucigalpa
NICARAGUA
Managua
Nicaragua L.
COSTA RICA
PANAMA
Panama
Colon
Trujillo
C. Gracias a Dios
G. of Tehuantepec
Statute Miles
0 100 200 300 400 500 1000
10
20
30
70
80
90
100
110
120

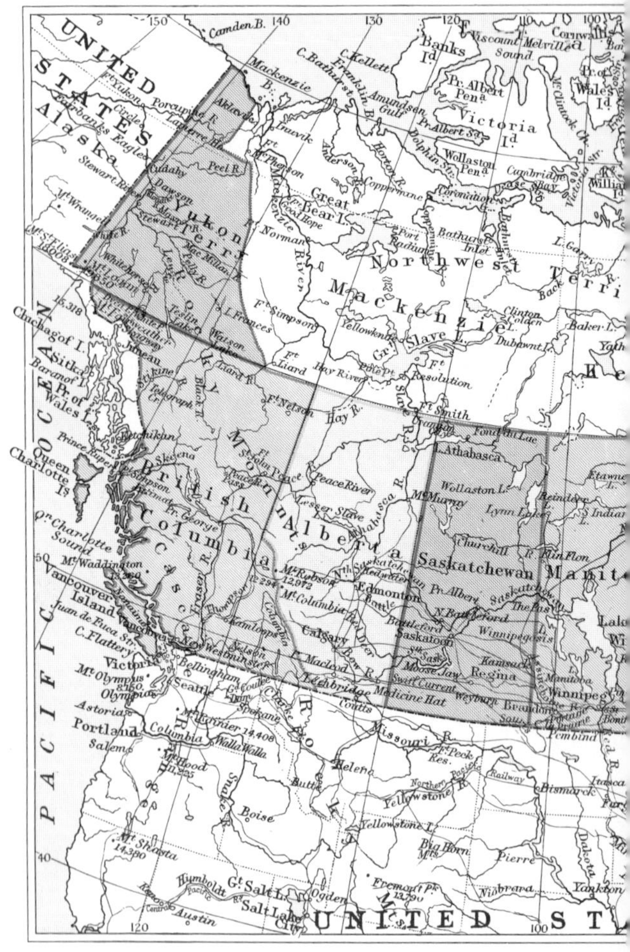

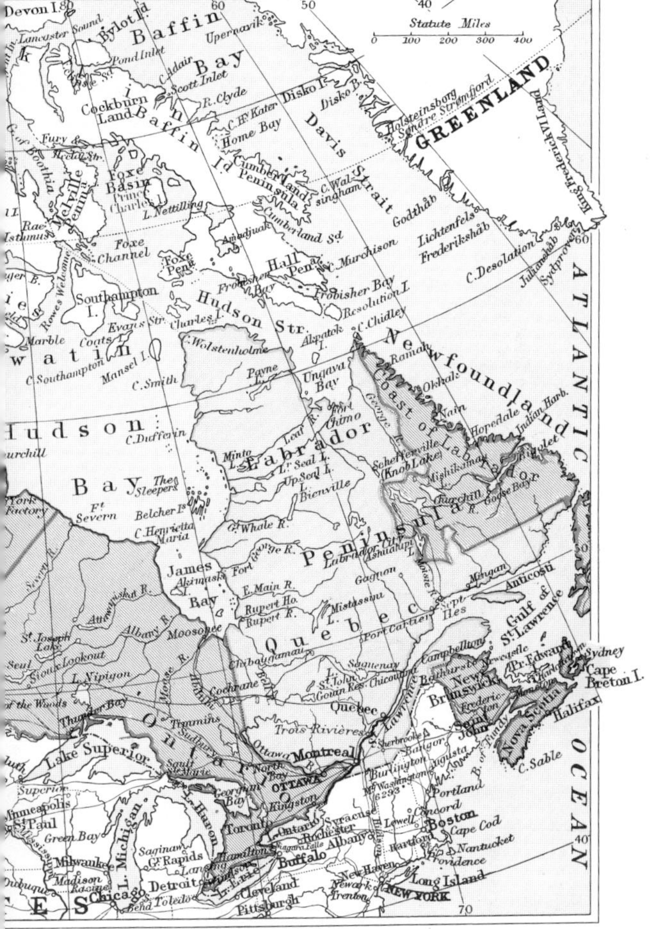

# WESTERN PROVINCES

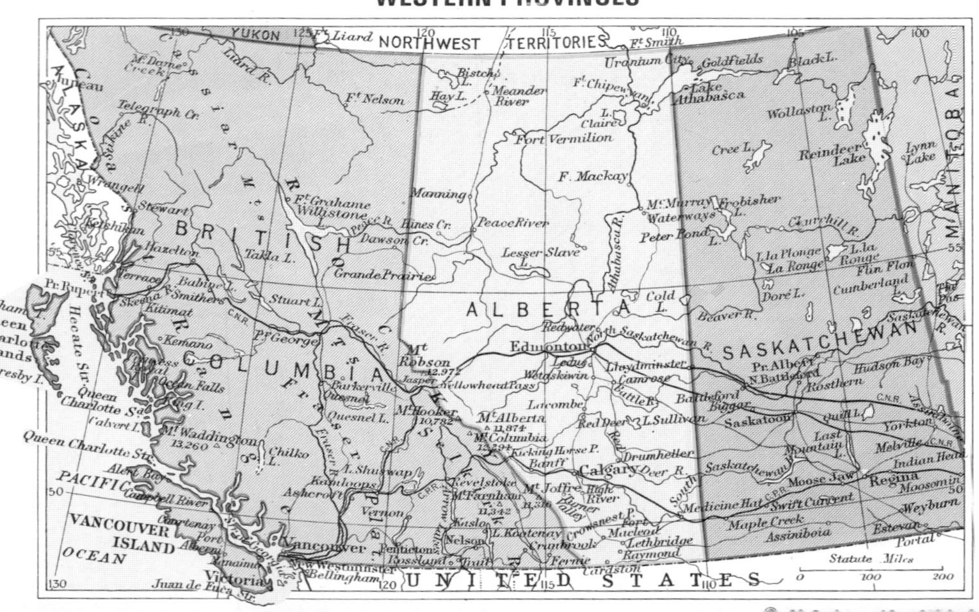

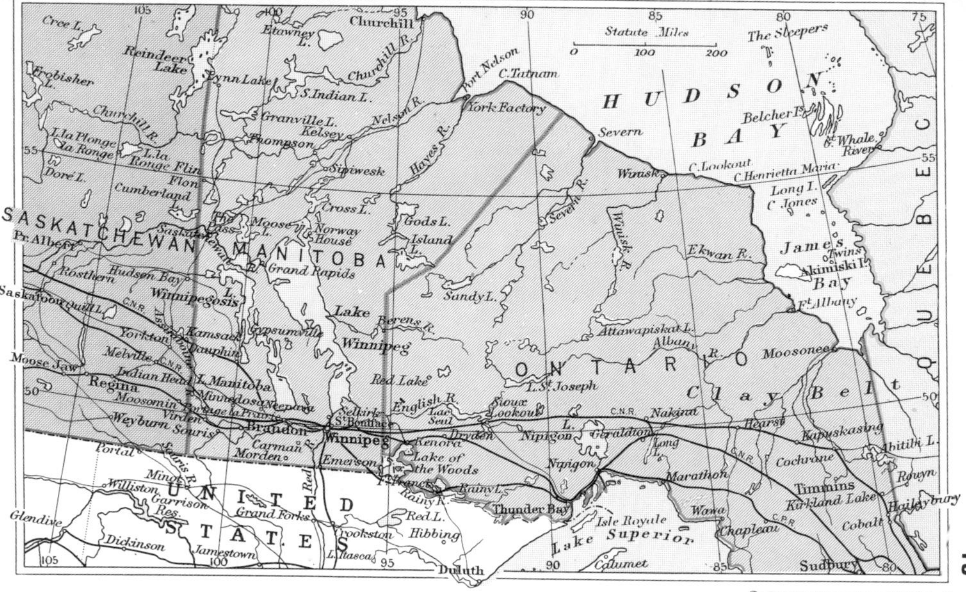
Statute Miles
0 100 200
H U D S O N
B A Y
James Bay
Q U E B E C
S A S K A T C H E W A N
M A N I T O B A
O N T A R I O
Clay Belt
U N I T E D
S T A T E S
Lake Superior
The Sleepers
Belcher Is.
Gt. Whale River
C. Lookout
C. Henrietta Maria
Long I.
C. Jones
Twins
Akimiski I.
Ft. Albany
Moosonee
Ekwan R.
Albany R.
Attawapiskat L.
Winisk R.
Winisk
Severn
Severn R.
C. Tatnam
Port Nelson
York Factory
Churchill
Churchill R.
Etawney L.
Cree L.
Reindeer Lake
Frobisher L.
Lynn Lake
S. Indian L.
Granville L.
Kelsey
Thompson
Nelson R.
Hayes R.
Sipiwesk
Churchill R.
L. la Plonge
La Ronge
L. la Ronge
Flin Flon
Doré L.
Cumberland L.
Cross L.
Gods L.
Island L.
Sandy L.
The Pas
Moose L.
Norway House
Grand Rapids
Pr. Albert
Rosthern
Hudson Bay
Saskatoon
Quill L.
L. Winnipegosis
Lake Winnipeg
Berens R.
Gypsumville
Kamsack
Yorkton
Dauphin
Melville
Moose Jaw
Indian Head
Regina
L. Manitoba
Minnedosa
Neepawa
Moosomin
Portage la Prairie
Virden
Weyburn
Souris
Brandon
Selkirk
St. Boniface
Winnipeg
Carman
Morden
Emerson
Portal
Souris R.
Red L. 
Red Lake
English R.
Lac Seul
Sioux Lookout
L. St. Joseph
Kenora
Dryden
Lake of the Woods
Rainy L.
Rainy R.
Nipigon
L. Nipigon
Geraldton
Long L.
Nakina
Hearst
Kapuskasing
Abitibi L.
Cochrane
Rouyn
Timmins
Kirkland Lake
Haileybury
Cobalt
Sudbury
Chapleau
Wawa
Marathon
Thunder Bay
Isle Royale
Calumet
Duluth
Hibbing
Red L.
Crookston
L. Itasca
Grand Forks
Red R.
Minot
Williston
Garrison Res.
Glendive
Dickinson
Jamestown
C.N.R.
C.P.R.
50
55
75
80
85
90
95
100
105

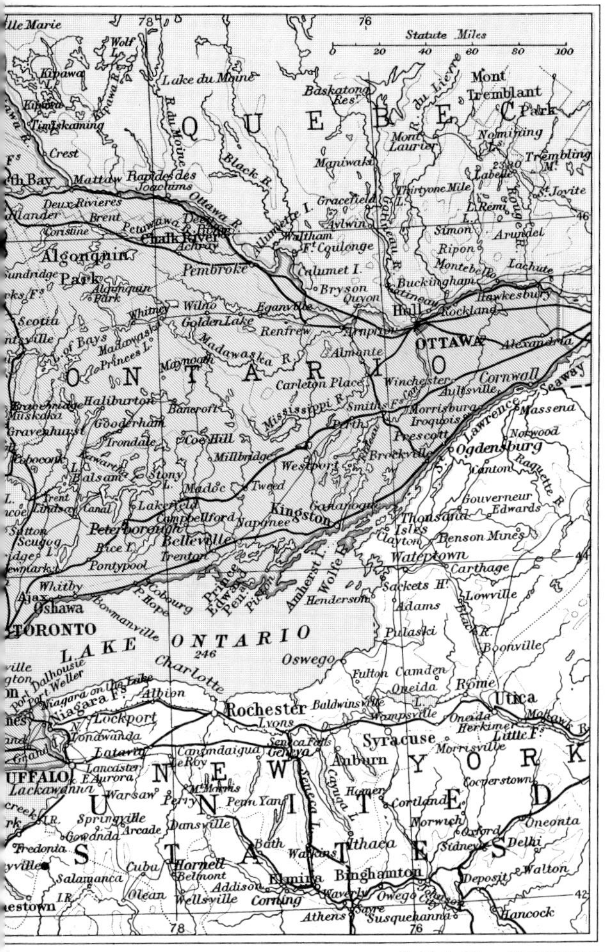
Statute Miles
0 20 40 60 80 100
78
76
Q U E B E C
O N T A R I O
LAKE ONTARIO
246
N E W Y O R K
U N I T E D S T A T E S
Lake du Moine
R. du Moine
Baskatong Res.
R. du Lievre
Mont Tremblant Park
Nominingue
Mont Laurier
Maniwaki
Trembling Mt.
Labelle
St. Jovite
Rouge R.
Black R.
Mattawa
Rapides des Joachims
Ottawa R.
Deux Rivieres
Brent
Petawawa
Deep River
Chalk River
Achray
Allumette I.
Gracefield
Gatineau R.
Thirtyone Mile L.
L. Remi
Waltham
Ft. Coulonge
Aylwin
Simon L.
Arundel
Ripon
Montebello
Lachute
Algonquin Park
Pembroke
Calumet I.
Bryson
Quyon
Buckingham
Gatineau
Hawkesbury
Hull
Rockland
OTTAWA
Alexandria
Whitney
Wilno
Golden Lake
Eganville
Renfrew
Arnprior
Almonte
Madawaska
Madawaska R.
L. of Bays
Princes L.
Maynooth
Carleton Place
Winchester
Cornwall
Aultsville
Seaway
Mississippi R.
Smiths Fs.
Morrisburg
Iroquois
Massena
Haliburton
Bancroft
Perth
Prescott
Norwood
Bracebridge
Muskoka
Gravenhurst
Gooderham
Irondale
Coe Hill
Millbridge
Westport
Brockville
Ogdensburg
St. Lawrence
Canton
Raquette R.
Kawartha
Balsam L.
Stony L.
Madoc
Tweed
Gouverneur
Edwards
Trent Canal
Lindsay
Lakefield
Campbellford
Napanee
Kingston
Gananoque
Thousand Isles
Clayton
Benson Mines
Sutton
Scugog L.
Peterborough
Belleville
Rice L.
Trenton
Pontypool
Watertown
Carthage
Whitby
Ajax
Oshawa
Cobourg
P. Hope
Bowmanville
Prince Edward Pen.
Picton
Amherst I.
Wolfe I.
Sackets H.
Henderson
Adams
Lowville
Black R.
TORONTO
Pulaski
Boonville
Oswego
Charlotte
Port Dalhousie
Port Weller
Niagara on the Lake
Niagara Fs.
Albion
Fulton
Camden
Oneida L.
Rome
Utica
Lockport
Rochester
Baldwinsville
Lyons
Wampsville
Oneida
Herkimer
Mohawk R.
Little Fs.
N. Tonawanda
Batavia
Seneca Falls
Syracuse
Morrisville
Canandaigua
Geneva
Auburn
Lancaster
E. Aurora
LeRoy
BUFFALO
Lackawanna
Warsaw
Mt. Morris
Perry
Penn Yan
Seneca L.
Cayuga L.
Homer
Cortland
Cooperstown
Springville
Arcade
Gowanda
Dansville
Norwich
Oxford
Oneonta
Fredonia
Bath
Watkins
Ithaca
Sidney
Delhi
Cuba
Hornell
Belmont
Salamanca
Addison
Elmira
Binghamton
Deposit
Walton
Olean
Wellsville
Corning
Waverly
Owego
Athens
Sayre
Susquehanna
Hancock
46
44
42

# QUEBEC



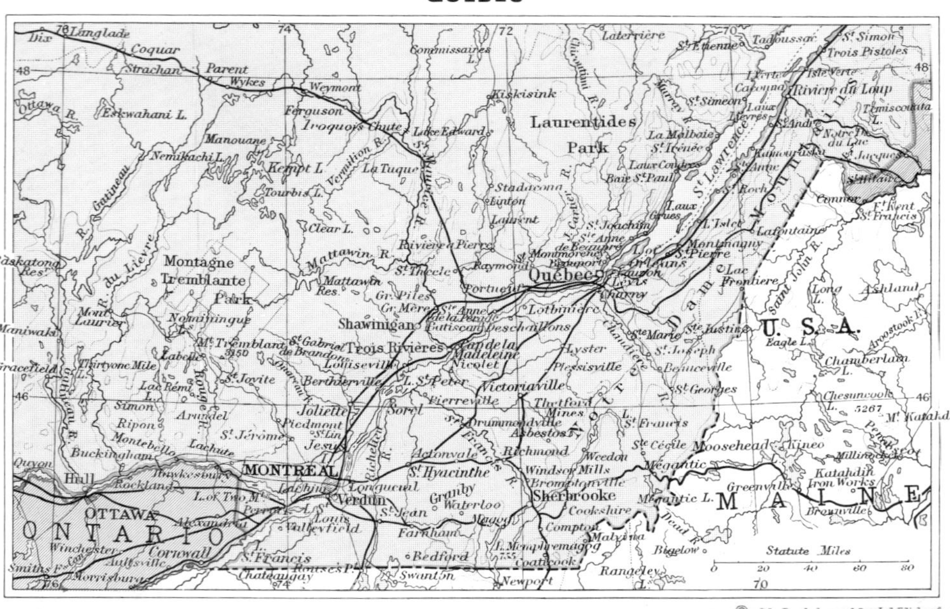

Laurentides
Park
Montagne
Tremblante
Park
Québec
MONTREAL
OTTAWA
Trois Rivières
Sherbrooke
Hull
Shawinigan
Victoriaville
Drummondville
St. Hyacinthe
Granby
Verdun
Lévis
La Tuque
Joliette
St. Jérôme
Sorel
Thetford Mines
Asbestos
Rivière du Loup
Trois Pistoles
La Malbaie
Baie St. Paul
Tadoussac
Magog
Cornwall
Kempt L.
Clear L.
Baskatong Res.
Mattawin R.
Chicoutimi R.
St. Maurice R.
Gatineau R.
Ottawa R.
Richelieu R.
Chaudière R.
Saint John R.
St. Lawrence
Notre Dame Mountains
ONTARIO
MAINE
U. S. A.
Moosehead L.
Chamberlain L.
Mt. Katahdin
Statute Miles
0 20 40 60 80

QUEBEC
NEWFOUNDLAND
Gulf of St Lawrence
ATLANTIC OCEAN
NEW BRUNSWICK
NOVA SCOTIA
Prince Edward I.
Cape Breton I.
Anticosti I.
Magdalen Is.
Cabot Str.
Northumberland Str.
Jacques Cartier Pass.
Gaspé Pen.
Long Ra.
White B.
Notre Dame Bay
Bonavista Bay
Trinity Bay
Conception Bay
Placentia Bay
St Mary's Bay
Avalon Pen.
ST. JOHN'S
Halifax
Fredericton
Moncton
Charlottetown
Sydney
Miquelon (Fr.)
St Pierre (Fr.)
U.S.A.
Quebec to Liverpool 2800m.
Halifax to St Johns 540m.
H. to Q. 737 m.
Statute Miles
0 50 100 150

Vancouver Island
Victoria
Seattle
Washington
Portland
Oregon
Idaho
Montana
Wyoming
Nevada
Utah
Colorado
California
Arizona
New Mexico
San Francisco
Sacramento
Los Angeles
San Diego
Salt Lake City
PACIFIC OCEAN
Gulf of California
Lower California
MEXICO
Statute Miles
0 100 200 300 400 500

C A N A D A
Winnipeg
Red L.
Lac Seul
St. Joseph Lake
Sioux Lookout
Attawapiskat
Albany R.
Moosonee
Moose R.
E. Main R.
Rupert Ho.
Rupert R.
Mistassini L.
L. Nipigon
L. of the Woods
Thunder Bay
Cochrane
Timmins
Sudbury
L. St. John
Gouin Res.
Chicoutimi
Saguenay
Quebec
Trois Rivières
Montreal
Ottawa R.
North Bay
OTTAWA
Gulf of St. Lawrence
Campbellton
Newcastle
Bathurst
St. Lawrence
Fredericton
St. John
B. of Fundy
Sherbrooke
Bangor
Augusta
Me.
Burlington
Mt. Washington 6293
Vt.
N.H.
Portland
Concord
Boston
Cape Cod
Lowell
Mass.
Hartford
Conn.
Nantucket
Providence & R.I.
Lake Superior
Duluth
Superior
Sault Ste. Marie
Minnesota
Minneapolis
St. Paul
Wis.
Green Bay
Mississippi
Milwaukee
Madison
Racine
Chicago
L. Michigan
Mich.
Saginaw
Gr. Rapids
Lansing
Detroit
Windsor
L. Huron
Georgian Bay
Kingston
Toronto
L. Ontario
Hamilton
Niagara Falls
Buffalo
Rochester
Syracuse
N.Y.
Albany
Hudson R.
L. Erie
Cleveland
Toledo
Sandusky
S. Bend
Gary
New Haven
Long Island
Newark
NEW YORK
Trenton
N.J.
Philadelphia
Atlantic C.
Delaware R. & Bay
Pittsburgh
Pa.
Harrisburg
Md.
Del.
Baltimore
WASHINGTON
Iowa
Dubuque
Des Moines
Davenport
Illinois
Ind.
Ohio
Columbus
Dayton
Springfield
Indianapolis
Cincinnati
Wheeling
W.Va.
Va.
Richmond
Newport News
Chesapeake Bay
Norfolk
Portsmouth
C. Hatteras
Keokuk
Missouri
St. Joseph
Kansas City
Jefferson City
Wichita
St. Louis
Cairo
Louisville
Lexington
Ky.
Cumberland
Petersburg
Winston Salem
Raleigh
N.C.
Mt. Mitchell 6710
C. Lookout
Nashville
Norris R.
Knoxville
Tenn.
Memphis
Tulsa
Muskogee
Ozark Mts.
Arkansas
Little Rock
Camden
Wilmington
C. Fear
Columbia
S.C.
Georgetown
Charleston
ATLANTIC
Tennessee
Columbus
Birmingham
Atlanta
Augusta
Ala.
Ga.
Macon
Beaufort
Savannah
Altamaha R.
Brunswick
Jacksonville
OCEAN
Dallas
Red R.
Sabine
Miss.
Vicksburg
Jackson
Tombigbee
Alabama
Montgomery
Albany
Natchitoches
Louisiana
Baton Rouge
Mobile
Tallahassee
Pensacola
New Orleans
Beaumont
Galveston
Apalachee Bay
Florida
Tampa
L. Okeechobee
Palm B.
Miami
C. Sable
Pine Is.
Key West
Florida Str.
Gr. Bahama
Lit. Bahama
Gr. Abaco
The Bahamas
New Providence
Eleuthera
Nassau
Cat I.
Watling I.
Andros Is.
Long I.
Acklins I.
Mariguana
Brownsville
Matamoras
GULF OF MEXICO
Havana
Matanzas
Bahia Honda
Pinar del Rio
C. San Antonio
Bahama Chan.
Nuevitas
CUBA
Gr. Inagua
Windward P.
C. Catoche
Yucatan Str.
Pinos I.
Trinidad
Camaguey
Manzanillo
Santiago de Cuba
Haiti
Port au Prince
Progreso
Triangulos
Valladolid
Merida
Cozumel I.
Lit. Cayman
90
80
70
50
40
30
20

# EASTERN STATES

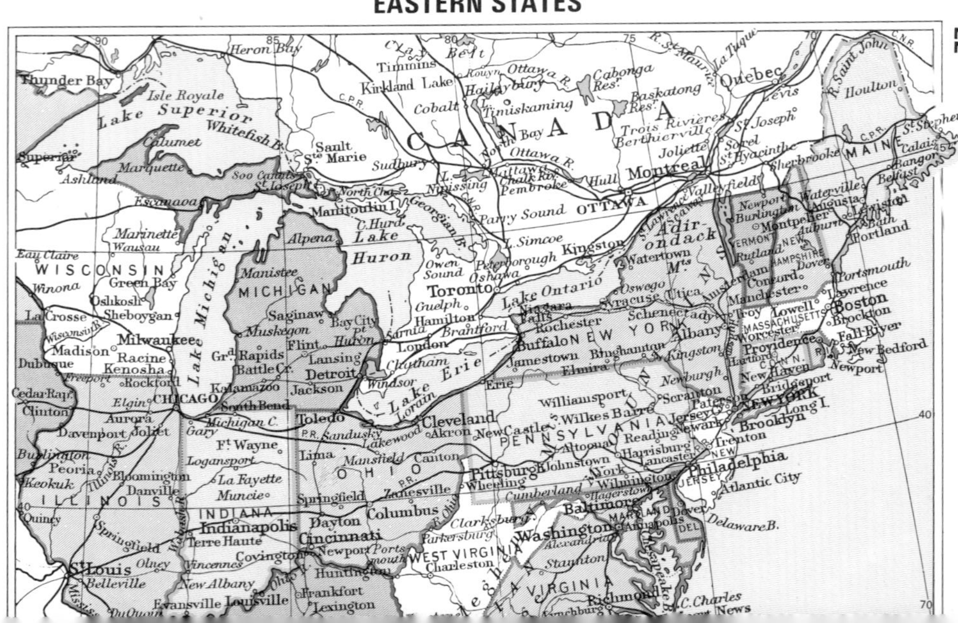

ATLANTIC
OCEAN
GULF OF MEXICO
TENNESSEE
NORTH CAROLINA
SOUTH CAROLINA
GEORGIA
ALABAMA
MISSISSIPPI
FLORIDA
APPALACHIAN
THE BAHAMAS
Paducah
Hopkinsville
Clarksville
Johnson City
Winston Salem
Greensboro
Durham
Raleigh
Pamlico Sd.
C. Hatteras
Raleigh B.
C. Lookout
Onslow B.
Long B.
Jonesboro
Paris
Milan
Newport
Jackson
Kentucky L.
Cumberland R.
Oak Ridge
Nashville
Knoxville
6710 Mt. Mitchell
Asheville
Charlotte
Columbia
Alcoa
Fayetteville
New Bern
Jacksonville
Memphis
Chattanooga
Tennessee R.
Huntsville
Pickwick L.
Holly Springs
Decatur
Dalton
Guntersville L.
Rome
Greenville
Gainesville
Florence
Wilmington
Columbia
Pontotoc
Gadsden
Athens
Clark Hill Res.
L. Marion
Greenwood
Grenada
Birmingham
Anniston
Atlanta
Madison
Augusta
Orangeburg
Greenville
Tuscaloosa
Savannah R.
Charleston
Macon
Dublin
Vicksburg
Selma
L. Martin
Columbus
Port Royal
Meridian
A.V.R.
Montgomery
Savannah
Jackson
Georgetown
St. Stephens
Monroeville
Darien
Brookhaven
Columbia
Albany
Brunswick
Natchez
Hattiesburg
Brewton
Thomasville
Waycross
Mobile
Daphne
Westville
Fernandina
Jacksonville
L. Pontchartrain
Pensacola
Tallahassee
Lake City
St. Augustine
New Orleans
Apalachicola
Apalachee B.
Gainesville
Ocala
Daytona Beach
Cedar Keys
Mississippi R.
Orlando
Titusville
C. Canaveral
Dade C.
Kissimmee
St. Petersburg
Tampa
Tampa B.
Fort Pierce
L. Okeechobee
Palm Beach
Gd. Bahama I.
Gt. Abaco
Berry Is.
Miami
Nassau
New Providence
Eleuthera
Ten Thousand Is.
C. Sable
Key Largo
Florida Bay
Key West
Florida Keys
Statute Miles
0 50 100 200 300
35
30
25
85
80
75

# MIDDLE ATLANTIC COAST

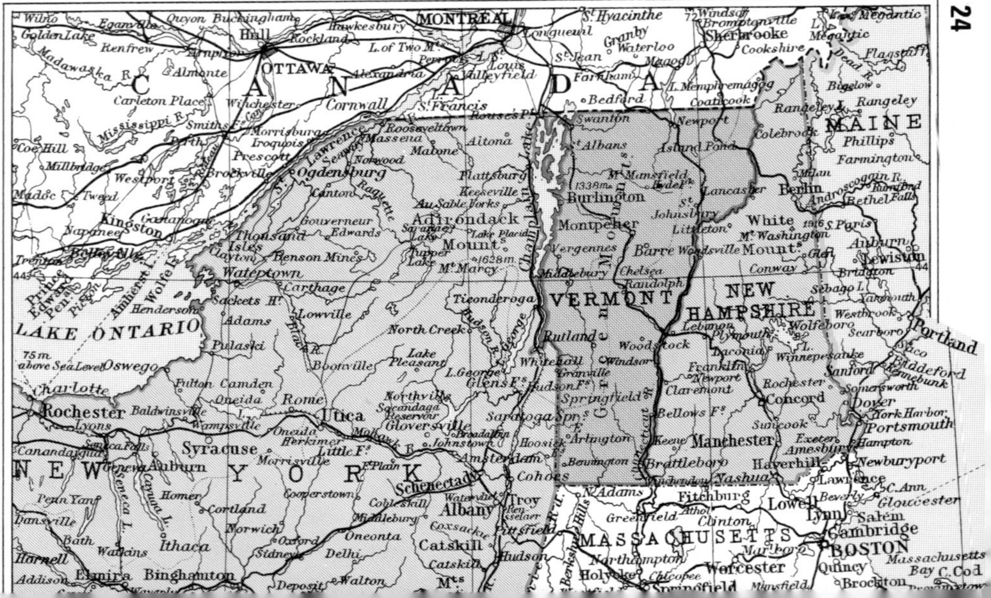

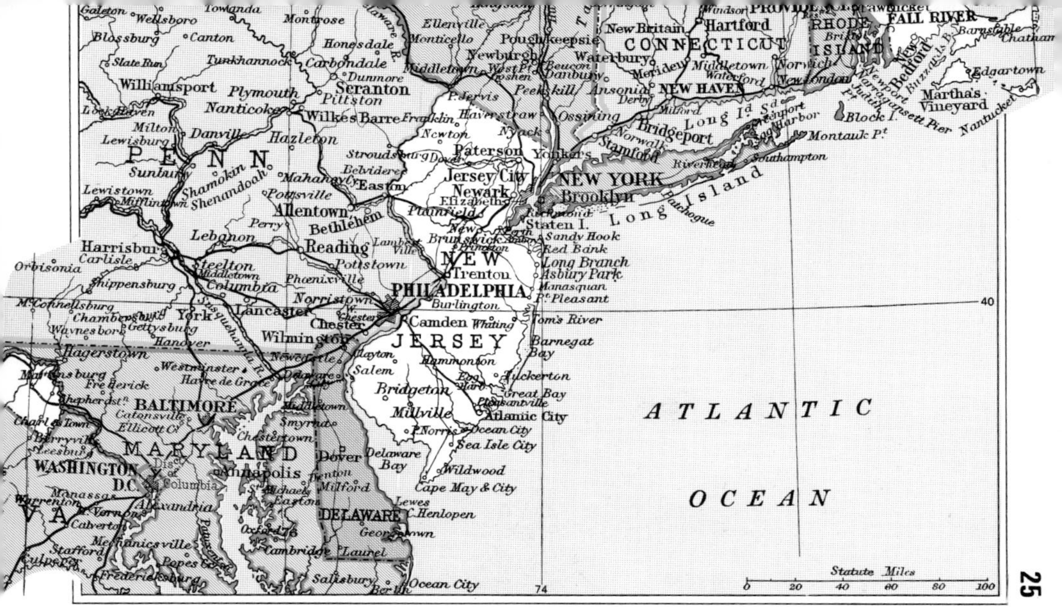
ATLANTIC
OCEAN
PENN
NEW JERSEY
MARYLAND
DELAWARE
CONNECTICUT
RHODE ISLAND
VA
NEW YORK
Brooklyn
PHILADELPHIA
BALTIMORE
WASHINGTON D.C.
Dist. of Columbia
NEW HAVEN
FALL RIVER
Hartford
New Britain
Waterbury
Meriden
Middletown
Norwich
New London
Bridgeport
Stamford
Norwalk
Ansonia
Derby
Milford
Danbury
Poughkeepsie
Newburgh
Peekskill
Ossining
Haverstraw
Nyack
Yonkers
Paterson
Jersey City
Newark
Elizabeth
Plainfield
New Brunswick
Princeton
Trenton
Camden
Burlington
Staten I.
Sandy Hook
Red Bank
Long Branch
Asbury Park
Manasquan
Pt. Pleasant
Tom's River
Barnegat Bay
Tuckerton
Great Bay
Atlantic City
Ocean City
Sea Isle City
Wildwood
Cape May & City
Millville
Bridgeton
Salem
Hammonton
Long Island
Long Id. Sd.
Patchogue
Riverhead
Southampton
Sag Harbor
Montauk Pt.
Block I.
Newport
Narragansett Pier
New Bedford
Martha's Vineyard
Edgartown
Nantucket
Barnstable
Chatham
Galeton
Wellsboro
Towanda
Montrose
Blossburg
Canton
Honesdale
Tunkhannock
Carbondale
Dunmore
Scranton
Pittston
Williamsport
Plymouth
Nanticoke
Wilkes Barre
Lock Haven
Milton
Danville
Hazleton
Lewisburg
Sunbury
Shamokin
Shenandoah
Mahanoy City
Pottsville
Stroudsburg
Belvidere
Easton
Allentown
Bethlehem
Lewistown
Mifflintown
Harrisburg
Carlisle
Lebanon
Reading
Pottstown
Phoenixville
Norristown
Steelton
Middletown
Columbia
Lancaster
York
Chester
Wilmington
Orbisonia
Shippensburg
McConnellsburg
Chambersburg
Gettysburg
Waynesboro
Hanover
Hagerstown
Westminster
Havre de Grace
Frederick
Catonsville
Ellicott City
Annapolis
Chestertown
Smyrna
Dover
Milford
Delaware Bay
Lewes
C. Henlopen
Georgetown
Easton
Oxford
Cambridge
Laurel
Salisbury
Berlin
Ocean City
Alexandria
Manassas
Warrenton
Culpeper
Stafford
Fredericksburg
Mechanicsville
Statute Miles
0
20
40
60
80
100
40
74

# ERIE AND OHIO BASINS

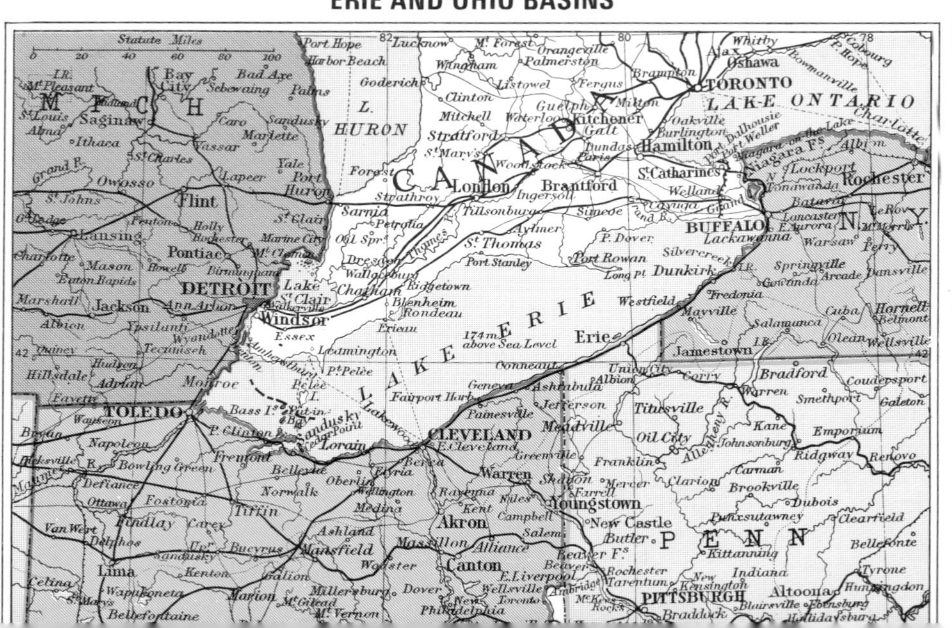

WEST VIRGINIA
V A.
K Y
COLUMBUS
CINCINNATI
Dayton
Springfield
Hamilton
Newark
Zanesville
Chillicothe
Portsmouth
Ironton
Wheeling
Parkersburg
Clarksburg
Fairmont
Charleston
Huntington
Lexington
Ashland
Roanoke
Lynchburg
Staunton
Charlottesville
Harrisonburg
Danville
Hagerstown
Cumberland
Martinsburg
Winchester
Bluefield
Princeton
Beckley
Welch
Williamson
Logan
Big Sandy R.
Kanawha R.
Greenbrier R.
Cheat R.
Ohio
Muskingum R.
Kentucky R.
Bristol
Middlesboro
Clinch Mts.
Cumberland Mts.

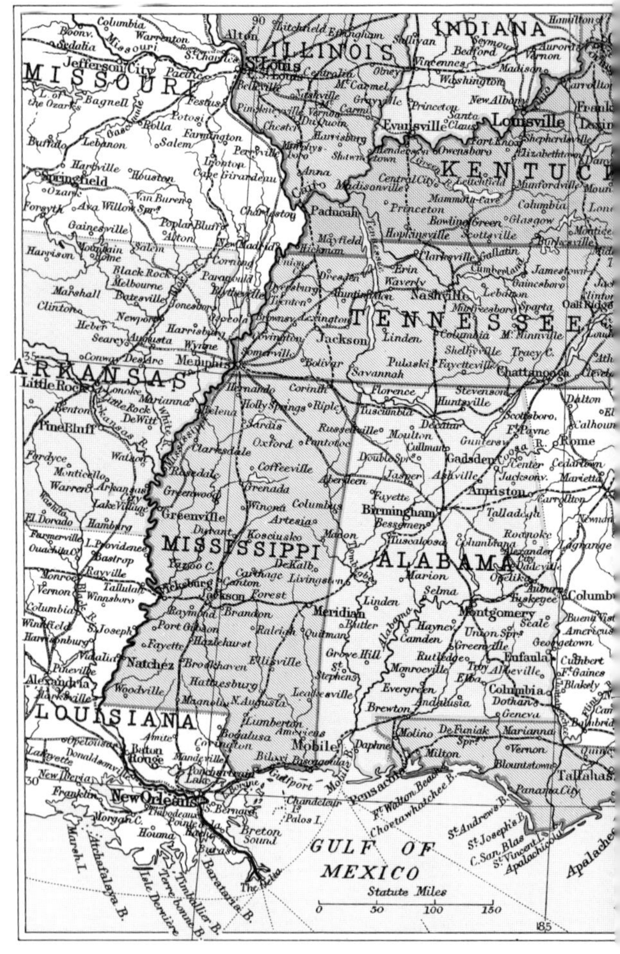
MISSOURI
ILLINOIS
INDIANA
KENTUCK
TENNESSEE
ARKANSAS
MISSISSIPPI
ALABAMA
LOUISIANA
GULF OF MEXICO
Statute Miles
0 50 100 150
90
35
30
85
Columbia
Boonv.
Sedalia
Jefferson City
St. Louis
Alton
Belleville
Springfield
Louisville
Evansville
Owensboro
Paducah
Cairo
Cape Girardeau
Poplar Bluff
New Madrid
Hickman
Nashville
Clarksville
Jackson
Memphis
Chattanooga
Little Rock
Pine Bluff
Helena
Corinth
Huntsville
Decatur
Gadsden
Anniston
Birmingham
Tuscaloosa
Greenville
Vicksburg
Natchez
Meridian
Montgomery
Selma
Mobile
Pensacola
Biloxi
Gulfport
New Orleans
Baton Rouge
Hattiesburg
Columbus
Panama City
Tallahas.
Dothan
Eufaula
Breton Sound
Chandeleur Is.
Mississippi
Tennessee
Alabama R.
Arkansas R.
Mobile B.
Choctawhatchee B.
St. Andrews B.
The Delta

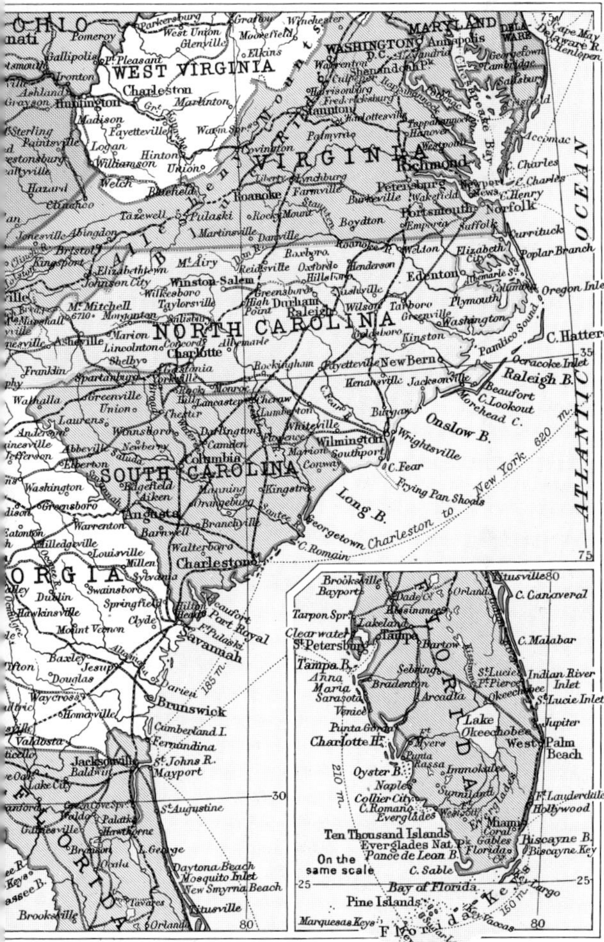
OHIO
WEST VIRGINIA
Charleston
MARYLAND
WASHINGTON D.C.
Annapolis
VIRGINIA
Richmond
Petersburg
Norfolk
Portsmouth
Roanoke
Lynchburg
NORTH CAROLINA
Raleigh
Durham
Winston-Salem
Greensboro
Charlotte
Wilmington
New Bern
Elizabeth City
Edenton
Plymouth
Washington
Pamlico Sound
C. Hatteras
Ocracoke Inlet
Oregon Inlet
Raleigh B.
Onslow B.
C. Lookout
C. Fear
Frying Pan Shoals
Long B.
SOUTH CAROLINA
Columbia
Charleston
Georgetown
C. Romain
Augusta
GEORGIA
Savannah
Brunswick
Cumberland I.
Fernandina
Jacksonville
St. Johns R.
Mayport
St. Augustine
Daytona Beach
Mosquito Inlet
New Smyrna Beach
Titusville
FLORIDA
Charleston to New York 620 m.
185 m.
ATLANTIC OCEAN
C. Canaveral
C. Malabar
Tampa
St. Petersburg
Clearwater
Tampa B.
Sarasota
Venice
Lake Okeechobee
West Palm Beach
Jupiter
St. Lucie Inlet
Indian River Inlet
Ft. Lauderdale
Hollywood
Miami
Coral Gables
Biscayne B.
Biscayne Key
Naples
Collier City
C. Romano
Everglades
Ten Thousand Islands
Everglades Nat. Pk.
Ponce de Leon B.
C. Sable
Bay of Florida
Pine Islands
Marquesas Keys
Key West
Sugar Loaf Key
Key Vacas
Key Largo
Florida Keys
On the same scale
210 m.
150 m.
35
30
25
75
80

# CENTRAL STATES

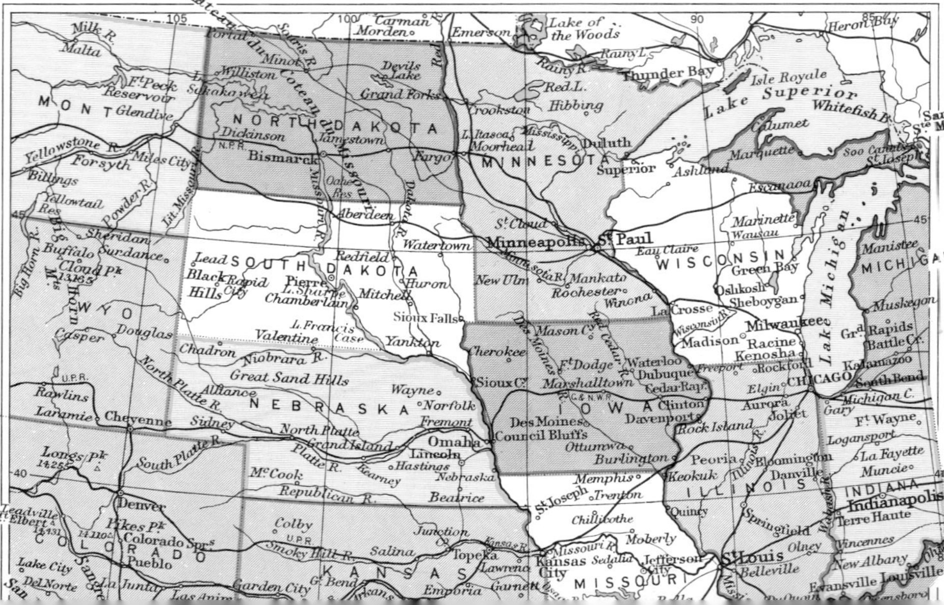

NEW MEXICO
TEXAS
OKLAHOMA
ARKANSAS
LOUISIANA
MISSISSIPPI
ALA
TENN
MEXICO
GULF OF MEXICO
Llano Estacado
Bolson de Mapimi
Santa Fe
Las Vegas
Albuquerque
Lincoln
Roswell
Rio Pecos
El Paso
Ciudad Juarez
Pecos
Midland
Colorado City
Marfa
Presidio
Amarillo
Canadian R.
Borger
Woodward
Farwell
Childress
Lubbock
Wichita Falls
Chickasha
Lawton
Red R.
Ardmore
Enid
Ponca City
Guthrie
Tulsa
Vinita
Muskogee
Oklahoma Cy
Shawnee
Mc Alester
Atoka
L. Texoma
Denison
Paris
Greenville
Dallas
Ft. Worth
Abilene
Cisco
Brazos R.
Sherwood
S. Angelo
Waco
Temple
Corsicana
Tyler
Longview
Texarkana
Kerrville
Colorado R.
Austin
Hearne
Trinity R.
Lufkin
Sabine R.
Brackettville
Eagle Pass
S. Antonio
Columbus
Houston
Beaumont
Orange
Port Arthur
Galveston
Rockport
Matagorda I.
Corpus Christi
Padre I.
L. Madre
Laredo
Brownsville
Pt. Isabel
Joplin
Carthage
Fayetteville
Tahlequah
Ft. Smith
Dardanelle
Little Rock
Hot Springs
Pine Bluff
Camden
Arkansas City
Jonesboro
Newport
Norfolk Lake
Shreveport
Monroe
Red R.
Alexandria
Donaldsonville
Lake Charles
Baton Rouge
Morgan C.
New Orleans
Mississippi R.
Memphis
Holly Springs
Greenwood
Greenville
Vicksburg
Jackson
Natchez
Brookhaven
Meridian
Hattiesburg
Mobile
Grenada
Pontotoc
St. Stephens
Selma
Montgomery
Monroeville
Brewton
Daphne
Pensacola
Birmingham
Tuscaloosa
Gadsden
Decatur
Huntsville
Nashville
Columbia
Jackson
Milan
Paris
Clarksville
Hopkinsville
Paducah
Charleston
Chihuahua
Conchos R.
Rio Bravo del Norte
Piedras Negras
Allende
Nueva Rosita
Sierra Mojada
Nuevo Laredo
Camargo
Jimenez
Hidalgo del Parral
Escalon
Mapimi
El Oro
Lerdo
Gómez Palacio
Monclova
Villaldama
Cerralvo
Monterrey
Statute Miles
0 50 100 200 300 400

MINNEAPOLIS
St. PAUL
Stillwater
Hudson
Chippewa Falls
Eau Claire
Menomonie
Ellsworth
Durand
Mondovi
Augusta
Medford
Stanley
Owen
Wausau
Greenwood
Marshfield
Neilsville
Stevens Pt.
Wisconsin Rapids
W I S C O N
Glencoe
Shakopee
Jordan
Hastings
Red Wing
Henderson
New Prague
Lesuear Cen.
Cannon R.
Pepin L.
Wabasha
Alma
St. Peter
Northfield
Lake City
Zumbrota
Faribault
Waseca
Owatonna
Plainview
Arcadia
Black R.
Black Riv. Falls
Rochester
Winona
Dodge Center
Tomah
Wautoma
Necedah
Mapleton
M I N N.
Hayfield
St. Charles
Wells
Winnebago
Blue Earth
Austin
Chatfield
Lanesboro
Spring Valley
Caledonia
Preston
Albert Lea
Elmore
La Crosse
Onalaska
Sparta
Mauston
Kilbourn
Elroy
Viroqua
Reedsburg
Baraboo
Richland Center
Northwood
Lyle
Cresco
Lansing
Titanka
Forest City
Osage
Decorah
Clear Lake
Charles City
Calmar
Waukon
Postville
Mason City
Britt
Mc. Gregor
New Hampton
Shell Rock R.
Belmond
Nashua
W. Union
Elkader
Hampton
Greene
Sumner
Waverly
Oelwein
Clarion
Iowa Falls
Ackley
Cedar Falls
Webster City
Waterloo
Dubuque
Eldora
Grundy Center
Independence
Manchester
Story City
Reinbeck
La Porte City
Cascade
Bellevue
Monticello
Vinton
Tama
Boone
Nevada
Marshallt
Marion
Anamosa
I O W A
Ames
State Center
Toledo
Cedar Rapids
Maquoketa
Iowa R.
Belle Plaine
Clinton
Madrid
Grinnell
Tipton
Dewitt
Newton
Brooklyn
Marengo
Coralville Res.
Iowa City
Cedar R.
Rochester Res.
Des Moines
Montezuma
W. Liberty
Davenport
Wilton Jc.
Red Rock
Pella
Indianola
What Cheer
Muscatine
Knoxville
Oskaloosa
Sigourney
Washington
Columbus
Eddyville
Osceola
Chariton
Lucas
Ottumwa
Wapello
Albia
Mt. Pleasant
Rathbun R.
Fairfield
New London
Corydon
Mystic
Eldon
Des Moines R.
Burlington
Leon
Centerville
Bloomfield
Ft. Madison
Cincinnati
Farmington
Keokuk
Prairie du Chien
Lancaster
Mineral Pt.
Platteville
Darlington
Monroe
Dodgeville
Madison
Boscobel
Wisconsin R.
Mississippi R.
Warren
Galena
Freeport
Mt. Carroll
Savanna
Polo
Morrison
Fulton
Sterling
Moline
Geneseo
Rock Island
Aleda
Princeton
Kewanee
Keithsburg
Galva
Galesburg
Monmouth
Abingdon
Knoxville
Chillicothe
Peoria
Lomax
Spoon R.
Canton
Bushnell
Nauvoo
Lewistown
Macomb
Colchester
Carthage
Havana
Warsaw
Astoria
I L L I
Rushville
Mt. Sterling
Beardstown
Virginia
Quincy
Palmyra
Barry
Jacksonville
Unionville
Lancaster
Lucerne
Princeton
Memphis
Queen City
Kahoka
Green C.
Kirksville
Milan
La Belle
Trenton
M O
Edina
La Grange
Linneus
La Plata
Chillicothe
Shelbyville
Chariton R.
Hannibal
Statute Miles
0 20 40 60 80 100

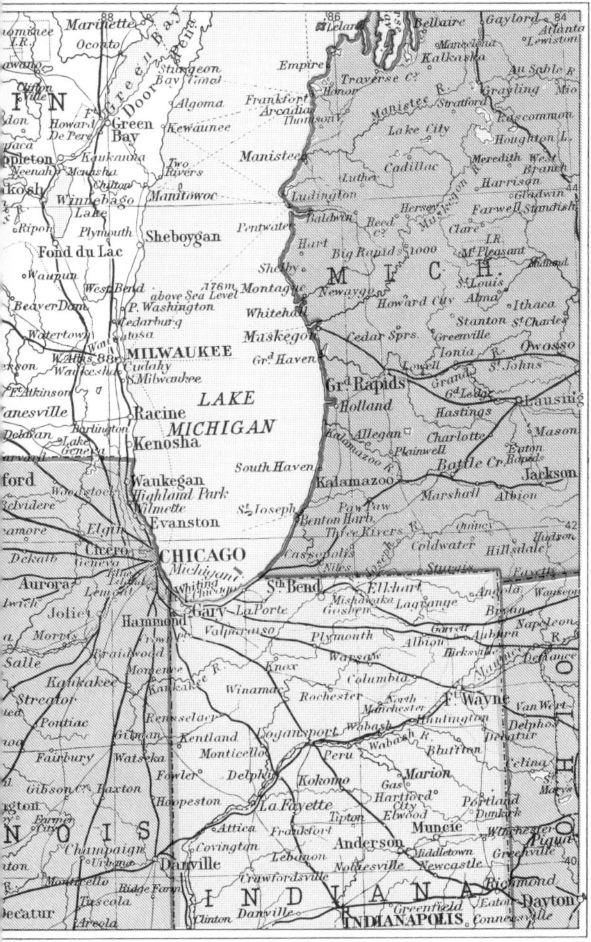
Green Bay
Door Pen.
Marinette
Oconto
Sturgeon Bay
Algoma
Kewaunee
Green Bay
Two Rivers
Manitowoc
Sheboygan
Fond du Lac
Winnebago Lake
Plymouth
Ripon
Waupun
West Bend
Beaver Dam
P. Washington
Cedarburg
Watertown
MILWAUKEE
Cudahy
S. Milwaukee
Racine
Kenosha
Burlington
Lake Geneva
Delavan
Janesville
Ft. Atkinson
LAKE
MICHIGAN
176m. above Sea Level
Waukegan
Highland Park
Wilmette
Evanston
Elgin
Cicero
CHICAGO
Aurora
Joliet
Hammond
Gary
Kankakee
Streator
Pontiac
Fairbury
Watseka
Gibson Cy.
Paxton
Champaign
Urbana
Danville
Tuscola
Arcola
Decatur
N O I S
Empire
Traverse Cy.
Frankfort
Arcadia
Manistee
Ludington
Pentwater
Hart
Shelby
Montague
Whitehall
Muskegon
Grd. Haven
Grd. Rapids
Holland
Allegan
Kalamazoo
South Haven
St. Joseph
Benton Harb.
Cassopolis
Niles
Bellaire
Gaylord
Atlanta
Lewiston
Kalkaska
Grayling
Au Sable R.
Roscommon
Houghton L.
Lake City
Cadillac
Manistee R.
Harrison
Gladwin
Farwell
Standish
Clare
Mt. Pleasant
Midland
Big Rapids
M I C H.
St. Louis
Alma
Ithaca
Howard City
Stanton
St. Charles
Greenville
Cedar Sprs.
Ionia
Owosso
St. Johns
Grand R.
Lansing
Hastings
Charlotte
Mason
Eaton Rapids
Battle Cr.
Jackson
Marshall
Albion
Coldwater
Hillsdale
Hudson
Sturgis
Three Rivers
Sth. Bend
Elkhart
Mishawaka
Goshen
Lagrange
Angola
La Porte
Valparaiso
Plymouth
Warsaw
Auburn
Garrett
Bryan
Napoleon
Defiance
Knox
Columbia
Winamac
Rochester
Ft. Wayne
Van Wert
Huntington
Logansport
Wabash
Peru
Bluffton
Decatur
Delphos
Celina
Kentland
Monticello
Delphi
Kokomo
Marion
Fowler
Hoopeston
La Fayette
Tipton
Elwood
Hartford City
Portland
Muncie
Anderson
Attica
Frankfort
Covington
Lebanon
Noblesville
Middletown
Newcastle
Crawfordsville
Greenfield
Richmond
Dayton
Greenville
Piqua
INDIANAPOLIS
Connersville
Danville
Clinton
I N D I A N A
O H I O
42
40
44
84
86
88

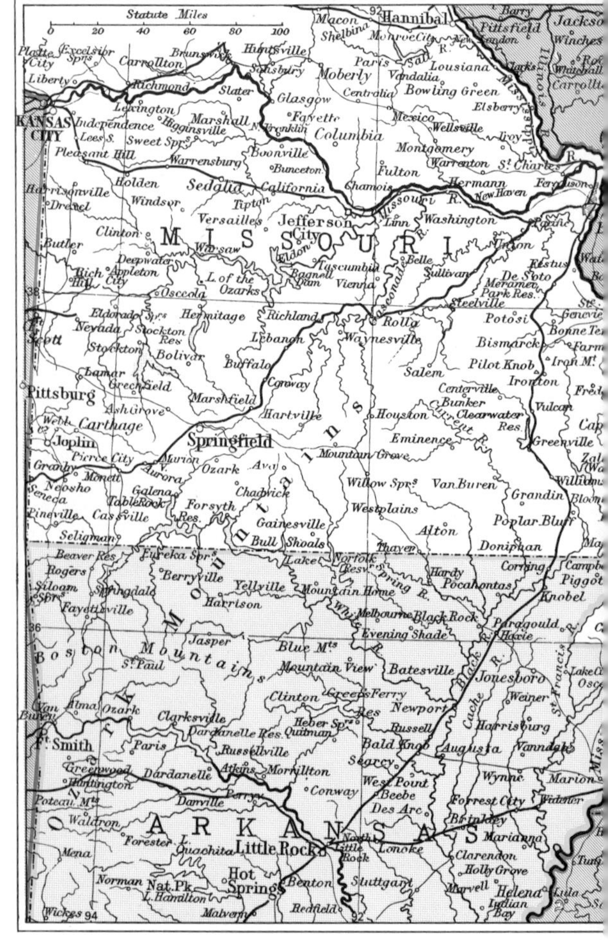
Statute Miles
0
20
40
60
80
100
MISSOURI
ARKANSAS
Ozark Mountains
Boston Mountains
Hannibal
Macon
Shelbina
Monroe City
New London
Barry
Pittsfield
Jackson
Winchester
Huntsville
Brunswick
Carrollton
Excelsior Sprs.
Platte City
Liberty
Richmond
Salisbury
Moberly
Paris
Salt R.
Lousiana
Vandalia
Bowling Green
Centralia
Slater
Glasgow
Lexington
Kansas City
Independence
Higginsville
Marshall
Fayette
Franklin
Columbia
Mexico
Wellsville
Troy
Elsberry
Lees S.
Sweet Sprs.
Pleasant Hill
Warrensburg
Boonville
Bunceton
Montgomery
Warrenton
St. Charles
Fulton
Harrisonville
Holden
Sedalia
California
Chamois
Hermann
New Haven
Ferguson
Dreasel
Windsor
Tipton
Missouri R.
Linn
Washington
Versailles
Jefferson City
Pacific
Clinton
Butler
Warsaw
Eldon
Union
Deepwater
Appleton City
Rich Hill
Tascumbia
Belle
Sullivan
Festus
De Soto
L. of the Ozarks
Bagnell Dam
Vienna
Meramec Park Res.
Osceola
Steelville
Gasconade R.
Eldorado Sprs.
Hermitage
Richland
Rolla
Potosi
Ste. Genevieve
Bonne Terre
Nevada
Stockton Res.
Stockton
Lebanon
Waynesville
Bismarck
Farmington
Ft. Scott
Bolivar
Buffalo
Pilot Knob
Iron Mt.
Salem
Ironton
Lamar
Greenfield
Conway
Centerville
Pittsburg
Marshfield
Bunker
Clearwater Res.
Vulcan
Ash Grove
Hartville
Houston
Current R.
Webb City
Carthage
Springfield
Eminence
Greenville
Joplin
Pierce City
Marion V.
Mountain Grove
Granby
Monett
Aurora
Ozark
Ava
Neosho
Galena
Chadwick
Willow Sprs.
Van Buren
Williamsville
Grandin
Seneca
Table Rock
Forsyth Res.
West Plains
Pineville
Cassville
Gainesville
Poplar Bluff
Alton
Seligman
Bull Shoals
Doniphan
Beaver Res.
Eureka Sprs.
Lake
Norfolk Resvr.
Thayer
Rogers
Berryville
Hardy
Corning
Piggott
Siloam Sprs.
Springdale
Yellville
Mountain Home
Spring R.
Pocahontas
Knobel
Fayetteville
Harrison
White R.
Melbourne
Black Rock
Paragould
Hoxie
Evening Shade
Jasper
Blue Mts.
Black R.
St. Francis R.
St. Paul
Mountain View
Batesville
Jonesboro
Clinton
Greers Ferry Res.
Weiner
Van Buren
Alma
Ozark
Newport
Cache R.
Clarksville
Heber Sprs.
Harrisburg
Dardanelle Res.
Quitman
Russell
Ft. Smith
Paris
Russellville
Bald Knob
Augusta
Vanndale
Searcy
Greenwood
Dardanelle
Atkins
Morrillton
Wynne
Marion
Huntington
West Point
Conway
Beebe
Perry
Forrest City
Poteau Mts.
Danville
Des Arc
Brinkley
Waldron
Marianna
Forester
Ouachita L.
Little Rock
North Little Rock
Lonoke
Mena
Clarendon
Holly Grove
Hot Springs
Benton
Stuttgart
Norman
Nat. Pk.
L. Hamilton
Marvell
Helena
Indian Bay
Lula
Malvern
Redfield
Wickes
92
94
38
36

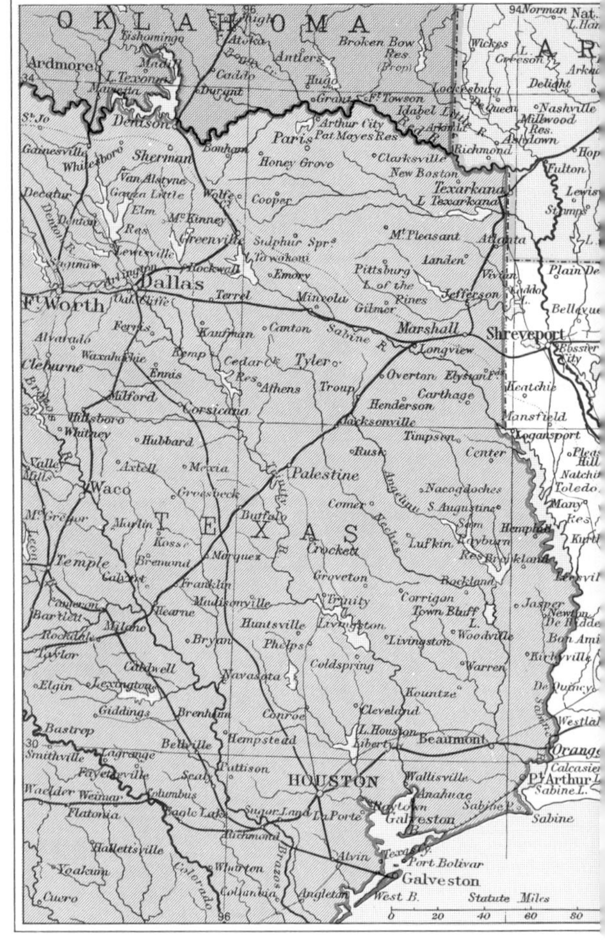
OKLAHOMA
TEXAS
Ardmore
Denison
Sherman
Gainesville
Paris
Clarksville
Texarkana
Dallas
Ft. Worth
Greenville
Mt. Pleasant
Marshall
Shreveport
Longview
Tyler
Corsicana
Palestine
Waco
Temple
Jacksonville
Henderson
Carthage
Nacogdoches
Lufkin
Crockett
Huntsville
Navasota
Brenham
Bryan
Conroe
Cleveland
Beaumont
Orange
Pt. Arthur
HOUSTON
Galveston
Port Bolivar
Angleton
Alvin
Hempstead
Bastrop
Giddings
Lexington
Caldwell
Cameron
Hearne
Madisonville
Hallettsville
Yoakum
Cuero
Wharton
Columbia
Columbus
Weimar
Flatonia
Lagrange
Smithville
Sabine
Statute Miles
0 20 40 60 80

# WESTERN STATES

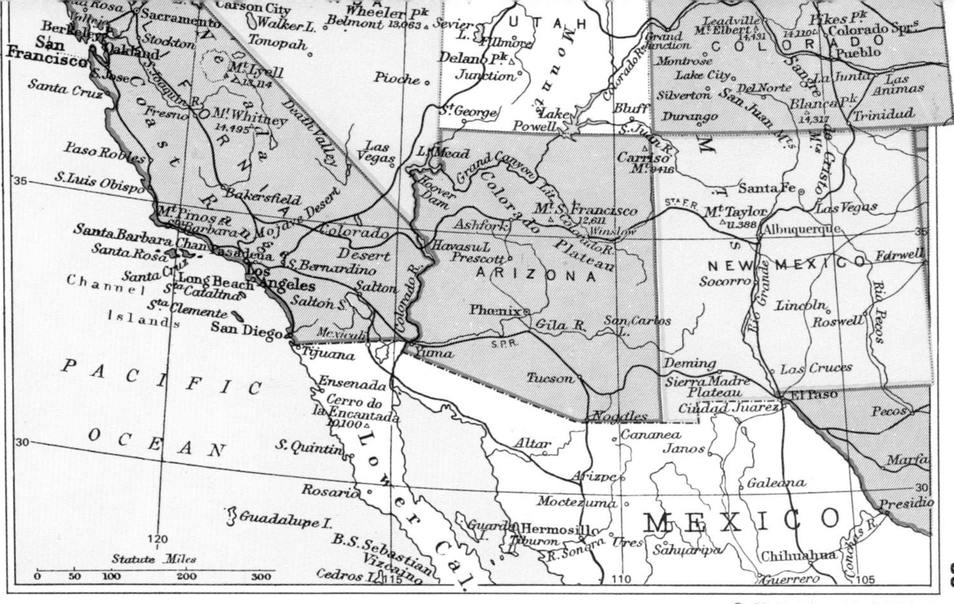
COLORADO
Pikes Pk.
Colorado Spr.s
Pueblo
Las Animas
Trinidad
La Junta
Leadville
Mt. Elbert
Lake City
Del Norte
San Juan Mts.
Silverton
Durango
Montrose
Grand Junction
Sangre de Cristo Mts.
Blanca Pk.
NEW MEXICO
Santa Fe
Las Vegas
Albuquerque
Mt. Taylor
Socorro
Rio Grande
Rio Pecos
Roswell
Lincoln
Las Cruces
El Paso
Deming
Sierra Madre Plateau
Ciudad Juarez
Pecos
Marfa
Presidio
Farwell
UTAH
Mounts
Fillmore
Delano Pk.
Junction
Sevier L.
St. George
Lake Powell
Bluff
S. Juan R.
Colorado R.
Carrizo Mts.
ARIZONA
Colorado Plateau
Grand Canyon
Mt. S. Francisco
Winslow
Ashfork
Prescott
Phoenix
Gila R.
San Carlos L.
Tucson
Nogales
Yuma
Havasu L.
Hoover Dam
L. Mead
S.P.R.
MEXICO
Chihuahua
Galeana
Janos
Cananea
Arizpe
Moctezuma
Hermosillo
Guerrero
Sahuaripa
Tres
R. Sonora
Altar
Tiburon I.
Guardia I.
Lower Cal.
Ensenada
Cerro de la Encantada
S. Quintin
Rosario
Guadalupe I.
B.S. Sebastian Vizcaino
Cedros I.
Tijuana
CALIFORNIA
Coast Range
Sierra Nevada
San Francisco
Berkeley
Oakland
S. Jose
Santa Cruz
Sacramento
Stockton
Fresno
S. Joaquin R.
Mt. Lyell
Mt. Whitney
Carson City
Walker L.
Tonopah
Belmont
Wheeler Pk.
Pioche
Las Vegas
Death Valley
Mojave Desert
Bakersfield
Paso Robles
S. Luis Obispo
Santa Barbara
Santa Rosa I.
Santa Cruz I.
Channel Islands
Sta. Catalina
Sta. Clemente
Long Beach
Los Angeles
Pasadena
S. Bernardino
Colorado Desert
Salton Sea
San Diego
PACIFIC OCEAN
Statute Miles
0 50 100 200 300

# PACIFIC COAST

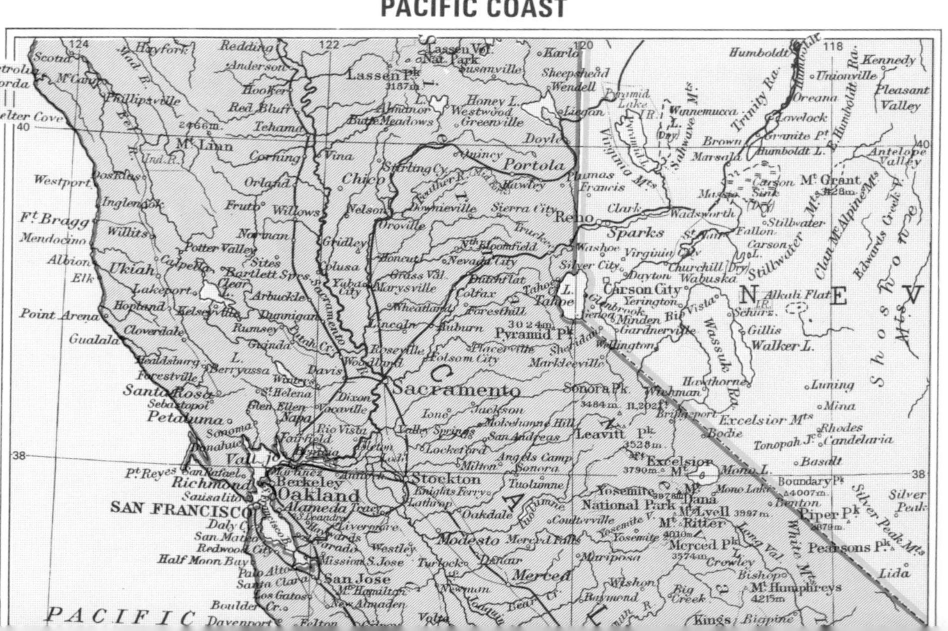

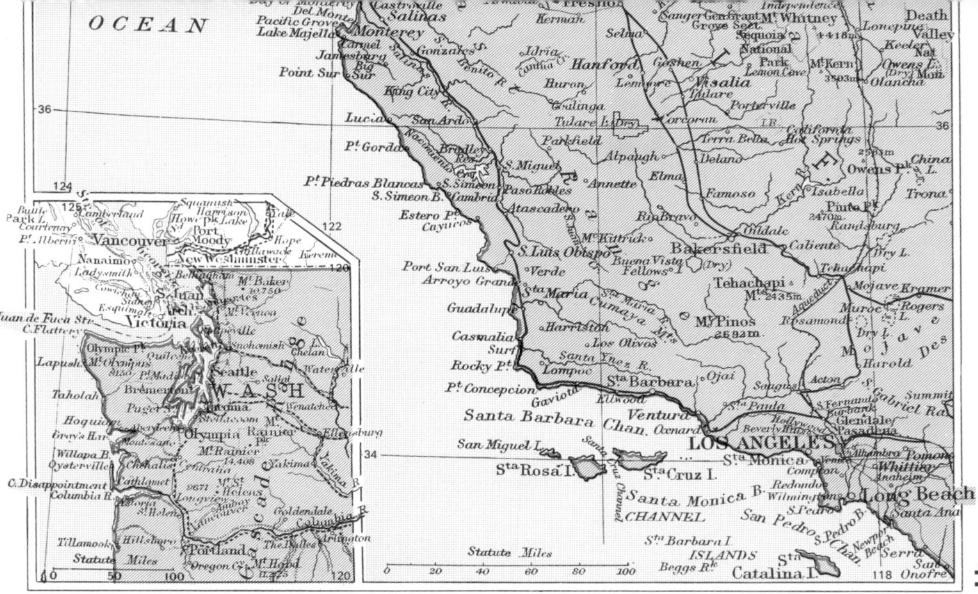
OCEAN
Monterey
Salinas
Castroville
Del Monte
Pacific Grove
Lake Majella
Carmel
Jamesburg
Point Sur
Big Sur
Gonzales
King City
San Ardo
Lucia
Pt. Gorda
Bradley
Pt. Piedras Blancas
S. Simeon
S. Simeon B.
Cambria
Paso Robles
Atascadero
Estero Pt.
Cayucos
S. Luis Obispo
Port San Luis
Arroyo Grande
Sta. Maria
Guadalupe
Casmalia
Surf
Rocky Pt.
Lompoc
Pt. Concepcion
Gaviota
Ellwood
Sta. Barbara
Ojai
Santa Barbara Chan.
Ventura
Oxnard
San Miguel I.
Sta. Rosa I.
Santa Cruz Channel
Sta. Cruz I.
Santa Monica B.
CHANNEL
Sta. Barbara I.
ISLANDS
Beggs Rk.
Sta. Catalina I.
San Pedro Chan.
S. Pedro B.
Newport Beach
San Onofre
LOS ANGELES
Sta. Monica
Redondo
Wilmington
Compton
Long Beach
Santa Ana
Anaheim
Whittier
Pomona
Alhambra
Pasadena
Glendale
Burbank
S. Fernando
Gabriel Ra.
Summit
Sta. Paula
Saugus
Acton
Kermah
Selma
Fresno
Hanford
Lemoore
Goshen
Visalia
Tulare
Porterville
Corcoran
Tulare L. (Dry)
Huron
Coalinga
Idria
Parkfield
Alpaugh
Delano
Terra Bella
California Hot Springs
Elma
Famoso
Annette
Rio Bravo
Mc Kittrick
Buena Vista
Fellows
Bakersfield
Oildale
Caliente
Tehachapi
Tehachapi Mts. 2435m
Mt. Pinos 2692m
Harriston
Los Olivos
Santa Ynez R.
Sanger
General Grant Grove Sect.
Sequoia National Park
Mt. Whitney 4418m
Lone Pine
Keeler
Owens L. (Dry)
Olancha
Mt. Kern 3503m
Lemon Cove
Independence
Death Valley
Isabella
Owens Pk.
China L.
Trona
Randsburg
Dry L.
Mojave
Kramer
Muroc
Rogers L.
Rosamond
Harold
Mojave Des.
Aqueduct
Vancouver
Victoria
Nanaimo
Ladysmith
Cumberland
Courtenay
Pt. Alberni
Squamish
Harrison Lake
Port Moody
New Westminster
Chilliwack
Hope
Yale
Juan de Fuca Str.
C. Flattery
Olympic Pt.
Mt. Olympus
Lapush
Seattle
Bremerton
Tacoma
Olympia
Mt. Rainier 14,408
Snohomish
Chelan
Waterville
Wenatchee
Ellensburg
Yakima
Yakima R.
W-A-S-H
Taholah
Hoquiam
Aberdeen
Gray's Har.
Willapa B.
Oysterville
Chehalis
Centralia
Cathlamet
C. Disappointment
Columbia R.
Astoria
St. Helens
Longview
Vancouver
Mt. St. Helens
Goldendale
The Dalles
Arlington
Tillamook
Hillsboro
Portland
Oregon City
Mt. Hood 11,225
Cascade
Statute Miles
0 50 100
Statute Miles
0 20 40 60 80 100
124 125 122 120 118 36 34

# ALASKA

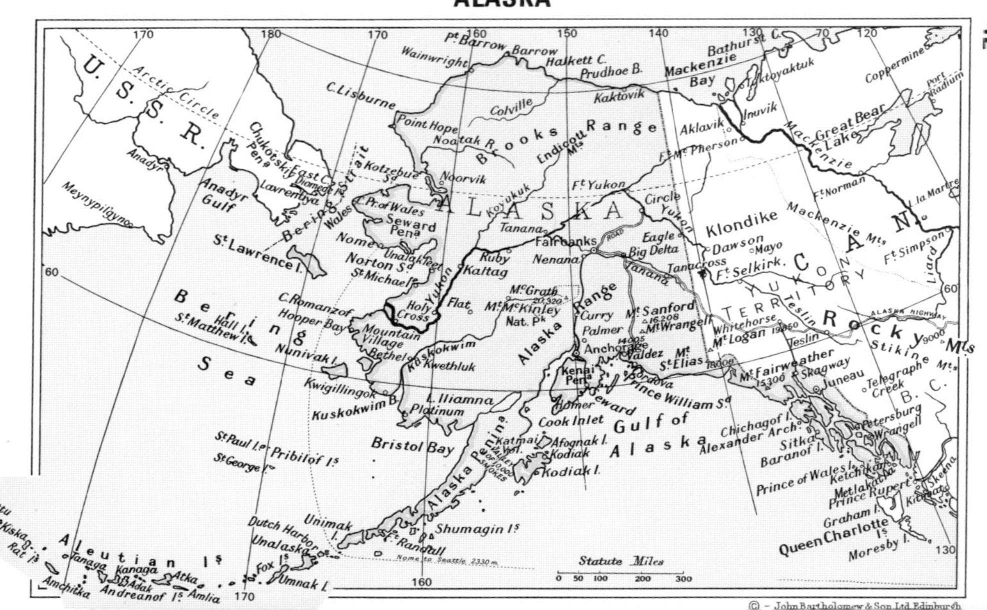
U. S. S. R.
Arctic Circle
Anadyr
Meynypil'gyno
Anadyr Gulf
Chukotski Pen.a
East C.
Diomede I.
Lavrentiya
Bering Strait
Wales
St. Lawrence I.
Bering Sea
St. Matthew I.
Hall I.
Nunivak I.
C. Lisburne
Point Hope
Noatak R.
Kotzebue Sd.
Noorvik
C. Pr. of Wales
Seward Pen.a
Nome
Unalakleet
Norton Sd.
St. Michael
C. Romanzof
Hooper Bay
Mountain Village
Bethel
Holy Cross
Yukon
Kwigillingok
Kuskokwim B.
Kuskokwim
Kwethluk
Pt. Barrow
Barrow
Wainwright
Halkett C.
Prudhoe B.
Kaktovik
Colville
Brooks Range
Endicott Mts.
Koyukuk
Ft. Yukon
ALASKA
Tanana
Fairbanks
Ruby
Kaltag
Nenana
Flat
McGrath
Mt. McKinley
20,320
Nat. Pk.
Alaska Range
Curry
Palmer
Anchorage
14005
Valdez
Mt. Sanford
16,208
Mt. Wrangell
Big Delta
Eagle
Circle
ROAD
L. Iliamna
Platinum
Bristol Bay
Alaska Pen.a
Katmai Vol.
VALLEY OF 10,000 SMOKES
Kenai Pen.a
Homer
Seward
Cook Inlet
Afognak I.
Kodiak
Kodiak I.
Cordova
Prince William Sd.
Gulf of Alaska
Mt. St. Elias
18008
Mt. Fairweather
15300
Skagway
Juneau
Chichagof I.
Alexander Arch.
Sitka
Baranof I.
Prince of Wales I.
Ketchikan
Metlakatla
Prince Rupert
Kitimat
Skeena
Petersburg
Wrangell
Graham I.
Queen Charlotte Is.
Moresby I.
Telegraph Creek
B. C.
Stikine Mts.
Rocky Mts.
9000
ALASKA HIGHWAY
Teslin
Whitehorse
Mt. Logan 19850
YUKON TERRITORY
Tanacross
Ft. Selkirk
Dawson
Mayo
Klondike
Mackenzie Mts.
CAN.
Ft. Simpson
Liard
Ft. Norman
L. la Martre
Great Bear Lake
Mackenzie
Port Radium
Coppermine
Bathurst C.
Mackenzie Bay
Tuktoyaktuk
Inuvik
Aklavik
Ft. McPherson
Shumagin Is.
Ft. Randall
Unimak I.
Dutch Harbor
Unalaska
Fox Is.
Umnak I.
Aleutian Is.
Atka
Amlia
Andreanof Is.
Adak
Kanaga
Tanaga
Amchitka
Kiska
Rat Is.
Agattu
Attu
Nome to Seattle 2330 m.
Statute Miles
0 50 100 200 300
170
180
170
160
150
140
130
70
120
60
60
130
160
170

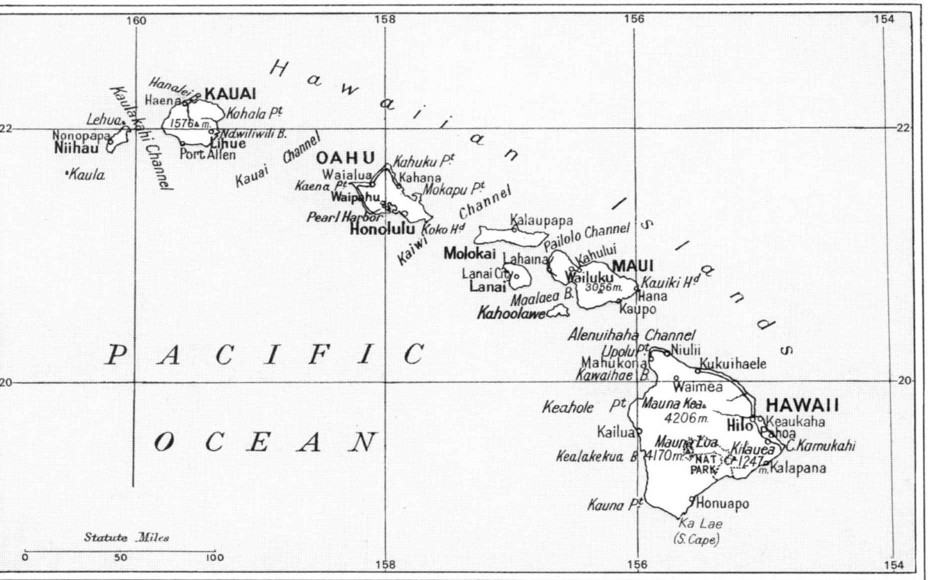
Hawaiian Islands
PACIFIC OCEAN
KAUAI
Hanalei
Haena
Kohala Pt
1576 m.
Nawiliwili B.
Lihue
Port Allen
Lehua
Nonopapa
Niihau
Kaula
Kaulakahi Channel
Kauai Channel
OAHU
Waialua
Kaena Pt
Waipahu
Pearl Harbor
Honolulu
Kahuku Pt
Kahana
Mokapu Pt
Koko Hd
Kaiwi Channel
Kalaupapa
Molokai
Pailolo Channel
Lahaina
Lanai City
Lanai
Kahului
MAUI
Wailuku
3056 m.
Kauiki Hd
Hana
Kaupo
Maalaea B.
Kahoolawe
Alenuihaha Channel
Upolu Pt
Niulii
Mahukona
Kawaihae B.
Kukuihaele
Waimea
Keahole Pt
Mauna Kea
4206 m.
HAWAII
Hilo
Keaukaha
Pahoa
C. Kamukahi
Kailua
Mauna Loa
4170 m.
Kilauea
1247 m.
NAT PARK
Kalapana
Kealakekua B
Kauna Pt
Honuapo
Ka Lae
(S. Cape)
Statute Miles
0
50
100
160
158
156
154
22
20

# MEXICO AND C. AMERICA

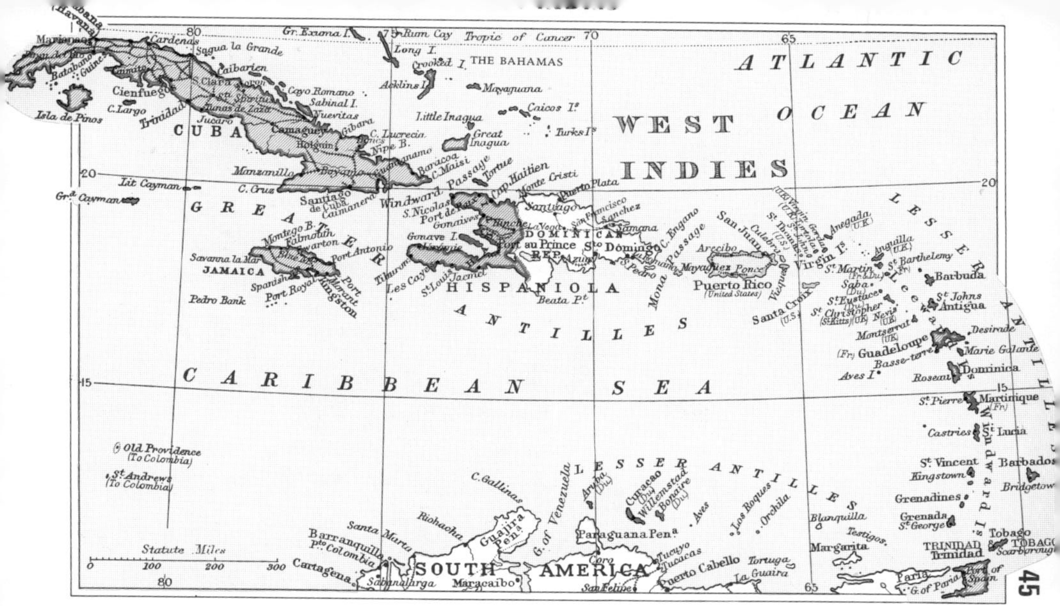
ATLANTIC OCEAN
WEST INDIES
THE BAHAMAS
Tropic of Cancer
CUBA
GREATER ANTILLES
HISPANIOLA
JAMAICA
DOMINICAN REP.
Puerto Rico
(United States)
CARIBBEAN SEA
LESSER ANTILLES
Leeward Is.
Windward Is.
SOUTH AMERICA
TRINIDAD & TOBAGO
Windward Passage
Mona Passage
Virgin Is.
G. of Venezuela
Guajira Pen.a
Paraguana Pen.a
Old Providence
(To Colombia)
St Andrews
(To Colombia)
Statute Miles
0 100 200 300
Cienfuegos
Santiago de Cuba
Kingston
Port au Prince
Sto Domingo
San Juan
Guadeloupe
Martinique
Barbados
Trinidad
Maracaibo
Cartagena
Barranquilla

# SOUTH AMERICA

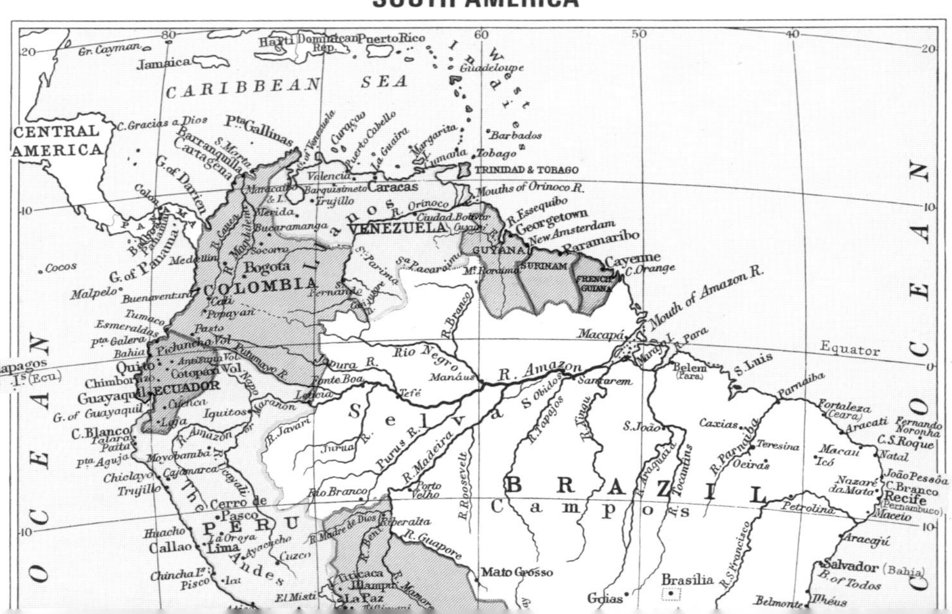

PACIFIC
ATLANT
Tropic of Capricorn
CHILE
The Andes
Patagonia
ARGENTINA
PARAGUAY
URUGUAY
Iquique
R. Loa
Tocopilla
Chuquicamata
Calama
Tarija
Mejillones
Antofagasta
Atacama Desert
Jujuy
Oran
Salta
R. Salado
R. Bermejo
R. Pilcomayo
Concepcion
Taltal
S. Miguel de Tucuman
Catamarca
Formosa
Asuncion
Posadas
S. Ambrosio
S. Felix
Chañaral
Caldera
Copiapo
Corrientes
La Rioja
R. Parana
R. Uruguay
La Serena
Coquimbo
Cordoba
Sta. Fé
Mt. Aconcagua
S. Juan
Uspallata Pass
Parana
Salto
Paysandu
L. Patos
Valparaiso
Mendoza
Gualeguaychu
Fray Bentos
Colonia
Juan Fernandez Is. (Chile)
Santiago
San Luis
Rosario
Chivilcoy
Maldonado
Montevideo
Chillan
Talca
Buenos Aires
Talcahuano
La Plata
Rio de la Plata
Concepcion
C. S. Antonio
Azul
Mar del Plata
Lebu
Colorado
Bahia Blanca
C. Corrientes
R. Negro
Valdivia
Corral
Puerto Montt
Chubut R.
Carmen de Patagones
G. of S. Matias
Chiloé I.
Rawson
Chonos Archo.
R. Chico
G. San Jorge
G. of Peñas
Deseado
Wellington I.
Santa Cruz
Falkland Is. (UK)
Stanley
Strait of Magellan
Str. of Magellan
Pta. Arenas
Tierra del Fuego
Staten I.
Cape Horn
Ouro Preto
Itatiaia
Vitória
Rio de Janeiro
Campos
S. Paulo
Niteroi
C. Frio
R. Parana
Curitiba
Santos
Iguapé
Cananéia
Paranaguá
S. Francisco do Sul
Sta. Catarina I.
Florianopolis
Pto. Alegre
Rio Grande
Statute Miles
0
500
1000
S. Georgia (UK)
20
30
40
50
100
90
80
70
60
50
40
30
20

# VENEZUELA, COLOMBIA, GUIANA

BOGOTA
VENEZUELA
COLOMBIA
Buenaventura
Gorgona I.
Cali
Neiva
Popayan
R.Patia
Tumaco
Pasto
Sotara
Esmeraldas
S.Francisco
Pedernales
Ibarra
Cayambe
QUITO
Antisana
Cotopaxi
Manta
Chimborazo
ECUADOR
Riobamba
Guayaquil
Salinas
Cuenca
Loja
Tumbes
Talara
Payta
Piura
Sechura
Jaen
Moyobamba
Chachapoyas
Cajamarca
Lambayeque
Chiclayo
Pacasmayo
Trujillo
Pataz
Uchiza
R.Santa
Chimbote
Huaraz
Casma
Huanuco
Huacho
Cerro de Pusco
LIMA
Callao
Chorillos
La Oroya
Huancavelica
Ayacucho
Chincha Is.
Pisco
Ica
Cuzco
Cusco
Pt. Maldonado
PERU
Andes
Iquitos
Nauta
Marañon
Ucayali
Yavari
(Javari)
Pucallpa
Pebas
Amazon
Leticia
Tabatinga
Equator
Japura
Ica
S.Paulo de Olivença
Tefe
Jurua
Jurua
R.Tapaua
BRAZIL
Acre
Purus
Rio Branco
Abuna
Cobija
Riberalta
Madidi
Reyes
Apolobamba
Lake Titicaca
Puno
Juliaca
Ayaviri
Arequipa
Misti
Atico
Mollendo
Moquegua
Ilo
Tacna
Arica
LA PAZ
Ancohuma
Illimani
Cochabamba
Sahama
Oruro
I. Poopo
SUCRE
Potosi
Pisagua
Iquique
Tarapaca
Huanchaca
Uyuni
Lagunas
Rio Loa
Tocopilla
CHILE
Tupiza
Calama
Atacama
Mejillones
BOLIVIA
PACIFIC OCEAN
Acari R.
Nazca
L.Villafro
Statute Miles
0 100 200 300 400
80
70
10
20
0

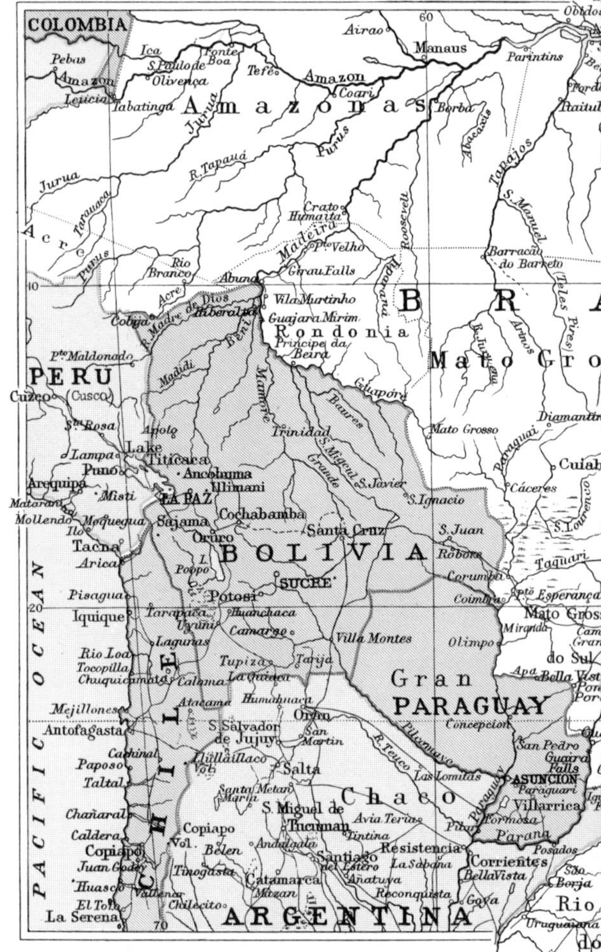
COLOMBIA
PERU
BOLIVIA
CHILE
ARGENTINA
Gran PARAGUAY
Chaco
Amazonas
Acre
Rondonia
Mato Grosso
PACIFIC OCEAN
Amazon
Manaus
Airao
Obidos
Parintins
Borba
Tefé
Coari
Pebas
Leticia
Tabatinga
S. Paulo de Olivença
Fonte Boa
Ica
Jurua
Purus
R. Tapauá
Abacaxis
Tapajos
S. Manuel
Crato
Humaita
Madeira
Pto Velho
Roosevelt
Barracão do Barreto
Rio Branco
Abuna
Girau Falls
Vila Murtinho
Guajara Mirim
Riberalta
Cobija
R. Madre de Dios
Beni
Principe da Beira
Guaporé
Mamoré
Baures
Madidi
Pto Maldonado
Cuzco (Cusco)
Sta Rosa
Apolo
Lake Titicaca
Lampa
Puno
Arequipa
Misti
Mataraní
Mollendo
Moquegua
Ilo
Tacna
Arica
Ancohuma
Illimani
LA PAZ
Sajama
Oruro
Cochabamba
Santa Cruz
Trinidad
S. Miguel
Grande
S. Javier
S. Ignacio
S. Juan
Roboré
Corumbá
Coimbra
Pto Esperança
Taquari
Cáceres
Cuiabá
S. Lourenço
Paraguai
Mato Grosso
Diamantino
Teles Pires
Arinos
R. Juruena
Juruena
L. Poopo
SUCRE
Potosi
Pisagua
Iquique
Tarapacá
Uyuni
Huanchaca
Camargo
Villa Montes
Olimpo
Miranda
Lagunas
Rio Loa
Tocopilla
Chuquicamata
Calama
Tupiza
Tarija
La Quiaca
Apa
Bella Vista
do Sul
Atacama
Humahuaca
Mejillones
Antofagasta
Oran
S. Salvador de Jujuy
San Martin
Concepcion
Pilcomayo
R. Teuco
Cachinal
Paposo
Taltal
Llullaillaco
Salta
Las Lomitas
San Pedro
Guaira Falls
ASUNCION
Paraguari
Villarrica
Santa Maria
Metan
S. Miguel de Tucuman
Chañaral
Caldera
Copiapo
Copiapo Vol.
Belen
Andalgala
Avia Teria
Tintina
Pilar
Formosa
Parana
Posados
Resistencia
Corrientes
Juan Godoy
Huasco
Tinogasta
Santiago del Estero
La Sabana
Añatuya
Catamarca
Mazan
Reconquista
BellaVista
Goya
Vallenar
El Toro
Chilecito
La Serena
Borja
Uruguaiana
Rio
60
10
20
70

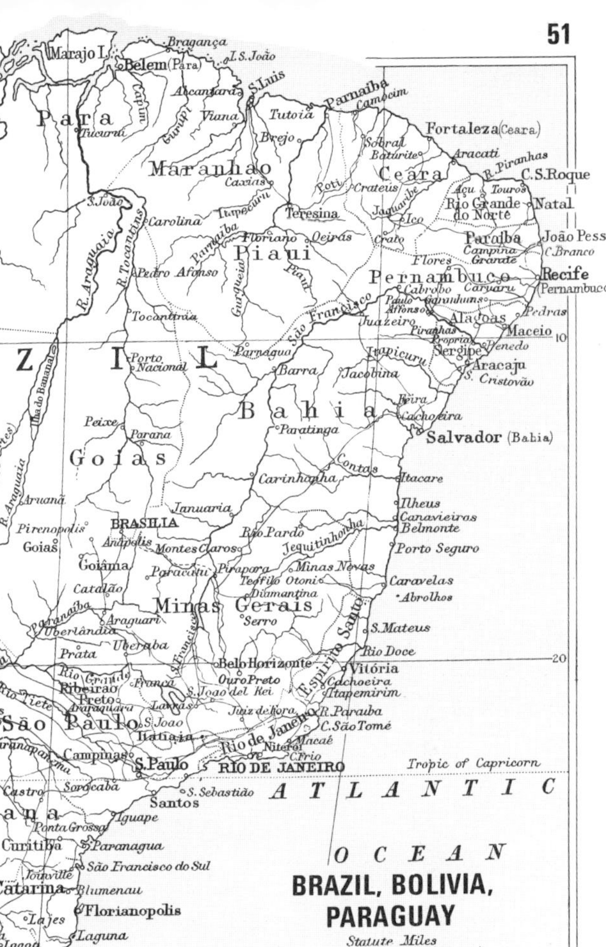
Marajo I.
Bragança
I. S. João
Belem (Para)
Para
Capim
Gurupi
Alcantara
S. Luis
Viana
Tucurui
Tutoia
Parnaiba
Camocim
Brejo
Fortaleza (Ceara)
Sobral
Baturite
Aracati
Maranhao
Caxias
R. Piranhas
C. S. Roque
Ceara
Poti
Crateus
Açu
Touros
Rio Grande do Norte
Natal
S. João
Itapecuru
Teresina
Jaguaribe
Ico
Carolina
Parnaiba
Floriano
Oeiras
Crato
Paraiba
João Pessôa
Campina Grande
C. Branco
Piaui
Flores
R. Araguaia
R. Tocantins
Pedro Afonso
Gurgueia
Piaui
Pernambuco
Recife (Pernambuco)
Cabrobo
Caruaru
Paulo Affonso
Garanhuns
Tocantins
São Francisco
Juazeiro
Alagoas
Pedras
Piranhas
Maceio
10
Propria
Penedo
Parnagua
Sergipe
Itapicuru
Aracaju
Z
I
L
Porto Nacional
Barra
Jacobina
S. Cristovão
Ilha do Bananal
Feira
Bahia
Cachoeira
Peixe
Paratinga
Salvador (Bahia)
Parana
Goias
Contas
Itacare
Carinhanha
R. Araguaia
Aruanã
Januaria
Ilheus
Canavieiras
BRASILIA
Belmonte
Pirenopolis
Rio Pardo
Jequitinhonha
Goias
Anapolis
Montes Claros
Porto Seguro
Goiâna
Paracatu
Pirapora
Minas Novas
Teofilo Otoni
Caravelas
Catalão
Diamantina
Abrolhos
Minas Gerais
Paranaiba
Araguari
Serro
Uberlândia
Espirito Santo
S. Mateus
Uberaba
S. Francisco
Prata
Rio Doce
Belo Horizonte
20
Vitória
Rio Grande
Ribeirao Preto
Franca
Ouro Preto
Cachoeira
Rio Tiete
S. Joao del Rei
Itapemirim
Araraquara
Lavras
Juiz de Fora
R. Paraiba
São Paulo
S. Joao
C. São Tomé
Itatiaia
Rio de Janeiro
Macaé
Paranapanema
Campinas
Niterói
C. Frio
S. Paulo
RIO DE JANEIRO
Tropic of Capricorn
Castro
Sorocaba
S. Sebastião
ATLANTIC
Santos
Iguape
Ponta Grossa
Curitiba
Paranagua
São Francisco do Sul
OCEAN
Joinville
Catarina
Blumenau
BRAZIL, BOLIVIA, PARAGUAY
Florianopolis
Lajes
Laguna
Statute Miles
Lagoa Vermelha
0
100
200
300
400
Torres
Porto Alegre
40
Lagoa dos Patos

Copiapo
Juan Godoy
Huasco
Vallenar
La Serena
Coquimbo
Ovalle
Illapel
Los Vilos
Viña del Mar
Valparaiso
SANTIAGO
S. Antonio
Pichilemu
Constitucion
Talca
Linares
Talcahuano
Tome
Concepcion
Chillan
Los Angeles
Lota
Arauco
Lebu
Angol
Mocha I.
Temuco
Valdivia
Corral
Osorno
L. Llanquihue
Puerto Montt
Ancud
I. of Chiloe
Guafo I.
G. of Corcovado
Chonos Archipelago
Taitao Peninsula
G. of Peñas
Great Wellington Island
Madre de Dios Archipelago
Hanover I.
Pto Natales
Q. Adelaide Ar.
Str. of Magellan
Desolation I.
Santa Ines I.
Cockburn Chan.
Londonderry I.
Hoste I.
Cape Horn
C H I L E
A n d e s
Belen
Andalgala
Tinogasta
Catamarca
Mazan
Chilecito
La Rioja
Jachal
Santiago del Estero
Añatuya
La Sabana
Resistencia
Corrientes
Bella Vista
Reconquista
Goya
Mercedes
Posadas
Sao Borja
BRAZIL
Uruguaiana
Livramento
Rivera
Porto
Bage
Pelotas
Salado
Parana
Dean Funes
L. Chiquita
Mortaros
S. Juan
Cruz del Eje
Cordoba
Santa Fe
Concordia
Salto
Aconcagua
V. Dolores
Villa Maria
Parana
Paysandu
Melo
Mendoza
S. Luis
Concepcion
Rosario
URUGUAY
ARGENTINA
Fray Bentos
Durazno
Treinta y Tres
Rancagua
S. Rafael
Villa Mercedes
Pergamino
Uruburu
Colonia
Lavalleja
Rocha
Canelones
Curico
Rufino
BUENOS AIRES
Junin
Ensenada
La Plata
Maldonado
MONTEVIDEO
Realico
Chivilcoy
Rio de la Plata
Sierra Nevado
Sta Rosa de Toay
Trenque Lauquen
9 de Julio
Chascomus
Pampas
Dolores
General Acha
Azul
Tandil
C. San Antonio
Salado
Olavarria
Callaqui Vol.
Neuquen
Tres Arroyos
Mar del Plata
C. Corrientes
Colorado
Bahia Blanca
Necochea
Zapala
Luro
Bahia Blanca
Villarrica Vol.
Neuquen
Rio Negro
Pto S. Antonio
Viedma
Carmen de Patagones
L. Nahuel Huapi
San Carlos de Bariloche
G. of San Matias
Minchinmavida Vol.
Pto Madryn
Peninsula of S. Jose
Esquel
Trelew
Bahia Nueva
Rawson
R. Chubut
Patagonia
ATLANTIC
OCEAN
Camarones B.
Senguerr
Comodoro Rivadavia
Dos Bahias C.
Pto Aisen
Sarmiento
G. San Jorge
Mt S. Valentin
Colonia Las Heras
L. Buenos Aires
R. Deseado
C. Blanco
Deseado
L. S. Martin
Chico
Port S. Julian
L. Viedma
S. Cruz
Port Santa Cruz
L. Argentino
Mt Stokes
Rio Gallegos
Coy Inlet
Falkland Islands (U.K.)
Jason Is
West Falkland
Stanley
East Falkland
Falkland Sd.
C. Virgenes
Str. of Magellan
Punta Arenas
Mt Darwin
Tierra del Fuego
Ushuaia
C. S. Diego
Staten I.
Navarino I.
Statute Miles
0
100
200
300
400
40
50
60
80

U.S.S.R.
ASIA
Amur R.
Sakhalin
Kuril Is.
Attu
Kiska
Dutch Harb.
Aleutian Islands
Yokohama to Vancouver 4262 m.
Yokohama to S. Francisco 4536 m.
Pr. Rupert
Queen Charlotte Is.
Vancouver I.
Victoria
Vancouver
Seattle
CANADA
Can. Pac. Rail.
Winnipeg
L. Superior
Quebec
Montreal
Ottawa
Toronto
North Pac. Rail.
NORTH AMERICA
Union Pac. Rail.
Chicago
New York
San Francisco
UNITED STATES
St. Louis
Washington
Los Angeles
South Pac. Rail.
Mississippi
S. Diego
Charleston
New Orleans
Harbin
Vladivostok
Changchun
Peking
Lushun
Sea of Japan
Wei-hai
KOREA
Hakodate
JAPAN
Tokyo
Kobe
Nanking
Nagasaki
Shanghai
Yokohama
Yokohama to Honolulu 3380 m.
Honolulu to Victoria 2840 m.
Honolulu to S. Francisco 2100 m.
CHINA
Taiwan (Formosa)
Ogasawara Gunto (Bonin Is.)
Tropic of Cancer
Midway Is.
NORTH
Hawaii
Honolulu
Pearl Harb.
MEXICO
Gulf of Mexico
Havana
Cuba
C.S. Lucas
Revilla Gigedo Is.
Mexico
Vera Cruz
Belmopan
Jamaica
Acapulco
Guatemala
Hong Kong
Luzon
PHILIPPINES
Manila
Northern Marianas
Wake I.
Guam
Manila to Honolulu 4840 m.
PACIFIC
OCEAN
Honolulu to Panama 4711 m.
3280 m.
CENTRAL AMERICA
NIC.
Colon
Panama
Clipperton I.
Marshall Is.
Mindanao
Fed. States of Micronesia
Truk
Palau Is.
Brisbane to Honolulu 4100 m.
Honolulu 2736 m.
3328 m.
Washington I.
Fanning I.
Christmas I.
Wellington to S. Francisco 6094 m.
COLOMBIA
Bogota
KIRIBATI
Gilbert Is.
Borneo
Equator
Baker Is.
Galapagos Is.
Quito
ECUADOR
Guayaquil
Celebes
INDONESIA
NEW GUINEA
Rabaul
Nauru I.
Ocean I.
Canton I.
Phoenix Is.
Jarvis I.
Malden I.
Starbuck I.
Jakarta
Java
Timor
Port Moresby
Solomon Is.
Tuvalu
Union Is.
Tongareva
Marquesas Is.
6593 m.
PERU
Lima
Callao
Timor Sea
Darwin
Thursday I.
Coral Sea
Santa Cruz
Rotumah
Western Samoa
Amer. Samoa
Manihiki
Suvarov I.
Panama
N. Terr.
VANUATU
Fiji Is.
Apia
Society Is.
Tahiti
Tuamotu Archipelago
Townsville
New Caledonia
Suva
Tonga or Friendly Is.
Cook Is.
Auckland
Iquique
Western Australia
Alice Spr.
Rockhampton
Queensl.
AUSTRALIA
Brisbane
Sydney to Suva 1750 m.
Norfolk I.
Austral Is.
Pitcairn I.
Ducie
Tropic of Capricorn
Easter I.
St. Felix
Kalgoorlie
South Australia
SOUTH
PACIFIC
Kermadec Is.
Perth
Fremantle
Albany
New South Wales
Adelaide
Sydney
Lord Howe I.
1280 m.
Valparaiso
Juan Fernandez
Victoria
Canberra
Melbourne
1240 m.
Tasman Sea
NEW ZEALAND
Auckland
Wellington
Christchurch
Dunedin
Bluff
Chatham Is.
OCEAN
Valdivia
Tasmania
Hobart
1200 m.

Mercator's Projection

BAFFIN BAY
GREENLAN
Boothia Pen.a
Gulf of Boothia
Baffin Island
Foxe Basin
Melville Peninsula
Pr. Charles I.
L. Nettilling
Davis Strait
Disko I.
Godhavn
Christianshåb
Jakobshavn
Holsteinsborg
Søndre Strømfjord
Southampton I.
Foxe Pen.a
L. Amadjuak
Hudson Strait
Baker L.
Chesterfield Inlet
Godthåb
Frederikshåb
KEEWATIN
C. Chidley
Julianehåb
Sydprøven
C. Farewell
Churchill
HUDSON BAY
Hebron
COAST OF LABRADOR
Churchill to Liverpool 2930 m.
Nain
Hopedale
Nelson
York Factory
Belcher Is.
CANADA
Hamilton Inlet
Goose Bay
Liverpool to Quebec
MANITOBA
L. Winnipeg
James Bay
Battle Harb.
Str. of Belle Isle
N.TH AMERICA
ONTARIO
Winnipeg
Can. Nat. Rail.
Thunder Bay
QUEBEC
Anticosti
Gulf of St. Lawrence
NEWFOUNDLAND
Gander
St. Johns
Quebec
Montreal
NEW BRUNSWICK
Fredericton
P. Edward
Cape Breton I.
Sydney
Bismarck
Duluth
St. Paul
Sudbury
Ottawa
Saint John
NOVA SCOTIA
Halifax
Minneapolis
Toronto
Augusta
L. Ontario
Milwaukee
Buffalo
Albany
Portland
Boston
C. Cod
Sable I.
Omaha
Chicago
Detroit
Niagara
Lincoln
Cleveland
Pittsburgh
New York
Kansas City
St. Louis
Cincinnati
Philadelphia
Baltimore
Washington
Richmond
UNITED STATES
Newport News
Memphis
Nashville
ATLANTIC
Atlanta
Wilmington
New York to Genoa 4055 m.
Charleston
Savannah
Bermuda
Mobile
San Antonio
New Orleans
Galveston
Gulf of Mexico
Tampa
Florida
Matamoras
Miami
The Bahamas
New Orleans to Liverpool 4530 m.
Key West
Nassau
Kingston to Liverpool
London to Georgetown
MEXICO
Tampico
Havana
Caicos Is.
WEST INDIES
OCEAN
Veracruz
Merida
Cuba
Mexico
Campeche
Jamaica
Hispaniola
St. Thomas
Nevis
Barbuda
Antigua
Montserrat
Dominica
Southampton to Barbados
Colon to Marseilles
Tehuantepec
BELIZE
Belmopan
Trujillo
GUATAMALA
HONDURAS
Kingston
CARIBBEAN SEA
St. Lucia
Barbados
Grenada
New York to Capetown
Acajutla
Salvador
NICARAGUA
Bluefields
S. Juan
Cartagena
Curaçao
La Guaira
CENTRAL AMERICA
COSTA RICA
Colon
Barranquilla
Caracas
Trinidad & Tobago
Punta Arenas
Orinoco
PACIFIC OCEAN
Panama & Balboa
COLOMBIA
VENEZUELA
New Amsterdam
Georgetown (Demerara)
Paramaribo
Cayenne
Buenaventura
Bogota
STH AMERICA
GUYANA
SURINAM
FR. GUIANA
Tumaco

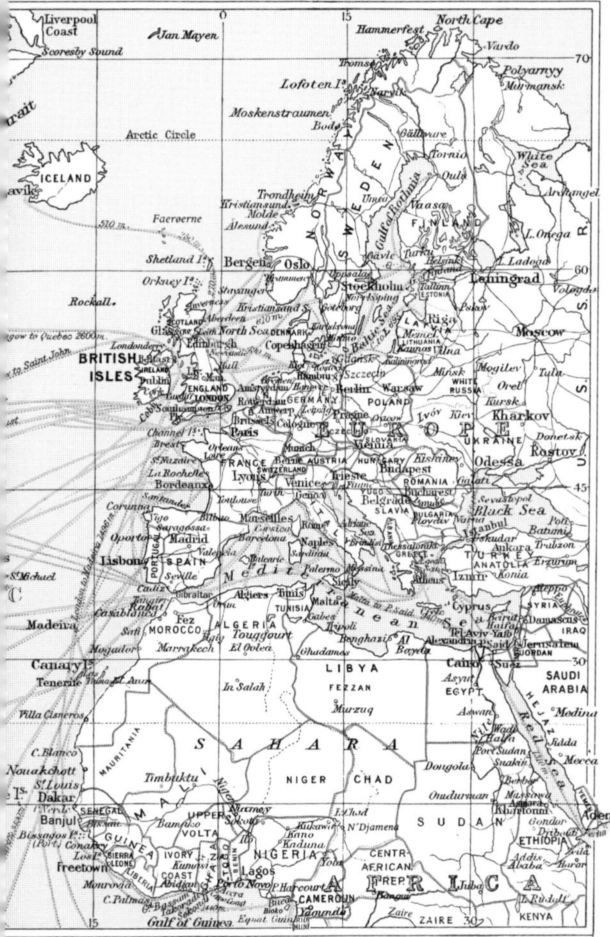
Liverpool Coast
Jan Mayen
Scoresby Sound
North Cape
Hammerfest
Vardo
Tromsø
Polyarnyy
Murmansk
Lofoten Is.
Narvik
Moskenstraumen
Bodø
Arctic Circle
Gällivare
Tornio
White Sea
ICELAND
Oulu
Archangel
Trondheim
Kristiansund
Molde
Ålesund
NORWAY
SWEDEN
Umeå
Gulf of Bothnia
Vaasa
FINLAND
L. Onega
Faerøerne
510 m.
Gävle
Turku
Helsinki
L. Ladoga
Shetland Is.
Bergen
Oslo
Uppsala
Leningrad
Orkney Is.
Stavanger
Stockholm
Tallinn
ESTONIA
Vologda
Rockall.
Norrköping
Kristiansand S.
Göteborg
Pskov
SCOTLAND
Aberdeen
Riga
LATVIA
Glasgow
North Sea
DENMARK
Moscow
Edinburgh
Copenhagen
Baltic Sea
LITHUANIA
Kaunas
Vilna
Londonderry
Malmö
BRITISH ISLES
Belfast
Gdansk
Kaliningrad
Mogilev
Tula
IRELAND
Dublin
Hull
Szczecin
Minsk
WHITE RUSSIA
Orel
Cork
ENGLAND
LONDON
Amsterdam
Hamburg
Bremen
Berlin
Warsaw
Rotterdam
GERMANY
POLAND
Kursk
Southampton
Antwerp
Leipzig
Brussels
Cologne
Prague
Lvov
Kiev
Kharkov
Channel Is.
Paris
EUROPE
SLOVAKIA
UKRAINE
Donetsk
Brest
Orleans
Munich
Vienna
Rostov
St. Nazaire
FRANCE
Berne
AUSTRIA
HUNGARY
Kishinev
Odessa
La Rochelle
Lyons
SWITZERLAND
Trieste
Budapest
ROMANIA
Galati
Bordeaux
Venice
Fiume
Bucharest
Genoa
Turin
YUGOSLAVIA
Belgrade
Santander
Toulouse
Sevastopol
Black Sea
Corunna
Vigo
Bilbao
Marseilles
BULGARIA
Plovdiv
Varna
Poti
Saragossa
Corsica
Rome
Adriatic Sea
ALBANIA
Batumi
Istanbul
Oporto
Madrid
Barcelona
Naples
Brindisi
Thessaloniki
Üsküdar
Ankara
Trabzon
PORTUGAL
SPAIN
Valencia
Sardinia
GREECE
TURKEY
Erzurum
Lisbon
Balearic Is.
Palermo
Messina
Aegean Sea
ANATOLIA
Seville
Mediterranean Sea
Athens
Izmir
Konia
St. Michael
Cadiz
Gibraltar
Algiers
Tunis
Sicily
Aleppo
Tangier
Rabat
Oran
TUNISIA
Malta
Malta to P. Said
Cyprus
SYRIA
Casablanca
London to Madeira 1496 m.
Fez
Gabes
Beirut
Damascus
Madeira
ALGERIA
Tripoli
Haifa
Tel Aviv-Yafo
IRAQ
Safi
MOROCCO
Touggourt
Benghazi
Al Bayda
Alexandria
P. Said
Jerusalem
Mogador
Marrakech
El Golea
Ghadames
JORDAN
Canary Is.
Cairo
Suez
LIBYA
SAUDI ARABIA
Tenerife
Las Palmas
Asyut
In Salah
FEZZAN
EGYPT
Villa Cisneros
Murzuq
Aswan
Medina
HEJAZ
MAURITANIA
SAHARA
Wadi Halfa
Red Sea
Jidda
C. Blanco
Port Sudan
Suakin
Mecca
Nouakchott
Dongola
Timbuktu
NIGER
CHAD
St. Louis
Dakar
MALI
Niger
Berber
Omdurman
C. Verde
SENEGAL
Niamey
Massawa
Khartoum
Aden
UPPER VOLTA
Sokoto
L. Chad
Banjul
Bamako
Kukawa
N'Djamena
SUDAN
Gondar
Bissagos Is.
Kano
Djibouti
Conakry
GUINEA
Kaduna
ETHIOPIA
Los Is.
SIERRA LEONE
IVORY COAST
GHANA
TOGO
BENIN
NIGERIA
CENTRAL AFRICAN REP.
Freetown
Lagos
Yola
Addis Ababa
Harar
Monrovia
LIBERIA
Abidjan
Porto Novo
AFRICA
P. Harcourt
Juba
C. Palmas
CAMEROUN
Bangui
L. Rudolf
Bioko
Yaounde
Zaire
Gulf of Guinea
Equat. Guin.
RIO MUNI
ZAIRE
KENYA
U.S.S.R.

jection

ATLANTIC OCEAN
ICELAND
Reykjavik
Hekla
Arctic Circle
Lofoten Is.
Faerøerne
Trondheim
NORWAY
SWEDEN
Shetland Is.
Orkney Is.
Rockall.
St. Kilda
C. Wrath
Bergen
Oslo
Stavanger
The Naze
GT BRITAIN & N. IRELAND
SCOTLAND
Edinburgh
Glasgow
REP. OF IRELAND
Belfast
Dublin
Cork
C. Clear
Irish Sea
NORTH SEA
Newcastle
Liverpool
Skagerrak
Kattegat
DENMARK
Göteborg
København
Kiel
BALTIC
Helgoland
St. Georges Ch.
Wales
ENGLAND
London
Portsmouth
Lands End
Amsterdam
Hamburg
Berlin
Gdansk
GERMANY
English Channel
Str. of Dover
C. la Hague
BELGIUM
Leipzig
Dresden
Köln
Bonn
Frankfurt
Brest
Paris
Strasbourg
Amiens
Nantes
Loire
Orleans
Bay of Biscay
FRANCE
Vichy
Genève
Lyon
St. Etienne
Bordeaux
Praha
München
Boden See
Wien
AUSTRIA
SWITZERLAND
Bern
The Alps
Trieste
Milano
Torino
Venezia
Bologna
Genova
C. Ortegal
C. Finisterre
La Coruña
Bayonne
Bilbao
Burgos
Douro
Porto
Pyrenees
Toulouse
Marseille
G. of Lions
G. of Genova
Lisboa
C. Roca
PORTUGAL
SPAIN
Zaragoza
Madrid
Tagus
Guadiana
Ebro R.
Barcelona
Valencia
Guadalquivir R.
C. St. Vincent
Cadiz
Sevilla
Granada
Strait of Gibraltar
Gibraltar
Tangier
Tarifa Pt.
Balearic Is.
Corsica
Elba
Sardinia
Firenze
ITALY
Roma
Napoli
Adriatic Sea
Zagreb
Zadar
Brindisi
Str. of Otranto
C. Leuca
Palermo
Sicily
C. Spartivento
C. Passero
MALTA
Alger
Algeria
Tunis
Morocco
AFRICA
MEDITERRANEAN
Tripoli
Benghazi
Statute Miles
0 100 200 300 400 500

C. Nordkyn
Kolguyev I.
Cheskaya B.
Pechenga
Murmansk
White Sea
Mezen
Timan Hills
Pechora
Ural Mounts
Ob
Tobolsk
Kem
Arkhangelsk
Oulu
Onega
Dvina
FINLAND
L. Onega
Sverdlovsk
Perm
Saimaa
L. Ladoga
Kronshtadt
Vologda
Leningrad
Rybinsk Res.
Volga
Tallinn
Chudskoye Oz. (L. Peipsi)
Gorkiy
Kazan
Kama
Valdai Hills
Riga
Moskva (Moscow)
U. S. S. R.
Ulyanovsk
Kuybyshev
Orenburg
Orsk
Kaunas
Vilnius
Minsk
Grodno
Mogilev
Tula
Ural
Saratov
Volga
Kursk
Aral Sea
Pripet R.
Kharkov
Don
Volgograd
Kiyev
Lvov
Dnieper
Donetsk
Astrakhan
Bug
Dniester
Taganrog
Rostov
Azov
Odessa
Prut
Iasi
Sea of Azov
Stavropol
CASPIAN SEA
ROMANIA
Galati
Crimea
Sevastopol
Caucasus Mts
Mt. Elbrus
Tbilisi
Baku
Bucuresti
BULGARIA
Varna
Sofiya
Balkan Mts
BLACK SEA
Sinop
Batumi
Kars
Yerevan
Bosporus
Trabzon
Istanbul
Sea of Marmara
Erzurum
Mt. Ararat
Tabriz
Tehran
Ankara
TURKEY
Dardanelles
Izmir
Aegean
Mosul
IRAN
Aleppo (Haleb)
Baghdad
Tigris
Rhodes
SYRIA
Euphrates
Damascus
IRAQ
Basra
Crete
CYPRUS
LEB.
Haifa
The Gulf
SEA
Port Said
ISRAEL
Jerusalem
JORDAN
SAUDI ARABIA
Alexandria
R. Nile
Suez Canal
Tobruk
40
60
70
80
50
40
30
50

# UNITED KINGDOM

# NORTHERN ENGLAND

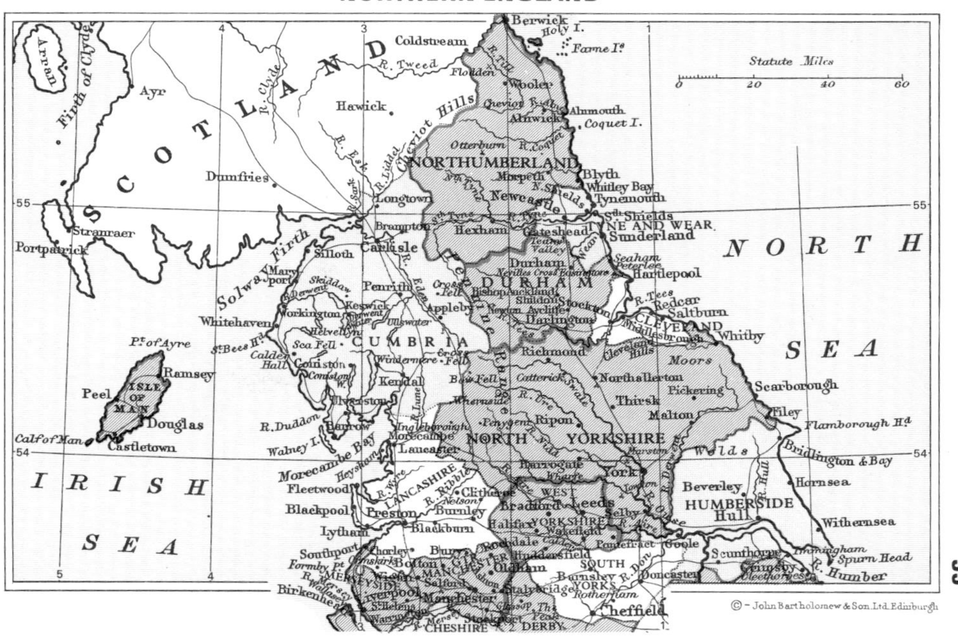

© – John Bartholomew & Son Ltd. Edinburgh

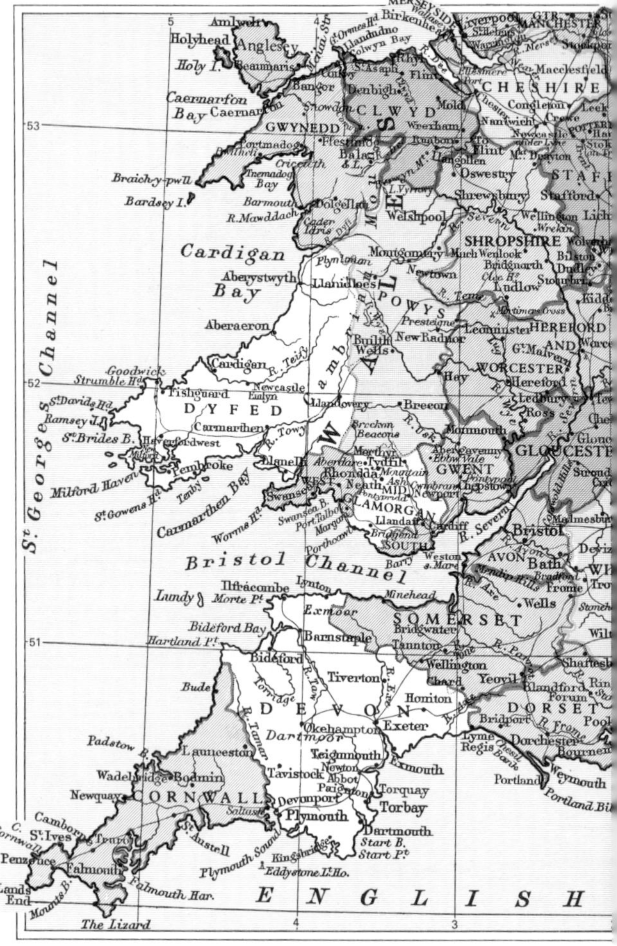
Holyhead
Anglesey
Holy I.
Beaumaris
Caernarfon Bay
Caernarfon
GWYNEDD
Portmadoc
Pwllheli
Criccieth
Tremadog Bay
Braich-y-pwll
Bardsey I.
Barmouth
R. Mawddach
Dolgellau
Cader Idris
Llandudno
Colwyn Bay
Conwy
Bangor
Snowdon
St. Asaph
Rhyl
Flint
Denbigh
CLWYD
Mold
Wrexham
Ruabon
Llangollen
Ffestiniog
Bala
L. Vyrnwy
Welshpool
Birkenhead
MERSEYSIDE
Liverpool
MANCHESTER
St. Helens
Warrington
Stockport
Macclesfield
Ellesmere Port
CHESHIRE
Chester
Congleton
Nantwich
Crewe
Newcastle under Lyme
Mt. Drayton
Oswestry
Shrewsbury
Stafford
Wellington
Wrekin
SHROPSHIRE
Much Wenlock
Bridgnorth
Bilston
Dudley
Clee Hs.
Ludlow
Montgomery
Newtown
Cardigan Bay
Plynlimon
Aberystwyth
Llanidloes
POWYS
Presteigne
New Radnor
Builth Wells
Aberaeron
Cardigan
R. Teify
Leominster
HEREFORD AND WORCESTER
Gt. Malvern
Hereford
Ledbury
Ross
Hay
Goodwick
Strumble Hd.
Fishguard
Newcastle Emlyn
DYFED
Llandovery
Brecon
Brecon Beacons
St. Davids Hd.
Ramsey I.
St. Brides B.
Haverfordwest
Carmarthen
R. Towy
Milford Haven
Pembroke
Tenby
St. Gowens Hd.
Carmarthen Bay
Llanelli
Swansea
Merthyr Tydfil
Aberdare
Rhondda
Neath
WEST
MID
GLAMORGAN
SOUTH
Pontypridd
Abergavenny
Ebbw Vale
GWENT
Monmouth
Pontypool
Newport
Chepstow
Cardiff
Llandaff
Bridgend
Port Talbot
Swansea B.
Worms Hd.
Porthcawl
Barry
St. George's Channel
Bristol Channel
R. Severn
Bristol
AVON
Bath
Weston s. Mare
GLOUCESTER
Malmesbury
Lundy
Morte Pt.
Ilfracombe
Lynton
Minehead
Exmoor
Bideford Bay
Barnstaple
SOMERSET
Bridgwater
Taunton
Wells
Frome
Hartland Pt.
Bideford
Tiverton
Wellington
Chard
Yeovil
Bude
Torridge
R. Taw
R. Exe
Honiton
DEVON
DORSET
Blandford Forum
Bridport
Dorchester
Lyme Regis
Chesil Bank
Weymouth
Portland
Portland Bill
Okehampton
Exeter
Dartmoor
R. Tamar
Padstow B.
Launceston
Teignmouth
Exmouth
Tavistock
Newton Abbot
Wadebridge
Bodmin
Paignton
Torquay
Newquay
CORNWALL
Devonport
Torbay
Saltash
Plymouth
Dartmouth
Start B.
Start Pt.
C. Cornwall
Camborne
St. Ives
Truro
St. Austell
Plymouth Sound
Kingsbridge
Penzance
Falmouth
Eddystone Lt. Ho.
Lands End
Mounts B.
Falmouth Har.
The Lizard
ENGLISH
53
52
51
5
4
3

Statute Miles
LINCOLN
NORFOLK
SUFFOLK
CAMBRIDGE
ESSEX
KENT
SURREY
HAMPSHIRE
BERKSHIRE
OXFORD
BEDFORD
HERTFORD
NORTHAMPTON
LEICESTER
WEST SUSSEX
EAST SUSSEX
GREATER LONDON
ISLE OF WIGHT
The Wash
Mouth of the Thames
Strait of Dover
CHANNEL
FRANCE

# SCOTLAND

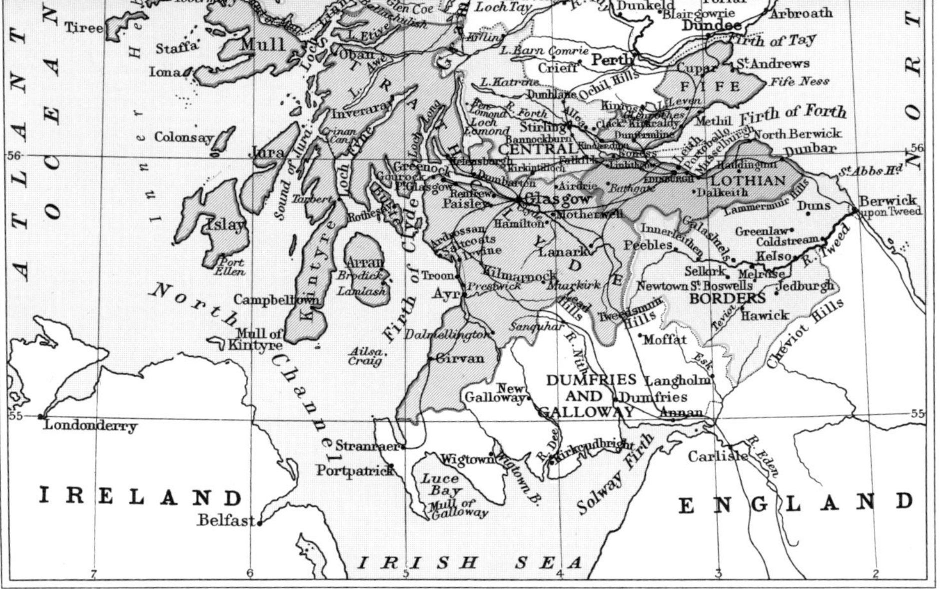
ATLANTIC OCEAN
NORTH
Inner Hebrides
Tiree
Staffa
Iona
Mull
Colonsay
Jura
Islay
Port Ellen
Sound of Jura
Oban
L. Etive
Glen Coe
Loch Tay
Killin
Dunkeld
Blairgowrie
Dundee
Arbroath
Firth of Tay
Perth
Comrie
Crieff
Ochil Hills
St. Andrews
Fife Ness
Cupar
FIFE
L. Leven
Kinross
Methil
Kirkcaldy
Dunfermline
Firth of Forth
North Berwick
Dunbar
St. Abbs Hd.
L. Katrine
Dunblane
Alloa
Stirling
Bannockburn
CENTRAL
Loch Lomond
Ben Lomond
R. Forth
Inveraray
L. Awe
STRATHCLYDE
Crinan Can.
Loch Fyne
Loch Long
Tarbert
Kintyre
Campbeltown
Mull of Kintyre
Rothesay
Bute
Greenock
Gourock
Pt. Glasgow
Helensburgh
Dumbarton
Kirkintilloch
Renfrew
Paisley
Glasgow
Airdrie
Bathgate
Motherwell
Hamilton
Ardrossan
Saltcoats
Irvine
Kilmarnock
Troon
Prestwick
Ayr
Muirkirk
Lanark
Arran
Brodick
Lamlash
Firth of Clyde
Ailsa Craig
Dalmellington
Girvan
Sanquhar
Lead Hills
Tweedsmuir Hills
Leith
Portobello
Musselburgh
Haddington
Edinburgh
LOTHIAN
Dalkeith
Lammermuir Hills
Duns
Berwick upon Tweed
Greenlaw
Coldstream
Kelso
R. Tweed
Galashiels
Innerleithen
Peebles
Selkirk
Melrose
Newtown St. Boswells
Jedburgh
BORDERS
Teviot
Hawick
Cheviot Hills
Moffat
Esk
Langholm
R. Nith
DUMFRIES AND GALLOWAY
Dumfries
Annan
New Galloway
R. Dee
Kirkcudbright
Wigtown
Wigtown B.
Luce Bay
Mull of Galloway
Stranraer
Portpatrick
Solway Firth
Carlisle
R. Eden
ENGLAND
North Channel
Londonderry
IRELAND
Belfast
IRISH SEA
56
55
7
6
5
4
3
2

# IRELAND

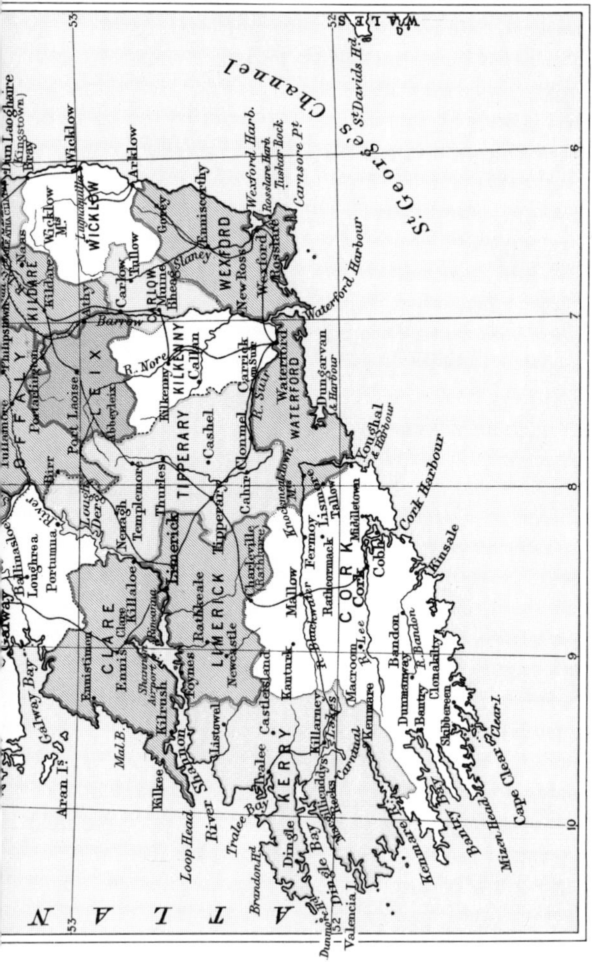
St George's Channel
St Davids Hd.
WALES
Dun Laoghaire (Kingstown)
Bray
Wicklow
Arklow
WICKLOW
Wicklow Mts.
Lugnaquilla
Naas
KILDARE
Kildare
Athy
Carlow
Tullow
Muine Bheag
Gorey
Enniscorthy
WEXFORD
New Ross
Wexford
Rosslare
Slaney
Barrow
Wexford Harb.
Rosslare Harb.
Tuskar Rock
Carnsore Pt.
Waterford Harbour
Philipstown
Tullamore
OFFALY
Portarlington
Port Laoise
LEIX
Abbeyleix
Birr
R. Nore
KILKENNY
Kilkenny
Callan
TIPPERARY
Cashel
Carrick on Suir
R. Suir
Clonmel
WATERFORD
Waterford
Dungarvan & Harbour
Youghal & Harbour
Cork Harbour
Kinsale
Thurles
Templemore
Nenagh
Lough Derg
Limerick
Tipperary
Cahir
Knockmealdown Mts.
Lismore
Tallow
Fermoy
Mitchelstown
Middleton
Cobh
Rathcormack
Charleville (Rathluirc)
Mallow
R. Blackwater
CORK
Cork
R. Lee
Macroom
Bandon
R. Bandon
Dunmanway
Clonakilty
Bantry
Skibbereen
Clear I.
Cape Clear
Mizen Head
Bantry Bay
Kenmare R.
Kenmare
Ballinasloe
Loughrea
Portumna
River Shannon
Galway
Galway Bay
Aran Is.
CLARE
Ennis
Killaloe
Ennistimon
Kilrush
Kilkee
Shannon Airport
Foynes
LIMERICK
Rathkeale
Newcastle
Listowel
Mal B.
Loop Head
Tralee Bay
Tralee
KERRY
Castleisland
Kanturk
Killarney
Lakes
Carrantual
Macgillicuddys Reeks
Dingle
Dingle Bay
Brandon Hd.
Dunmore Hd.
Valencia I.
ATLANTIC
53
52
6
7
8
9
10

# SCANDINAVIA

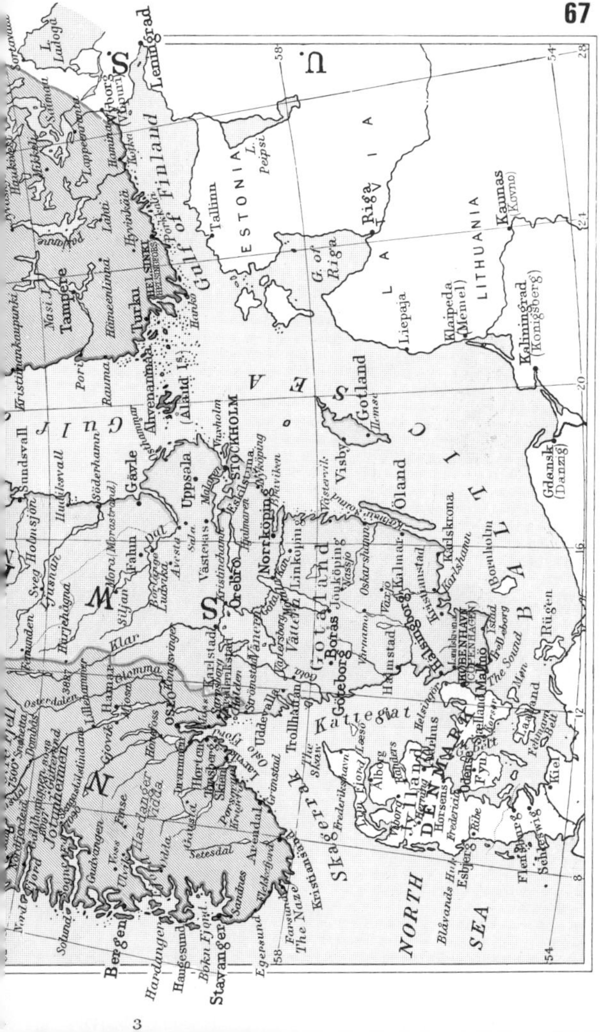

© – John Bartholomew & Son Ltd Edinburgh

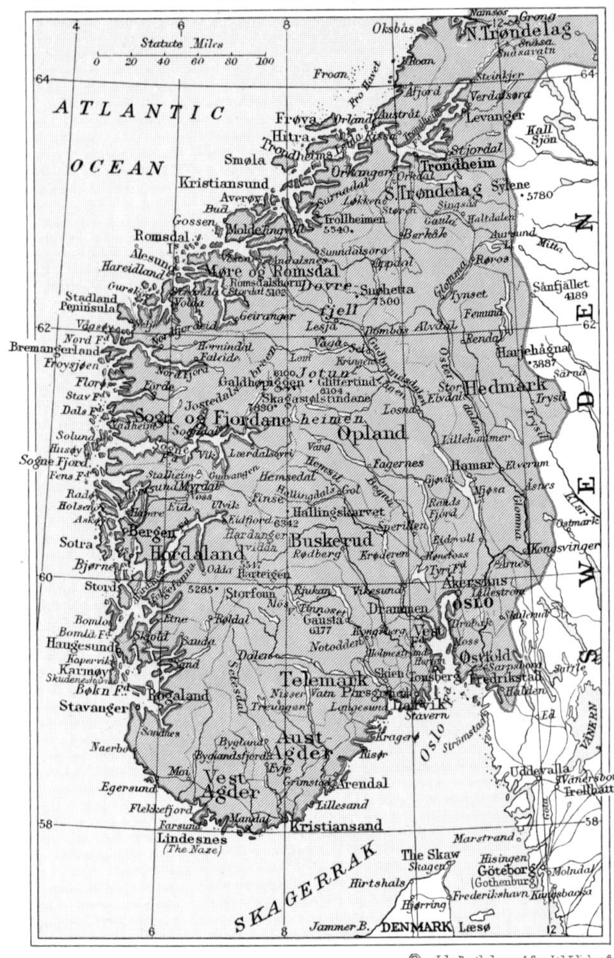
Statute Miles
0 20 40 60 80 100
ATLANTIC
OCEAN
N.Trøndelag
S.Trøndelag
Trondheim
Kristiansund
Smøla
Hitra
Frøya
Romsdal
Ålesund
Møre og Romsdal
Dovre fjell
Snøhetta 7500
Sogn og Fjordane
Jotun heimen
Galdhøpiggen
Opland
Hedmark
Hamar
Lillehammer
Bergen
Hordaland
Buskerud
Hardanger vidda
Drammen
OSLO
Akershus
Østfold
Fredrikstad
Telemark
Stavanger
Rogaland
Aust Agder
Vest Agder
Arendal
Kristiansand
Lindesnes
(The Naze)
SKAGERRAK
The Skaw
Skagen
Hirtshals
Hjørring
Frederikshavn
DENMARK
Læsø
Göteborg
(Gothenburg)
Uddevalla
SWEDEN
Oslo Fd.

Statute Miles
0 20 40 60
NORWAY
Kragerø
Risør
Tvedestrand
Evje
Arendal
Tromøy
Otra
Grimstad
Lillesand
Mandal
Kristiansand
Stjernoy
SKAGERRAK
Strömstad
Ed
Mellerud
VÄNERN
Lidköping
Uddevalla
Vänersborg
Skara
Lysekil
Orust
Trollhättan
Göta
Herrljunga
Tjörn
Alingsås
Marstrand
Kungalv
The Skaw
Skagen
Göteborg
(Gothenburg)
Borås
Hirtshals
Styrsö
Ugerby
Hjørring
Hirsholmene
Kungsbacka
Svendjunga
Lokken
Vendsyssel
Frederikshavn
SWEDEN
Jammer Bay
Læsø
Sæby
Læsø Rende
Hanstholm
Nørresundby
Åby
Kungsbacka F.
Ätran
Varberg
Hals
Thisted
Løgstør
Alborg
Lim Fjord
Falkenberg
Torup
Lim Fd
Aars
KATTEGAT
Agger
Nykøbing
Hadsund
Mariager Fd
Halmstad
Glyngøre
Lemvig
Skive
Hobro
Randers Fd
Anholt
Laholm B.
Struer
Viborg
Randers
Torekov
Lagan
Langå
Fornæs
Grenå
JYLLAND
JUTLAND
Skälder Bay
Vemb
Holstebro
Kullen Lt
Ängelholm
Rönde
Höganäs
Ringkøbing
Herning
Silkeborg
Ebeltoft
Hesselø
Gilleleje
Ringkøbing Fjord
Himmel B.
482
Århus
Hjelm
Helsingør
Hälsingborg
Skern
Skanderborg
Ise
Landskrona
Tarm
Brande
Gudenå
Tovs
Tunø
Samsø
Sejerø
Frederikssund
Hillerød
Ven
The Sound
Give
Horsens
Endelave
Samsø Belt
Zyngby
Grindsted
Vejle
Kalundborg
Holbæk
KØBENHAVN
(COPENHAGEN)
Varde
Bogense
Roskilde
Kastrup
Saltholm
Blåvands Huk
Amager
Malmö
Esbjerg
Fredericia
Store Belt
Brammunge
Kolding
Middelfart
SJÆLLAND
(ZEALAND)
Køge B.
Skanör
Fanø
Vamdrup
Odense
Slagelse
Soro
Ringsted
Ribe
Nyborg
Vojens
FYN
(FUNEN)
Falsterbo
Trelleborg
Östratorp
Haderslev
Assens
Korsör
Næstved
Mandø
Rømø
Lit Belt
Faborg
Svendborg
Skælskør
Fakse B.
Åbenrå
Præstø
Vordingborg
Tönder
Als
Tåsinge
Langeland
Orehoved
Stege
Møn
Sylt
Dybbøl
Sønderborg
Nakskov
Stubbekøbing
Westerland
Flensburg
Ærø
Maribo
Lolland
(Laaland)
Nykøbing
Falster
N. Frisian Islands
Alsen
Rødby
Rødbyhavn
Gedser
Husum
Schlei
Longeland Belt
Friedrichsort
Fehmarn Belt
Schleswig
Kiel Bay
Puttgarden
Fehmarn
Warnemünde
Tönning
Kiel
Grossenbrode
Lübeck B.
Rendsburg
Helgoland
Kanal
Heide
Neustadt
Stralsund
Neumünster
Eutin
Rostock
Itzehoe
WEST
Hammeren Lt
Sandvig
Christiansø Lt
Neuwerk
Elbe
Wismar
BORNHOLM
(to Denmark)
Glückstadt
Lübeck
Cuxhaven
GERMANY
Rønne
Neksø
HAMBURG
EAST
same scale
8
10
12
54
56
58

# NETHERLANDS, BELGIUM, LUXEMBOURG

BELGIUM
GERMANY
FRANCE
Rhein
Moselle
Wuppertal
Dusseldorf
Krefeld
Mönchen-Gladbach
Neuss
Köln
(Cologne)
BONN
Trier
Roer
Venlo
Roermond
Weert
Sittard
Heerlen
Maastricht
Aachen
Eupen
Verviers
Malmedy
St Vith
Herve
Spa
Amblève
LIÈGE
Liège
Seraing
Huy
LIMBURG
Maaseik
Genck
Hasselt
Bilzen
Tongeren
St Truiden
LUXEMBOURG
Luxembourg
Clervaux
Diekirch
Ettelbruck
Esch
Cruchten
Our
Sauer
Houffalize
Bastogne
St Hubert
Neufchâteau
Arlon
Virton
Chiny
Semois
Bouillon
Sedan
Meuse
Marche
Rochefort
Lesse
NAMUR
Namur
Dinant
Givet
Philippeville
Marienbourg
Couvin
Chimay
Thuin
Chatelet
Charleroi
Nivelles
Wavre
BRABANT
Leuven
(Louvain)
Tienen
Diest
Geel
Turnhout
ANTWERPEN
Antwerpen
(Anvers)
Lier
Nete
Mechelen
(Malines)
Dyle
BRUXELLES
BRUSSEL
Halle
Soignies
HAINAUT
Mons
Sambre
Valenciennes
Cambrai
Douai
Arras
Oise
Lille
Roubaix
Tourcoing
Tournai
Leuze
Ath
Ronse
(Renaix)
Oudenaarde
(Audenarde)
Kortrijk
(Courtrai)
Escaut
Menen
Ieper
(Ypres)
Poperinge
Roeselare
Tielt
Torhout
Diksmuide
Veurne
(Furnes)
Nieuwpoort
Oostende
(Ostende)
Blankenberge
Zeebrugge
Brugge
(Bruges)
Eeklo
Gent
(Gand)
Schelde
Dendermonde
Aalst
St Niklaas
Lokeren
Sas van Gent
Terneuzen
WEST
OOST
VLAANDEREN

ENGLAND
Dover
Calais
Boulogne
Montreuil
St Valery
Dieppe
Fécamp
Rouen
Elbeuf
Evreux
Mantes
Versailles
Chartres
Portsmouth
Plymouth
Falmouth
Lands End
Isles of Scilly
ENGLISH CHANNEL
C. de la Hague
Alderney
Cherbourg
Le Havre
Channel Islands
Guernsey
Sark
Jersey
Caen
St Lo
Granville
Normandy
Argentan
Pt de Talbert
St Malo
Dinard
St Servan
Avranches
I. de Ouessant (Ushant I.)
Brest
Morlaix
St Brieuc
Pt St Mathieu
Fougeres
Mayenne
Alençon
Brittany
Pontivy
Rennes
I. de Sein
Quimper
Maine
Laval
Le Mans
Lorient
Vannes
Châteaubriant
Vilaine
Angers
Loir
Tours
Loire
Blois
Belle Ile
Anjou
St Nazaire
R. Loire
Nantes
Saumur
Chinon
I. Noirmoutier
Châtellerault
I. d'Yeu
Poitou
La Roche s-Yon
Poitiers
Les Sables d'Olonne
Vienne
I. de Ré
Niort
Civray
La Rochelle
I. d'Oléron
Rochefort
Angoumois
St Junien
Limousin
Saintes
Royan
Cognac
Angoulême
Saintonge
BAY OF BISCAY
Pauillac
Perigueux
Tulle
Blaye
Brive
Bordeaux
Libourne
Dordogne
Bergerac
Statute Miles
0
50
100
Arcachon
Guyenne
Villeneuve s-Lot
Garonne
Landes
Bazas
Cahors
Agen
Mont de Marsan
Gascony
Dax
Bayonne
Biarritz
San Sebastian
Santander
Orthez
Adour
Auch
Muret
Bilbao
Pau
Oloron
Tarbes
Lourdes
Carcassonne
Garonne
Foix
St Girons
Pyrenees
Ebro
Pamplona
Luz
Perdido
Maladeta
Andorra
SPAIN
50
48
46
44
6
4
2
0

BELGIUM
BRUXELLES
Liège
BONN
Koblenz
Rhein (Rhine)
WEST GERMANY
Frankfurt am M
Main
Tourcoing
Roubaix
Lille
Douai
Mons
Valenciennes
Cambrai
St Quentin
Mézières
Sedan
Laon
Oise
Luxembourg
Mannheim
Thionville
R. Meuse
Verdun
Reims
Soissons
Saarbrücken
Karlsruhe
Stuttgart
Metz
Sarreguemines
Epernay
Denis
Châlons sur Marne
Bar le Duc
Nancy
Saverne
Strasbourg
PARIS
Lunéville
Ulm
Melun
Marne
Lorraine
Alsace
Champagne
Troyes
Sens
Joigny
Chaumont
Epinal
Colmar
Remiremont
Boden See (L. of Constance)
Montargis
Seine
Langres
Mulhouse
Auxerre
Belfort
Rhein
Zürich
Saône
Basel
Dijon
Aare
Clamecy
Besançon
Biel
Luzern
Loire
Nivernais
Burgundy
Comté
Franche
Neuchâtel
Salins
BERN
Nevers
Le Creusot
Lons-le-Saunier
SWITZERLAND
Moulins
Chalon sur Saône
R. Ain
Lausanne
L. Leman (L of Geneva)
Bourbonnais
Alps
Mâcon
Genève (Geneva)
R. Rhône
Bourg
Lugano
Vichy
Roanne
Mte Rosa
Annecy
Mont Blanc
Lyonnais
Lyon (Lyons)
Aix les Bains
Milano
Vienne
Chambéry
Issoire
Voiron
Mt Cenis
St Etienne
Po
Isère
Torino
Grenoble
ITALY
Le Puy
Mt Mezenc
Dauphiné
Briançon
Valence
Genova (Genoa)
Privas
Mt Viso
Gap
Embrun
Mende
Montelimar
Cuneo
Gulf of Genoa
Rhône
Florac
Durance
Orange
Digne
Millau
Alès
Avignon
Tarn
Nîmes
Provence
Nice
Monte Carlo
Monaco
Montpellier
Arles
Aix
Draguignan
Marseille (Marseilles)
Cannes
Côte d'Azur
Béziers
Sète
St Tropez
Toulon
Gulf of Lions
Aude
Narbonne
Is d'Hyères
MEDITERRANEAN SEA
Port Vendres
Bastia
Mt Cinto
Mte Rotondo
CORSICA (CORSE)
Ajaccio
Sartene
Bonifacio

C. Ortegal
BAY OF
La Coruna (Corunna)
El Ferrol del Caudillo
Villalba
Ribadeo
Gijon
Villaviciosa
Santander
Tineo
Oviedo
Llanes
Torrelavega
Portugalete
Carballo
Asturias
C. Finisterre
Muros
Santiago
Lugo
Cangas de Tineo
Reinosa
Galicia
Sarria
Cantabrian Mts
La Estrada
Monforte de Lemos
Leon
Herrera de Pisuerga
R. Arosa
Pontevedra
Astorga
Burgo
Vigo
Orense
Sahagun
Tuy
Minho
Benavente
Esla
Viana do Castelo
Entre Minho e Douro
Medina de Rioseco
Palencia
Braga
Tras os Montes
Braganca
Valladolid
Aranda
Porto (Oporto)
Vila Real
Zamora
Douro
Lamego
Medina del Campo
Sepulveda
R. Tormes
Salamanca
Ovar
Pinhel
Segovia
Aveiro
Viseu
Sierra de Guadarrama
Beira
Guarda
Ciudad Rodrigo
Coimbra
Sa da Estrela
Avila
MADRID
Figueira da Foz
Sa de Gata
Bejar
Sa de Gredos
Getafe
SPAIN
PORTUGAL
Plasencia
Aranjuez
Leiria
Castelo Branco
Talavera de la Reina
Toledo
Tomar
Tejo (Tagus)
Tajo (Tagus)
Arzobispo
Mts of Toledo
C. Carvoeiro
Abrantes
Caceres
Trujillo
Madridejos
Santarem
Valencia de Alcantara
Torres Vedras
Portalegre
R. Zancara
LISBOA (LISBON)
Sintra
Estremoz
Elvas
Merida
Guadiana
Belem
Setubal
Badajoz
Don Benito
Olivenza
Evora
Puertollano
Valdepe
Zafra
Pozoblanco
Extremadura
Alentejo
Jerez de los Caballeros
Sierra Morena
Belmez
Linares
Moura
C. Sines
Sines
Beja
Andujar
Córdoba
Minas de Rio Tinto
Jaén
Odemira
Ourique
Valverde
Guadalquivir
Sa de Monchique
Ecija
Andalusia
Alcala la Real
Aljezur
Algarve
Huelva
Sevilla (Seville)
Lucena
C. St Vincent
Loule
Osuna
Genil
Utrera
Mulhaçen
Lagos
Faro
Tavira
Ayamonte
Antequera
Granada
Sanlucar de Barrameda
Velez Malaga
Jerez de la Frontera
Puerto de Sta Maria
Torremolinos
Cadiz
San Fernando
Torrox
Motril
Malaga
Medina Sidonia
Marbella
Estepona
La Linea
C. Trafalgar
Gibraltar (U.K.)
Tarifa
Algeciras
Strait of Gibraltar
Tanger (Tangier)
Ceuta (Sp)
MOROCCO
ATLANTIC OCEAN
Statute Miles
0
50
100
10
8
6
4
42
40
38
36

FRANCE
Bayonne
Adour
Dax
Toulouse
Carcassonne
Gulf of Lions
Irun
Tolosa
Pamplona
Navarra
Pyrenees
Perpignan
Mt. Perdido
Mt. Maladeta
Andorra
Port Bou
C. Creus
Jaca
Tafalla
Seo de Urgel
Figueras
Rosas
Huesca
Barbastro
Berga
Gerona
Tudela
Vich
Balaguer
Manresa
Blanes
Ebro
Segre
Lerida
Igualada
Mataro
Zaragoza (Saragossa)
Catalonia
Sabadell
Badalona
Barcelona
Calatayud
Aragon
Reus
Tarragona
Alcañiz
Molina
Tajo (Tagus)
Montalban
Tortosa
R. Ebro
Morella
Albarracin
Vinaroz
Teruel
Balearic Isles
Menorca (Minorca)
Alcala
Cuenca
Castellon de la Plana
Pollensa
Alcudia
Mahon
Burriana
Palma
Manacor
Mallorca (Majorca)
Sagunto
Utiel
Valencia
Requena
Ibiza (Iviza)
Cabrera
La Roda
Cullera
Jucar
Alcira
Albacete
Almansa
Jativa
Denia
Ibiza
C. Nao
Formentera
Villena
Murcia
Alcoy
Hellin
Elche
Alicante
Segura
Cieza
Orihuela
Murcia
Totana
Mar Menor
C. de Palos
Lorca
La Union
Cartagena
Baza
Aguilas
Cuevas de Vera
Sorbas
Dellys
Alger (Algiers)
Almeria
C. Gata
MEDITERRANEAN SEA
Wadi Sheliff
AFRICA
Oran

# SWITZERLAND

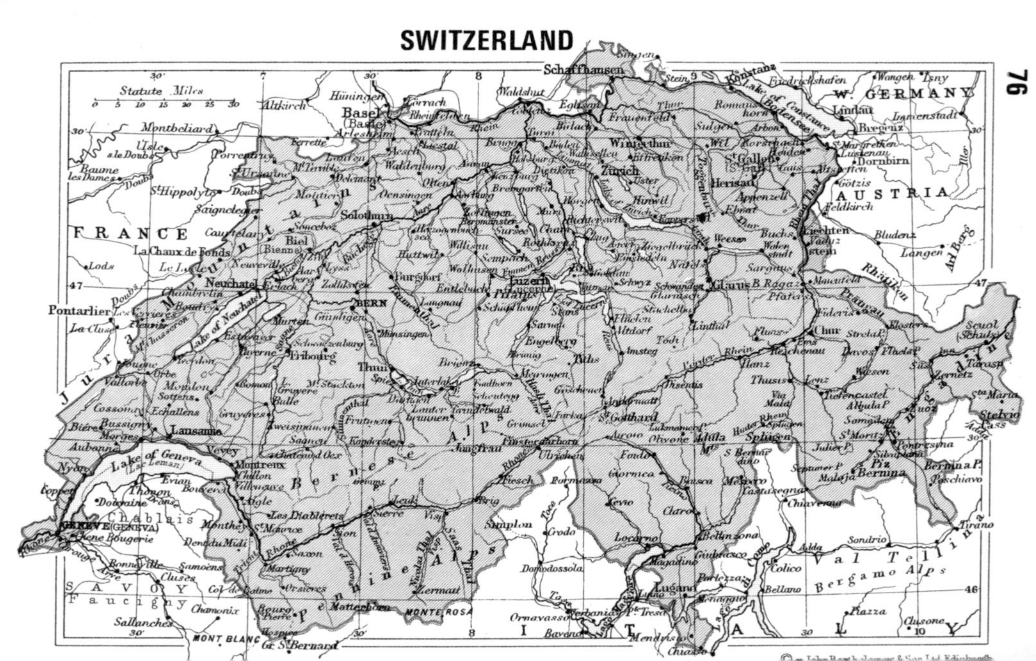

Münster
Bocholt
Nijmegen
Borken
Warendorf
Gütersloh
Detmold
Holzminden
Seesen
NIEDER
Einbeck
Clausthal
NORDRHEIN-
WESTFALEN
Rhein
Kleve
Wesel
Lippe
Hamm
Lippstadt
Höxter
Karlshafen
Northeim
Maas
Paderborn
Gelsenkirchen
Oberhausen
Essen
Dortmund
Soest
Warburg
SACHSEN
Geldern
Göttingen
Duisburg
Bochum
Ruhr
Warstein
Diemel
Worbis
Venlo
Krefeld
Mulheim
Witten
Arnsberg
Arolsen
Hann Münden
Iserlohn
Hagen
Düsseldorf
Wuppertal
Korbach
Kassel
M. Gladbach
Rheydt
Neuss
Remscheid
Sauerland
Eschwege
Solingen
Rothaar G.
Fritzlar
Eder
Fulda
Rotenburg
Olpe
KÖLN
(COLOGNE)
Mulheim
Kalk
Frankenberg
Jülich
Siegen
HESSEN
Hersfeld
Düren
Siegburg
Vacha
Aachen
Aix-la-Chapelle
BONN
Beuel
Marburg
Alsfeld
Bad Godesberg
Linz
Giessen
Vogels
Berg
Fulda
Ahrweiler
E. GERMANY
Gemünd
Westerwald
Wetzlar
Wetter
Malmedy
Neuwied
Schlüchtern
St Vith
Koblenz
Ems
Lahn
Bad Nauheim
Nidda
Rhön Geb.
R. Saale
Limburg
Nassau
Homburg
Friedberg
Bad Kissingen
Prum
Eifel
Kinzig
Cochem
St Goar
Hunsruck
Wiesbaden
Taunus
Hanau
Offenbach
Spessart
Schweinfurt
Zell
Rheingau
Bingen
FRANKFURT AM M.
Gemünden
RHEINLAND
Bitburg
Wittlich
Bernkastel
Mainz
Aschaffenburg
Mosel
Kreuznach
Darmstadt
Würzburg
Main
LUXEMBOURG
Trier
(Treves)
Idarwald
Alzey
Meldbokus
PFALZ
Alsenz
Worms
Bensheim
Wertheim
BAYERN
Luxembourg
Saarburg
Birkenfeld
Odenwald
Tauber
Ludwigshafen
Mannheim
Katzenbuckel
S. Wendel
Kaiserslautern
Hardt Geb.
Eberbach
Merzig
Saar
Neckar
SAAR
Heidelberg
Saarlouis
Neunkirchen
Homburg
Künzelsau
Speyer
Kocher R.
Jagst
Saarbrücken
Zweibrücken
GERMANY
Landau
Metz
Pirmasens
Germersheim
Bruchsal
Schwäbisch Hall
LORRAINE
Karlsruhe
Heilbronn
Pforzheim
Enz R.
Ludwigsburg
BADEN
Gmünd
Rastatt
Wildbad
Esslingen
Göppingen
Nancy
Baden-Baden
STUTTGART
Moselle
Meurthe
STRASBOURG
Kehl
WÜRTTEMBERG
Tübingen
Reutlingen
Swabian Alps
Offenburg
Freudenstadt
Hechingen
Ulm
Hohenzollern
Vosges Mts
ALSACE
Schwarzwald
St Dié
Ebingen
Danube
Iller R.
Epinal
Colmar
Waldkirch
Villingen
Sigmaringen
Biberach
FRANCE
Ill
Breisach
Freiburg
Tuttlingen
Waldsee
Feld Berg
Neustadt
Stockach
Zell
Singen
Überlingen
Ravensburg
Mulhouse
Badenweiler
Schaffhausen
Friedrichshafen
Isny
Lörrach
Waldshut
Bodensee
Konstanz
Lindau
Statute Miles
0
20
40
60
Basel
Rhein
SWITZERLAND
AUSTRIA
50
48
6
8
10

Statute Miles
0 20 40 60 100
NORTH SEA
Helgoland
West & East Frisian Is.
Nh. Frisian Is.
Westerland
Flensburg
Schleswig
Kiel B.
Fehmarn
Kiel
Holstein
Lübeck B.
Stralsund
Warnemünde
Greifswald
Rostock
Wismar
Lübeck
Cuxhaven
Wilhelmshaven
Bremerhaven
Hamburg
Altona
Wilhelmsburg
Harburg
Schwerin
Emden
Groningen
Leeuwarden
Oldenburg
Bremen
Lüneburg
Elbe
Weser
Niedersachsen
Verden
Celle
Wittenberge
Neustrelitz
Fehrbellin
Havel
EAST
Spandau
NETHERLANDS
AMSTERDAM
Zwolle
Utrecht
Enschede
Zutphen
Arnhem
R. Ems
Lingen
Osnabrück
Minden
Hannover
Aller
Wolfburg
Braunschweig
(Brunswick)
Brandenburg
Potsdam
Magdeburg
Hildesheim
Bielefeld
Nordrhein
Münster
Salzgitter
WEST
Westfalen
Wesel
Gelsenkirchen
Hamm
Harz Mts
Dessau
Wittenberg
GERMANY
Krefeld
Mönchengladbach
Essen
Dortmund
Duisburg
Wuppertal
Ruhr
Göttingen
Nordhausen
Halle
Kassel
Mühlhausen
Köln
Cologne
Düsseldorf
GERMANY
Leipzig
Maas
Maastricht
Aachen
BONN
Siegen
Hessen
Eisenach
Erfurt
Weimar
Gotha
Altenburg
Gera
Karl-Marx-Stadt
(Chemnitz)
Marburg
Taufstein Mt.
Giessen
Fulda
Meiningen
Zwickau
Plauen
Koblenz
Rheinland
Rhein
Coburg
Thüringer Wald
Erz Geb.
Karlovy Vary
(Karlsbad)
BELGIUM
Wiesbaden
Frankfurt am M.
Hanau
Bingen
Mosel
Mainz
Offenbach
Darmstadt
Bamberg
Schweinfurt
Schnee Berg
Fichtel Geb.
Trier
Luxembourg
Pfalz
Worms
Würzburg
Main
Bayreuth
Böhmer Wald
Plzen (Pilsen)
Saarland
Kaiserslautern
Ludwigshafen
Mannheim
Saarbrücken
Speyer
Rothenburg
Nürnberg
Fürth
Metz
LORRAINE
Heidelberg
Ansbach
Bayern
Haguenau
Heilbronn
Karlsruhe
Regensburg
Nancy
Baden-Baden
Stuttgart
Nördlingen
Strasbourg
Baden-
Donau
(Danube)
Ingolstadt
Straubing
Bayrischer W.
Kehl
Tübingen
Württemberg
Ulm
Augsburg
Isar
Passau
Landshut
Vosges Mts.
ALSACE
Schwarzwald
Colmar
Danube
München
(Munich)
FRANCE
Sigmaringen
Freiburg
Tuttlingen
Inn
Wels
Mulhouse
Feld B.
Schaffhausen
Bodensee
(L. Constance)
Rosenheim
Traunstein
Salzburg
Berchtesgaden
Doubs
Basel
Rhein
Konstanz
Kempten
Oberammergau
Aare
Zurich
Dornbirn
Kufstein
Schwaz
Neuchâtel
Luzern
Liechtenstein
Landeck
Innsbruck
Zell
BERN
Glarus
Gr. Glockner
Tamsweg
SWITZERLAND
Chur
Brenner Pass
Drava
Villach
6
10
12
54
52

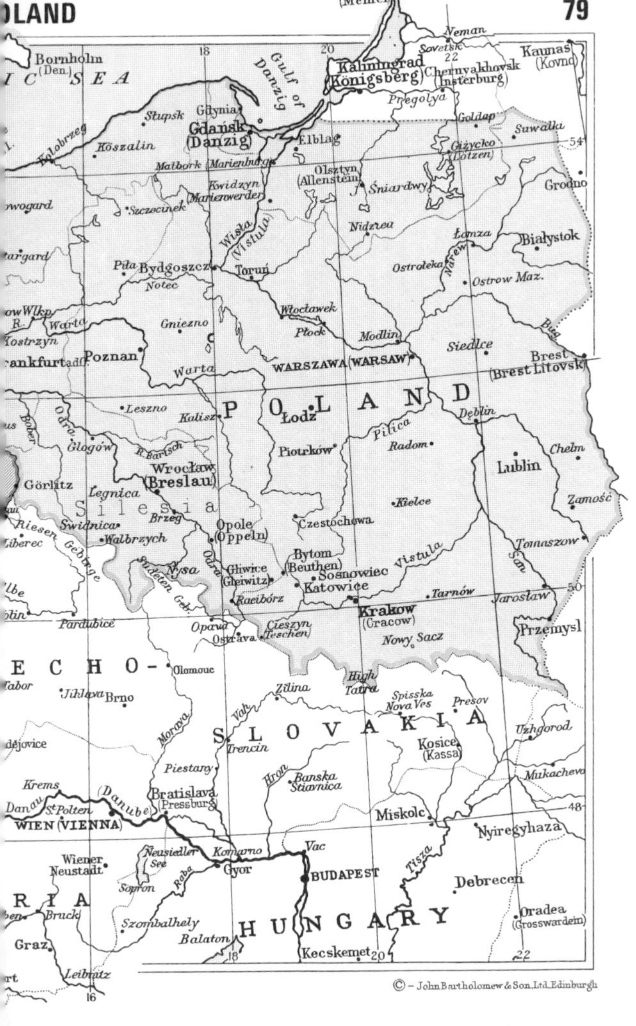
Memel
Neman
Sovetsk
Kaunas (Kovno)
Bornholm (Den.)
SEA
Gulf of Danzig
Kaliningrad Königsberg
Chernyakhovsk (Insterburg)
Pregolya
Goldap
Suwałki
Słupsk
Gdynia
Gdańsk (Danzig)
Elbląg
Kołobrzeg
Koszalin
Giżycko (Lötzen)
Malbork (Marienburg)
Olsztyn (Allenstein)
Grodno
Kwidzyn (Marienwerder)
Śniardwy
Szczecinek
Nidzica
Wisła (Vistula)
Łomża
Białystok
Piła
Bydgoszcz
Toruń
Ostrołęka
Narew
Ostrow Maz.
Notec
Włocławek
Płock
Modlin
Gniezno
Warta
Siedlce
Bug
Poznan
Frankfurt a.d.O.
Kostrzyn
WARSZAWA (WARSAW)
Brest (Brest Litovsk)
POLAND
Leszno
Kalisz
Łodz
Odra
Bober
Pilica
Dęblin
Głogów
R. Barisch
Piotrków
Radom
Chełm
Wrocław (Breslau)
Lublin
Görlitz
Legnica
Kielce
Zamość
Silesia
Brzeg
Świdnica
Opole (Oppeln)
Częstochowa
Riesen Gebirge
Wałbrzych
Liberec
Tomaszow
Bytom (Beuthen)
Nysa
Gliwice (Gleiwitz)
Sosnowiec
Vistula
San
Sudeten Geb.
Katowice
Raciborz
Tarnów
Jarosław
Krakow (Cracow)
Pardubice
Opava
Cieszyn (Teschen)
Przemysl
Ostrava
Nowy Sacz
Olomouc
Tabor
High Tatra
Jihlava
Brno
Zilina
Spisska Nova Ves
Presov
Vah
Morava
SLOVAKIA
Uzhgorod
Trencin
Kosice (Kassa)
Piestany
Mukacheva
Hron
Banska Stiavnica
Krems
Danube
Bratislava (Pressburg)
St. Polten
Miskolc
WIEN (VIENNA)
Nyiregyhaza
Neusiedler See
Komarno
Vac
Wiener Neustadt
Gyor
BUDAPEST
Tisza
Sopron
Raba
Debrecen
Bruck
Oradea (Grosswardein)
Szombathely
HUNGARY
Balaton
Graz
Kecskemet
Leibnitz
18
20
22
16
54
50
48

E. GERMANY
Dresden
Karl Marx Stadt (Chemnitz)
Zwickau
Plauen
Erfurt
Coburg
Main
Bamberg
Würzburg
Nürnberg
Amberg
Ansbach
W. GERMANY
Regensburg
Straubing
Ingolstadt
Danube
Landshut
Passau
Ulm
Augsburg
München (Munich)
Inn
Lech
Kempten
Bodensee (L. Constance)
Rosenheim
Dornbirn
VORARLBERG
Liechtenstein
Landeck
Innsbruck
TIROL
Brenner P.
Solbad Hall
Kitzbühel
SALZBURG
Salzburg
Ischl
Salzach
AUSTRIA
Tauern
Alps
Rhatian
Ortles
Adige
Bolzano
Mt Adamello
Trento
Dolomites
Riva
Rovereto
L. d'Iseo
L. di Garda
Brescia
Verona
Cremona
Mantua
Po
Padova (Padua)
Venezia (Venice)
Treviso
Belluno
Udine
Gorizia
Carnic Alps
Lienz
Gr. Glockner
CARINTHIA
Villach
Klagenfurt
Karawanken
Julian Alps
Tamsweg
Leoben
STYRIA
Graz
Leibnitz
Maribor
Drava
Sava
Celje
Ljubljana (Laibach)
Postumia
Trieste
Istra
Rijeka (Fiume)
Krk
Pula
Kapela Mts
Velebit
Pag
Zadar
Dugi Otok
Sibenik
Split (Spalato)
Brac
Hvar
Dinaric Alps
Knin
Imotski
Bihac
Banja Luka
Una
Bos Novi
Vrbas
Sisak
Karlovac
Zagreb (Agram)
Virovitica
Varaždin
Kaposvár
Nagykanizsa
Balaton
Mur
Körmend
Szombathely
Sopron
BURGENLAND
Neunkirchen
Bruck
Wiener Neustadt
Neusiedler See
Leitha
Baden
UPPER
LOWER
AUSTRIA
Linz
Wels
Steyr
Enns
Chain
St. Pölten
Krems
Freistadt
Gmünd
Znojmo
Břeclav
WIEN VIENNA
Bratislava (Pressburg)
Moravia
Brno (Brünn)
Prostejov
Olomouc
Přerov
Jihlava (Iglau)
Tabor
Písek
Vltava
České Budějovice (Budweis)
Böhmer Wald
Plzen (Pilsen)
Cheb (Eger)
Karlovy Vary (Karlsbad)
Jáchymov
Chomutov
Most
Ohre
Erz Geb.
Ústí (nad Labem)
Děčín
Liberec
Litoměřice
Elbe
Ml. Boleslav
PRAHA PRAGUE
Kolín
BOHEMIA
ČESKÉ ZEMĚ
CZECHOSLOVAKIA
Pardubice
Hradec Králové
Riesen Geb.
Glatz
Sudeten Mts
Šumperk
Sternberk
Opava (Troppau)
Silesia
Wrocław (Breslau)
Moravian Mts
Morava
White Carpathians
Little Carpathians
Papa
Raba
Veszprém
Bakony
HUNGARY
Leghorn
Livorno
Lucca
Firenze (Florence)
Arno
Arezzo
San Marino
Rimini
Ancona
Perugia
ITALY
Parma
Modena
Ferrara
Bologna
Ravenna
ADRIATIC SEA
YUGOSLAVIA
Travnik
10
12
14
16
50
48
46
44

POLAND
Statute Miles
0 50 100
Kielce
Częstochowa
Zamosc
Rovno
Sokal
Vistula
San
Bug
Katowice
Krakow
Brody
Jaroslaw
Rzeszów
Tarnów
Bochnia
Przemysl
Lvov (Lemberg)
U.S.S.R.
Galicia
Ternopol
Cieszyn
Nowy Sącz
Carpathian Mountains
Sambor
Drogobych
Stryy
Dniester
Buczacz
Zbrucz
High Tatra
Žilina
Ružomberok
Prešov
Ondava
Ivano-Frankovsk (Stanislav)
Kamenets Podolskiy
Kolomyya
SLOVAKIA
SLOVENSKO
Ban Bystrica
Kosice (Kassa)
Uzhgorod (Ungvar)
Latorica
Mukachevo
Chernovtsy
Banska Stiavnica
Hernad
Khust
Yasinya
Miskolc
Tokaj
Tisza
Satu Mare
Sighet
Nyiregyhaza
Szamos
Eger
Vac
Esztergom
Baia Mare
Cimpulung
Botosani
Debrecen
BUDAPEST
Jászberény
Tasnad
HUNGARY
Bistrita
Cegled
Piatra Neamt
Szolnok
Oradea
Dej
Dunanjváros
Kecskemét
Cluj (Kolozsvár)
Transylvania
Bekes
Szentes
T.Mures
Kiskunfélegyháza
Békéscaba
Gyula
Bihor Mts
Aiud
Mures
Danube
Hodmezovasarhely
Szeged
Mako
Arad
Alba Julia
Sighisoara
Mures
Olt
Subotica
Senta
Sombor
Timisoara
Lugoj
Sibiu
Brasov
Tisa
ROMANIA
Timis
Transylvanian Alps
Novi Sad
Zrenjanin
Tirgu Jiu
Ploiesti
Vršac
Pitesti
Sava
Pancevo
Olt
Zemun
Bazias
Iron Gate
Orsova
Turnu Severin
BUCURESTI (BUCHAREST)
Tuzla
Sabac
BEOGRAD (BELGRADE)
Slatina
Arges
R. Drina
Valjevo
Craiova
YUGOSLAVIA
Morava
Vidin
Giurgiu
Ruse
Kragujevac
Zajecar
Dunarea (Danube)
Lom
Dunav
Užice
Krusevac
BULGARIA
Pleven
Foca
Pljevlja
Novi Pazar
Niš (Nish)
Pirot
Vratsa
Isker
Veliko Turnovo
50
48
46
44
20
22
24
26

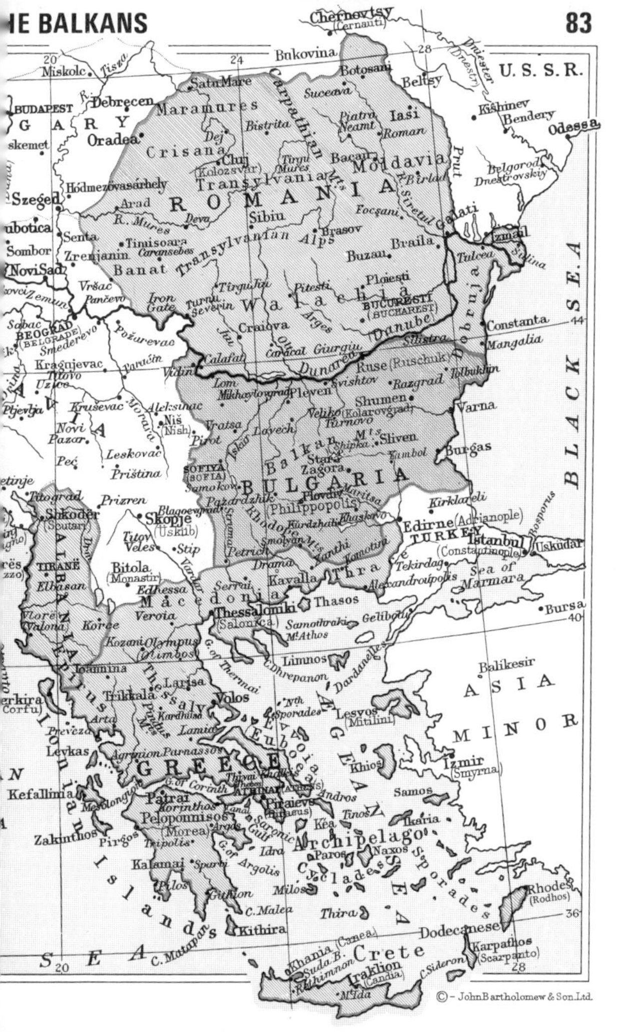

# NORTH ITALY

SWITZERLAND
Bern
Lausanne
Montreux
Sion
Martigny
Thun
Brig
Chur
Tunnel
Lepontine Alps
R. Rhine
R. Rhône
Rhætian Alps
Splügen Pass
Pennine Alps
ALPS
M. Blanc
Gr. St Bernard
Matterhorn
Monte Rosa
Simplon Pass
Domodossola
Locarno
L. di Maggiore
Lugano
L. di Como
Chiavenna
Maloja Pass
Bernina
Sondrio
Adda
Bormio
Tonale Pass
Stelvio P.
Ortles
Malles Venosto
Merano
Bolzano
Bressanone
Brenner Pass
Hochfeiler
Dobbiaco
Carnic Alps
Villach
Auronzo
Pieve di Cadore
Pontebba
Tarvisio
Tolmezzo
Julian Alps
Tolmino
Marmolada
TRENTINO
ALTO ADIGE
Dolomites
Edolo
Adamello
Trento
Belluno
FRIULI
Udine
VENEZIA GIULIA
Gorizia
Monfalcone
Grado
G. of Trieste
TRIESTE
Rijeka
Kopar
Piran
Istra
Poreč
Rovinj
Pula
Rt. Kamenjak
Kvarner
Cres
VALLE D'AOSTA
Aosta
Gr. Paradiso
Ivrea
Biella
M. la Levanna
Cuorgnè
Mt Cenis
Chivasso
TORINO (TURIN)
Dora Riparia
Rivoli
Pinerolo
Chieri
Casale
Asti
Carmagnola
Cottian Alps
M. Viso
Saluzzo
Bra
Savigliano
Alba
Fossano
Cuneo
Mondovì
Col di Tenda
Maritime Alps
PIEMONTE
Vercelli
Novara
Varallo
Arona
Varese
Como
Lecco
Busto Arsizio
Malpensa
Monza
Bergamo
LOMBARDIA
MILANO (MILAN)
Treviglio
Vigevano
Lodi
Pavia
Crema
Clusone
BRESCIA
Iseo
Garda
Riva
Rovereto
Peschiera
Pontevico
Cremona
Mantova
Villafranca
VERONA
Legnago
Schio
Asiago
Bassano
Vicenza
Castelfranco
Feltre
Vittorio
Treviso
Mestre
VENETO
PADOVA
Este
VENEZIA (VENICE)
Chioggia
GULF OF VENICE
Piave
Brenta
Adige
Rovigo
Adria
Cavarzere
Mouths of the Po
Po
Voghera
Piacenza
Valenza
Tanaro
Alessandria
Tortona
Bobbio
Novi
Acqui
Fidenza
Parma
Viadana
Guastalla
Mirandola
Reggio
Modena
FERRARA
Comacchio
Panaro
EMILIA
ROMAGNA
BOLOGNA
Vergato
Imola
Lugo
Faenza
Forlì
Ravenna
Cesenatico
Cesena
Rimini
M. Cimone
Pontremoli
LIGURIA
GENOVA (GENOA)
Voltri
Savona
Noli
Finale Marina
Albenga
Imperia
C. Mele
(Oneglia & Pto Maurizio)
Sanremo
Ventimiglia
Mentone
Nice
Monaco
Cannes
Var
Roja
Rapallo
Chiavari
GULF OF GENOA
LA SPEZIA
Palmaria
Carrara
Massa
Viareggio
Serchio
Pisa
LIVORNO (LEGHORN)
Lucca
Pescia
Pistoia
Prato
FIRENZE (FLORENCE)
Empoli
Arno
Etruscan Apennines
TOSCANA
SAN MARINO
Urbino
MARCHE
Fossombrone
M. Catria
Jesi
Pesaro
Fano
Senigallia
Ancona
ADRIATIC SEA
Statute Miles
0
20
40
60
46
44
8
10
12
14

YUGOSLAVIA
ALBANIA
Thessaloniki
THESSALONIKI
(SALONICA)
CHALCIDICE
Kozani
Grevena
Ioannina
EPIRUS
THESSALY
Larisa
Karditsa
Arta
Preveza
Acarnania & Ætolia
CENTRAL GREECE
Evvoia
Phocis
Boeotia
Attica
ATHINAI
(ATHENS)
Achaia
Elis
PELOPONNISOS
(MOREA)
Argolis
Arcadia
Messenia
Laconia
Kefallinia
Zakinthos
Levkas
Ithaka
Kithira
(Cerigo)
Nthn Sporades
G. of Thermai
G. of Patras
G. of Corinth
Saronic G.
Gulf of Messenia
G. of Laconia
G. of Argolis
C. Matapan
C. Maléa
Statute Miles
0 20 40 60 80

# WESTERN U.S.S.R.

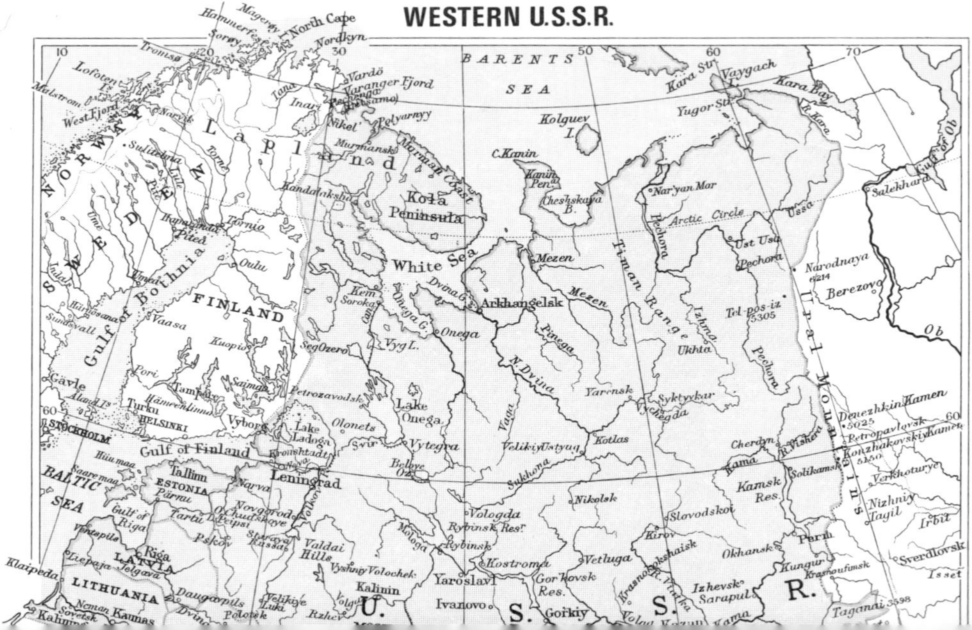

CASPIAN SEA
BLACK SEA
Sea of Azov
Aral Sea
Ust Urt
Kara Bogaz G.
Caspian Depression
KAZAKH
TURKMEN
TURKEY
ROMANIA
BULGARIA
GEORGIA
ARMENIA
AZERBAIJAN
MOLDAVIA
WHITE RUSSIA
UKRAINE
CRIMEA
Caucasus Mountains
R. Ural
Volga
Don
Donets
Dnepr
Dnestr
Prut
R. Bug
Pripyat
Desna
Manych
Kuban R.
Uzen R.
Orenburg
Orsk
Guryev
Uralsk
Kuybyshev
Syzran
Saratov
Engels
Volgograd
Volzhskiy
Leninsk
Astrakhan
Kamyshin
Penza
Tambov
Voronezh
Saransk
Tula
Orel
Kursk
Belgorod
Kharkov
Poltava
Kremenchug
Kirovograd
Dnepropetrovsk
Zaporozhye
Donetsk
Makeyevka
Voroshilovgrad
Gorlovka
Rostov
Novocherkassk
Taganrog
Zhdanov
Berdyansk
Kherson
Nikolayev
Odessa
Kishinev
(Chisinau)
Kiyev
Zhitomir
Berdichev
Uman
Chernigov
Gomel
Bryansk
Roslavl
Mozyr
Bobruysk
Pinsk
Brest
Lvov
Chernovtsy
Simferopol
Sevastopol
Yalta
Kerch
Krasnodar
Novorossiysk
Tuapse
Anapa
Yeysk
Stavropol
Armavir
Elista
Tsimlyansk Res.
Millerovo
Elbrus
18,481
Mt. Kazbek 16,558
Ordzhonikidze
Groznyy
Makhachkala
Derbent
Baku
Tbilisi
Kutaisi
Batumi
Poti
Sukhumi
Gori
Leninakan
Kirovabad
Yerevan
Nakhichevan
Mt. Ararat
16,946
Kars
Erzurum
Trabzon
Sinope
Ankara
Istanbul
Edirne
Bursa
Uskudar
Sea of Marmara
Bosporus
Varna
Burgas
Ruse
Silistra
Shumen
Constanta
Galati
Braila
Bucuresti
Brasov
Iasi
Mouths of Danube
Krasnovodsk
C. Shakhova
Lenkoran
Statute Miles
0 100 200 300
50
40
30

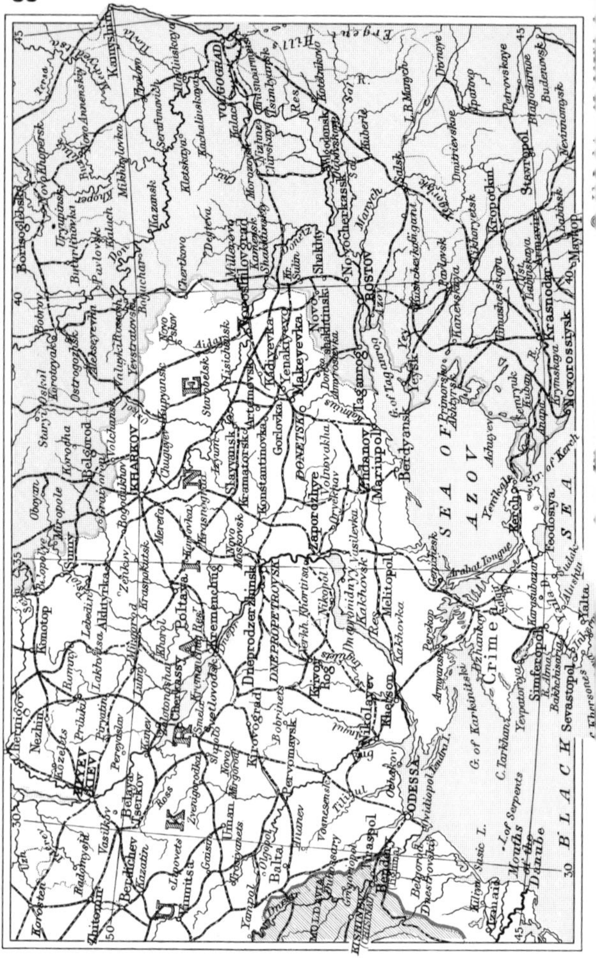
U K R A I N E
KIEV
KHARKOV
DONETSK
DNEPROPETROVSK
ODESSA
VOLGOGRAD
ROSTOV
Krasnodar
SEA OF AZOV
BLACK SEA
Crimea
Simferopol
Sevastopol
Yalta
Feodosiya
Kerch
Yevpatoriya
Arabat Tongue
Zaporozhye
Kirovograd
Nikolayev
Kherson
Poltava
Kremenchug
Cherkassy
Zhitomir
Vinnitsa
Berdichev
Chernigov
Nezhin
Sumy
Konotop
Belgorod
Taganrog
Zhdanov (Mariupol)
Berdyansk
Melitopol
Krivoy Rog
Nikopol
Kakhovka
Makeyevka
Gorlovka
Kramatorsk
Slavyansk
Konstantinovka
Lisichansk
Voroshilovgrad
Novorossiysk
Maykop
Stavropol
Kropotkin
Yeysk
MOLDAVIA
KISHINEV
Bendery
Tiraspol
Balta
Uman
Pervomaysk
Voznesensk
Ochakov
Novocherkassk
Shakhty
Kamensk
Millerovo
Borisoglebsk
Kamyshin
Mouths of the Danube

THE CAUCASUS

# SOVIET CENTRAL ASIA

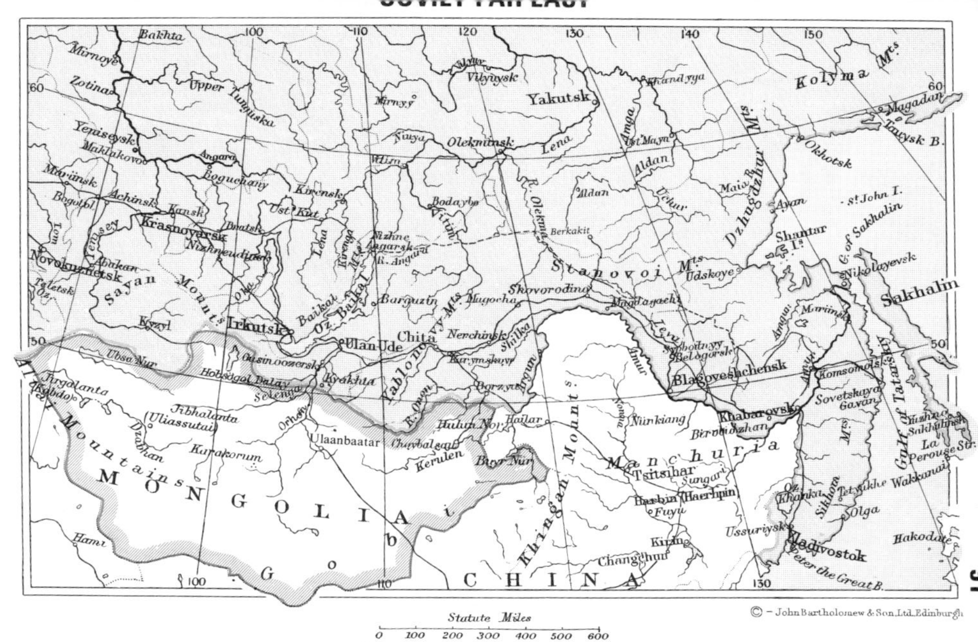
Bakhta
Mirnoye
Zotinas
Upper Tunguska
Mirnyy
Vilyuysk
Yakutsk
Khandyga
Kolyma Mts
Magadan
Tauysk B.
Yeniseysk
Maklakovo
Angara
Boguchany
Nuya
Olekminsk
Lena
Amga
Ust Maya
Aldan
Okhotsk
Mariinsk
Bogotol
Achinsk
Kansk
Kirensk
Ust' Kut
Bodaybo
Vitim
R. Olekma
Uchur
Maia R.
Dzhugdzhur Mts
Ayan
St John I.
Tom
Yenisey
Krasnoyarsk
Bratsk
Nizhneudinsk
Nizhne Angarsk
R. Angara
Berkakit
Shantar Is.
G. of Sakhalin
Novokuznetsk
Abakan
Teletsk Oz.
Sayan Mounts
Kyzyl
Oka
Irkutsk
Baikal Mts
Oz. Baikal
Barguzin
Yablonovyy Mts
Mogocha
Skovorodino
Stanovoi Mts
Udskoye
Nikolayevsk
Sakhalin
Magdagachi
Mariinsk
Ulan Ude
Chita
Nerchinsk
Shilka
Amur
Svobodnyy
Belogorsk
Blagoveshchensk
Komsomolsk
Gulf of Tatarskiy
Ubsa Nur
Gusinoozersk
Hobsogol Dalay
Kyakhta
Selenga
Karymskoye
Borzya
Argun
Sovetskaya Gavan
Jirgalanta (Kobdo)
Altai Mountains
Jibhalanta (Uliassutai)
Dzabhan
Orhon
Ulaanbaatar
R. Onon
Hulun Nor
Hailar
Nonni
Nunkiang
Khabarovsk
Birobidzhan
Yuzhno Sakhalinsk
La Perouse Str.
Karakorum
Choybalsan
Kerulen
Buyr Nur
Khingan Mounts
Manchuria
Tsitsihar
Sungari
Harbin (Haerhpin)
Fuyu
Oz. Khanka
Sikhote Alin Mts
Wakkanai
MONGOLIA
Gobi
Hami
Kirin
Changchun
CHINA
Ussuriysk
Vladivostok
Olga
Hakodate
Peter the Great B.
Statute Miles
0 100 200 300 400 500 600

ARCTIC
BRITISH ISLES
London
North Sea
SCANDINAVIA
North Cape
Novaya Zemlya
Kara Sea
Paris
Baltic Sea
Berlin
Leningrad
Arkhangelsk
Salekhard
EUROPE
Wien (Vienna)
Roma
Moskva (Moscow)
UNION OF SOVIET
Ural Mts
Ob
Surgut
Tobolsk
Sverdlovsk
Petropavlovsk
Omsk
Volga
Sicily
Istanbul
GREECE
Black Sea
Astrakhan
Caucasus Mts
Mediterranean Sea
Trabzon
Erzurum
Ankara
Izmir
TURKEY
Taurus M.
Rhodes
CYPRUS
Tbilisi
Caspian Sea
Orsk
R. Ural
Kirghiz Steppes
Karaganda
R. Irtysh
KAZAKH
Oz. Balkhash
Aral Sea
Syr Darya
UZBEK
Khiva
TURKMEN
Ashkhabad
Tashkent
KIRGIZ
Kokand
Kashgar
Bukhara
Samarkand
Mary
Dushanbe
TADZHIK
SINKI
Yarkand
Jerusalem
Cairo
Suez
SYRIA
JORDAN
Damascus
Mosul
Euphrates
Tigris
Damavand
Elburz Mts
Mashhad
Tehran
Baghdad
Babylon
IRAQ
EGYPT
Mt Sinai
Basra
Esfahan
IRAN (PERSIA)
Shiraz
Bushehr (Bushire)
The Gulf
Herat
Hindu Kush
Kabul
AFGHANISTAN
Peshawar
Srinagar
KASHMIR
Karakorum
Rawalpindi
Lahore
Kandahar
Kalat
PAKISTAN
R. Indus
Multan
Simla
Himalaya
Jumna
SAUDI ARABIA
Medina
Hejaz
Hasa
Riyadh
Nejd
Red Sea
Jiddah
Mecca
R. Nile
Str. of Hormuz
G. of Oman
Muscat
OMAN
Karachi
Ras al Junaiz
Delhi
Agra
Kanpur
Allahabad
Nepal
Lucknow
INDIA
G. of Kachchh
Baroda
Narmada
Surat
Nagpur
YEMEN
Mocha
SOUTH YEMEN
Kuria Muria Is
G. of Khambat
Bombay
Godavari
Aden
G. of Aden
Str. of Babel Mandeb
Arabian Sea
Panaji
Hyderabad
Krishna
Sokotra I. (S. Yemen)
C. Guardafui
Lakshadweep (Ind.)
Bangalore
Madras
Calicut
Mysore
Palk Str.
L. Victoria
Cape Comorin
Trincomalee
SRI LANKA
Maldive Is
G. of Mannar
Colombo
Galle
AFRICA
INDIAN OCEAN
Zanzibar
Statute Miles
0 500 1000
Gan
40 60 80

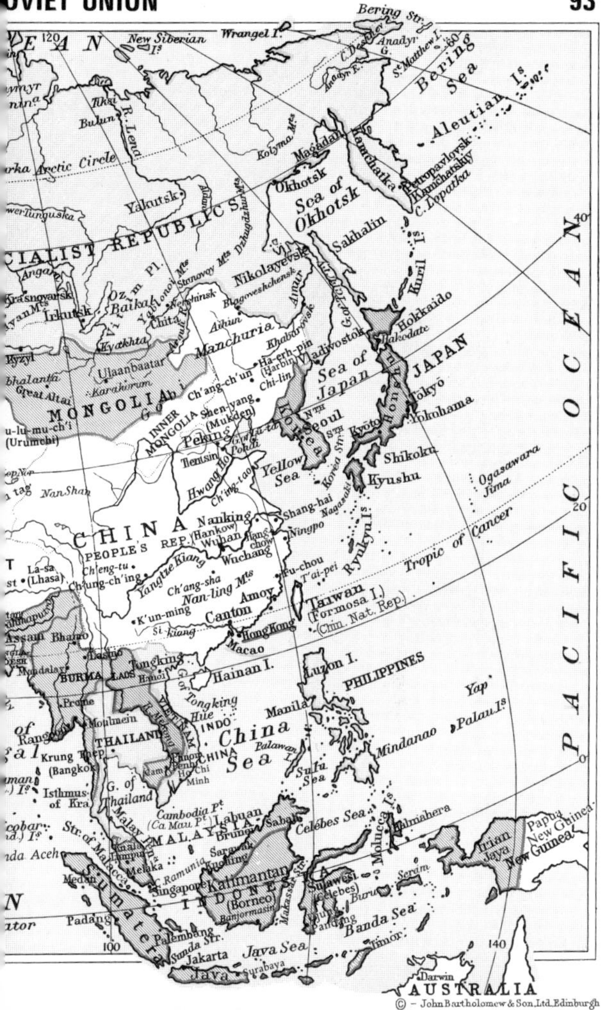
Bering Str.
Wrangel I.
New Siberian Is
Anadyr G.
St Matthew I.
Bering Sea
Aleutian Is
Tiksi
Bulun
R. Lena
Kolyma Mts
Magadan
Kamchatka
Petropavlovsk Kamchatskiy
C. Lopatka
Arctic Circle
Okhotsk
Sea of Okhotsk
Yakutsk
SOCIALIST REPUBLICS
Sakhalin
Kuril Is
Stanovoy Mts
Nikolayevsk
Blagoveshchensk
Amur
Krasnoyarsk
Irkutsk
Baikal
Chita
Aihun
Manchuria
Khabarovsk
Vladivostok
Hokkaido
Hakodate
JAPAN
Kyzyl
Ulaanbaatar
Karakorum
Great Altai
MONGOLIA
Ha-erh-pin (Harbin)
Ch'ang-ch'un
Chi-lin
Sea of Japan
Honshu
Tokyo
Yokohama
INNER MONGOLIA
Shen-yang (Mukden)
Korea
Seoul
Kyoto
Peking
Tientsin
Hwang Ho
Yellow Sea
Korea Str.
Shikoku
Kyushu
Ogasawara Jima
Nan Shan
Ch'ing-tao
Shang-hai
Nagasaki
Nanking
Ningpo
CHINA
PEOPLE'S REP.
(Hankow)
Wuhan
Wuchang
Ryukyu Is
Tropic of Cancer
La-sa (Lhasa)
Ch'eng-tu
Ch'ung-ch'ing
Yangtze Kiang
Ch'ang-sha
Nan-ling Mts
Fu-chou
T'ai-pei
Amoy
Taiwan (Formosa I.) (Chin. Nat. Rep.)
K'un-ming
Canton
Hong Kong
Macao
Si Kiang
Assam
Bhamo
Mandalay
BURMA
LAOS
Hanoi
Tongking
Hainan I.
Luzon I.
PHILIPPINES
Yap
Prome
G. of Tongking
Hue
Manila
Moulmein
Rangoon
THAILAND
VIETNAM
INDO CHINA
China Sea
Palawan I.
Mindanao
Palau Is
Krung Thep (Bangkok)
Phnom Penh
Ho Chi Minh
Sulu Sea
G. of Thailand
Isthmus of Kra
Cambodia Pt (Ca Mau Pt)
Labuan
Brunei
Sabah
Celebes Sea
Molucca Is
Halmahera
Irian Jaya
Papua New Guinea
New Guinea
Str. of Malacca
MALAYSIA
Kuala Lumpur
Melaka
Sarawak
Aceh
Medan
Singapore
Kalimantan (Borneo)
Banjarmasin
INDONESIA
Makassar Str.
Sulawesi (Celebes)
Buru
Seram
Sumatera
Padang
Palembang
Sunda Str.
Banda Sea
Timor
Jakarta
Java Sea
Java
Surabaya
Darwin
AUSTRALIA
PACIFIC OCEAN
120
100
140
40
20
0
© – John Bartholomew & Son, Ltd. Edinburgh

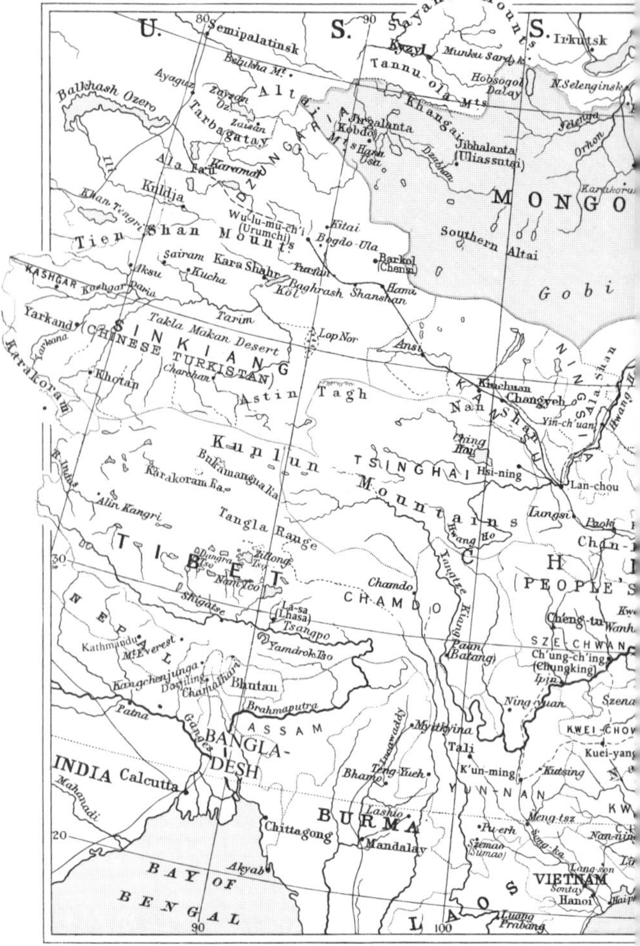

U. S. S. R.
Semipalatinsk
Sayansk Mounts.
Irkutsk
Kyzyl
Munku Sardyk
Tannu-ola Mts.
Belukha Mt.
Ayaguz
Zaysan Oz.
Altai
Hobsogol Dalay
N. Selenginsk
Balkhash Ozero
Tarbagatay
Zaisan
Jirgalanta (Kobdo)
Khangai
Selenga
Orhon
Ili
Ala Tau
Karamai
DZUNGARIA
Mts
Hara Usa
Dzabhan
Jibhalanta (Uliassutai)
Kuldja
Khan Tengri
Wu-lu-mu-ch'i (Urumchi)
Kitai
MONGO
Karakorum
Tien Shan Mounts
Bogdo Ula
Southern Altai
Sairam
Kara Shahr
Barkol (Chensi)
Aksu
Kucha
Turfan
KASHGAR
Kashgar Daria
Baghrash Köl
Shanshan
Hami
Gobi
Yarkand
Tarim
Takla Makan Desert
SINKIANG
(CHINESE TURKISTAN)
Yarkand
Lop Nor
Karakoram
Khotan
Charchan
Ansi
NINGSIA
Ala Shan
Astin Tagh
Kiuchuan
Changyeh
KANSU
Nan Shan
Yin-ch'uan
Hwang
Kunlun Mountains
Bukamangna Ra.
Ching Hai
TSINGHAI
Hsi-ning
Karakoram Ra.
Lan-chou
R. Indus
Alin Kangri
Tangla Range
Lungsi
Paoki
Hwang Ho
Chan-
TIBET
Dangra Tso
Ziling Tso
Nam Tso
Yangtze Kiang
CH
PEOPLE'S
Chamdo
CHAMDO
Shigatse
La-sa (Lhasa)
Tsangpo
NEPAL
Kathmandu
Mt. Everest
Yamdrok Tso
Paan (Batang)
SZECHWAN
Ch'eng-tu
Wanh
Kangchenjunga
Darjiling
Chamalhari
Bhutan
Ch'ung-ch'ing (Chungking)
Ipin
Patna
Brahmaputra
Ning-yuan
Szena
Ganges
ASSAM
Myitkyina
Tali
KWEICHOW
Kuei-yang
BANGLA-DESH
INDIA
Calcutta
Irrawaddy
Bhamo
Teng-Yueh
K'un-ming
Kutsing
Mahanadi
YUNNAN
Lashio
BURMA
Meng-tsz
Chittagong
Pu-erh
Nan-ning
Mandalay
Szemao (Sumao)
Song-ka
Akyab
BAY OF BENGAL
Lang-son
VIETNAM
Sontay
Hanoi
Hai-p
LAOS
Luang Prabang
80
90
30
20
90
100

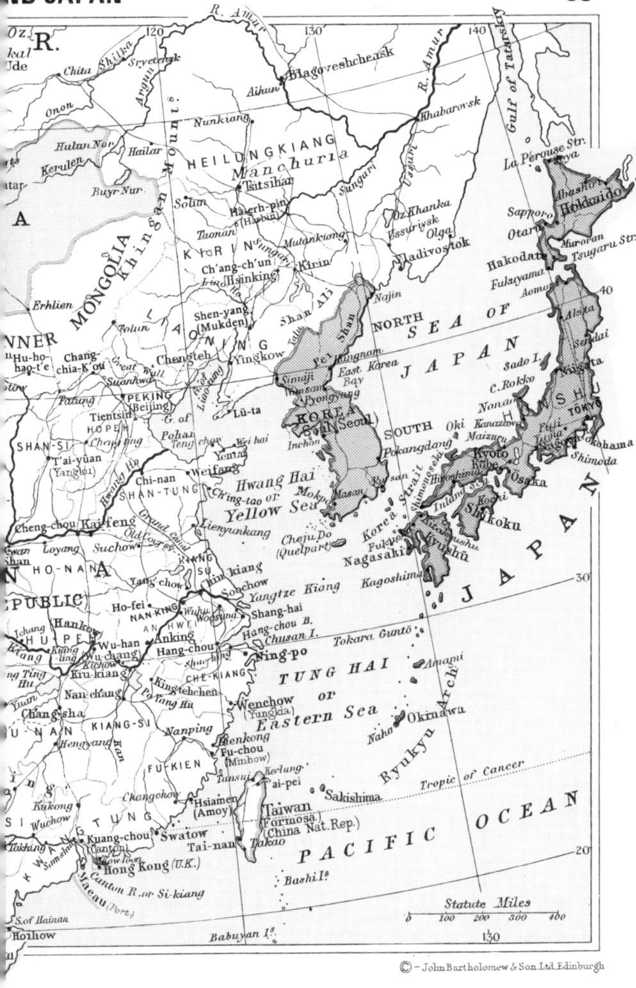
R. Amur
Chita
Shilka
Sryetensk
Argun
Onon
Blagoveshchensk
Aihun
R. Amur
Khabarovsk
Gulf of Tatarsky
Nunkiang
Hulun Nor
Hailar
HEILUNGKIANG
Manchuria
Kerulen
Tsitsihar
Buyr Nur
Solun
Sungari
Ussuri
La Pérouse Str.
Abashiri
Hokkaido
Sapporo
Otaru
Muroran
Tsugaru Str.
Hakodate
Fukuyama
Aomori
Akita
Sendai
Niigata
Sado I.
C. Rokko
HONSHU
Kanazawa
TOKYO
Yokohama
Shimoda
Kyoto
Kobe
Osaka
Maizuru
Oki
Hiroshima
Inland Sea
Kochi
Shikoku
Kyushu
Kagoshima
Nagasaki
Shimonoseki
Korea Strait
Fukuoka
Taonan
Mutankiang
Khanka
Ussuriysk
Olga
Vladivostok
KIRIN
Ch'ang-ch'un
(Hsinking)
Kirin
Liao Ho
Najin
MONGOLIA
Khingan Mounts
Erhlien
Shen-yang
(Mukden)
LIAONING
NORTH
SEA OF JAPAN
Chengteh
Yingkow
Hungnam
East Korea Bay
Sinuiju
Pyongyang
KOREA
Seoul
SOUTH
Inchon
Pokangdang
Pusan
Masan
Mokpo
Cheju Do
(Quelpart)
Hu-ho-hao-t'e
Chang-chia-K'ou
Great Wall
PEKING
(Beijing)
Tatung
Tientsin
HOPEH
G. of Pohai
Lü-ta
Wei hai
Yentai
SHAN-SI
T'ai-yüan
Weifang
Chi-nan
SHAN-TUNG
Ch'ing-tao
Hwang Hai
or Yellow Sea
Hwang Ho
Cheng-chou
Kai-feng
Lienyunkang
Loyang
Suchow
Grand Canal
HO-NAN
KIANG SU
Chin-kiang
Yang-chow
Soochow
Yangtze Kiang
Shang-hai
Ho-fei
NAN-KING
Wuhu
Woosung
Hang-chou B.
Chusan I.
Tokara Guntō
Hankow
HUPEH
Wu-han
Wu-chang
Anking
Hang-chou
Ning-po
TUNG HAI
or Eastern Sea
Amami
Kiu-kiang
CHE-KIANG
Nan-chang
Wenchow
(Yungkia)
Okinawa
Naha
Ryukyu Arch
Changsha
KIANG-SI
Nanping
Fu-chou
(Minhow)
FU-KIEN
Keelung
T'ai-pei
Sakishima
Tropic of Cancer
Changchow
Hsiamen
(Amoy)
Taiwan
(Formosa)
(China Nat. Rep.)
Swatow
Tai-nan
Takao
PACIFIC OCEAN
Kuang-chou
(Canton)
Kow-loon
Hong Kong (U.K.)
Canton R. or Si-kiang
Macau (Port.)
Bashi Is
Babuyan Is
S. of Hainan
Hoihow
Statute Miles
0 100 200 300 400
120
130
140
40
30
20

# JAPAN

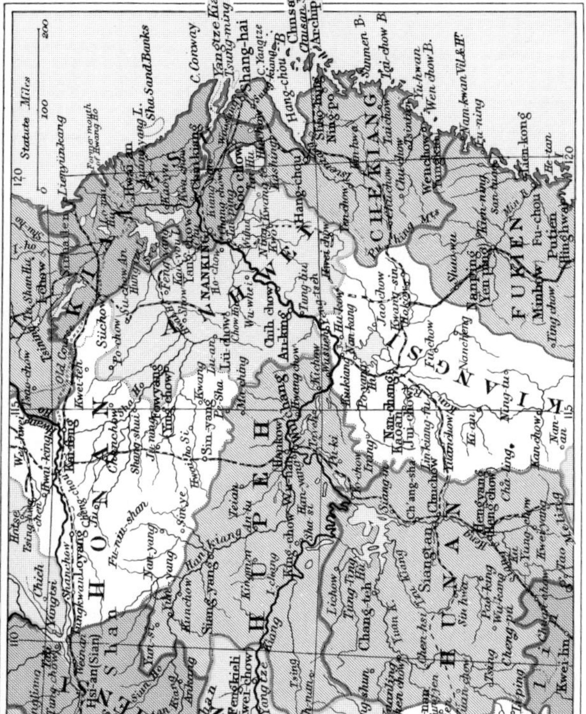
Statute Miles
0
100
200
HONAN
HUPEH
HUNAN
KIANGSI
CHEKIANG
FUKIEN
KWEICHOW
SZECHWAN
NANKING
Shang-hai
Hang-chow
Hankow
Chung-ch'ing
Yangtze Kiang
Chusan Archipelago
C. Conway
Fu-chou
Ning-po
Wenchow
Sin-yang
Kai-feng
Loyang
Hsi-an (Sian)
An-king
Nan-chang
Siangtan
Kuei-yang

# INDO-CHINA

TIBET
Statute Miles
CHINA
Tali
K'un-ming
Kweilin
INDIA
Imphal
Tropic of Cancer
BURMA
Mandalay
Hanoi
Haiphong
Gulf of Tongking
Hainan I.
THAILAND
Bangkok
Krung Thep
Rangoon
BAY OF BENGAL
G. of Martaban
Andaman Islands
(To India)
Port Blair
Mergui Archipelago
Gulf of Thailand
CAMBODIA
Phnom Penh
Ho Chi Minh
COCHIN CHINA
Nicobar Is
(To India)
SOUTH CHINA SEA
PENINSULAR MALAYSIA
Kuala Lumpur
SUMATERA
SINGAPORE
BORNEO
Anambas Is
Bunguran Is (Natuna)

PACIFIC OCEAN
INDIAN OCEAN
INDONESIA
SOUTH CHINA SEA
CELEBES SEA
SULU SEA
JAVA SEA
BANDA SEA
ARAFURA SEA
TIMOR SEA
CORAL SEA
Molucca Sea
Equator
NORTHERN MARIANAS (USA)
Pagan
Guguan
Anatahan
Saipan
Rota
Guam (U.S.)
Challenger Deep +36,161 ft
FED. STATES OF MICRONESIA
Caroline Is. (USA)
Yap
Ulithi
Fais
Sorol
Ngulu
Faraulep
Woleai
Lamotrek
Eauripik
Palau Is.
Babelthuap
Sonsorol Is.
Helen Reef
Mapia Is.
PHILIPPINES
Babuyan Is.
C. Bojeador
C. Engaño
Laoag
Dagupan
Luzon
Manila
Quezon City
Polillo
Palanan Pt.
Legaspi
Lubang Is.
Mindoro
Calamianes
Panay
Iloilo
Negros
Samar
Leyte
Siargao
Bislig
Mindanao
Davao
Davao Gulf
Dipolog
Zamboanga
Sulu Is.
Jolo
Basilan
Tawitawi
Palawan I.
Puerto Princesa
Taytay
Balabac I.
Balabac Str.
Talaud Is.
Sangihe Is.
Hainan I.
Hue
VIETNAM
LAOS
THAILAND
CAMBODIA
INDO-CHINA
Rangoon
Bangkok (Krung Thep)
Ho Chi Minh
Cochin China
Gulf of Thailand
Malay Peninsula
MALAYSIA
PEN. MALAYSIA
Kota Kinabalu (Jesselton)
Kudat
Sandakan
Labuan I.
SABAH
BRUNEI
Bandar Seri Begawan
Bintulu
Sibu
Sarawak
Kuching
Tawau
Darvel B.
Tarakan
Tanjungredeb
KALIMANTAN
(BORNEO)
Samarinda
Balikpapan
Banjarmasin
Pontianak
Singkawang
Karimata Is.
Bangka
Belitung
Palembang
Jakarta
Anambas Is.
Bunguran Is.
Riouw Is.
Singapore
Kuala Lumpur
Melaka
Malacca Strait
George Town
Pinang
Banda Aceh
Sabang
Aceh
Medan
Sibolga
Simeulue
Nias
Padang
Mentawai Is.
Bengkulu
Enggano
Sunda Str.
Telukbetung
Bandung
Cirebon
Semarang
Surabaya
Madura
Semeru
Yogyakarta
Cilacap
JAVA
Bali
Lombok
Mataram
Singaraja
Sumbawa
Raba
Sumba
Flores
Ende
Waingapu
Timor
Kupang
Roti
Sawu
Alor Is.
Solor Is.
Wetar
SULAWESI (CELEBES)
G. of Tomini
Gorontalo
Donggala
G. of Tomori
Manado
Ujung Pandang
Kabia I.
Butung
Baubau
Str. of Makassar
Halmahera
Morotai
Ternate
Bacan
Sula Is.
MOLUCCAS
Buru
Kajeli
Seram
Ambon
Banda Is.
Kai Is.
Aru Is.
Tanimbar Is.
Waigeo
Vogelkop
Manokwari
Fakfak
Biak
Yapen
Irian Bay
IRIAN JAYA
P. Jaya
Jayapura (Sukarnapura)
Pt. d'Urville
Humboldt B.
Aitape
Wewak
Tanahmerah
Merauke
Kolepom
NEW GUINEA
PAPUA
Madang
Mt. Hagen
Mendi
Kikori
Lae
Huon G.
Bulolo
Mt. Albert Edward
Mt. Victoria
Astrolabe B.
Port Moresby
Gulf of Papua
Daru
Torres Strait
Thursday I.
Admiralty Is.
Manus
Bismarck Archipelago
New Britain
New Ireland
Samarai
AUSTRALIA
Darwin
Melville I.
Statute Miles
0
200
400
600
800
100
110
120
130
140
150
10
0
10

# MALAY PENINSULA

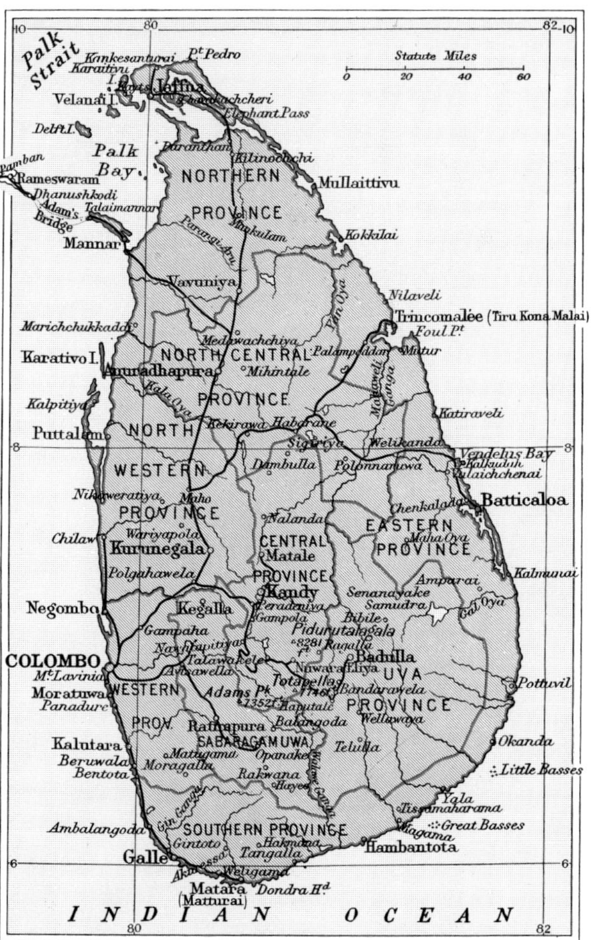
Palk Strait
Kankesanturai
Pt Pedro
Karaitivu I.
Jaffna
Chavakachcheri
Elephant Pass
Velanai I.
Delft I.
Palk Bay
Pamban
Rameswaram
Dhanushkodi
Adam's Bridge
Talaimannar
Mannar
Paranthan
Kilinochchi
NORTHERN PROVINCE
Mullaittivu
Parangi Aru
Kokkilai
Vavuniya
Nilaveli
Yan Oya
Trincomalee (Tiru Kona Malai)
Foul Pt
Marichchukkaddi
Medawachchiya
NORTH CENTRAL PROVINCE
Palampoddaru
Mutur
Karativo I.
Anuradhapura
Mihintale
Mahaweli Ganga
Kala Oya
Kalpitiya
Katiraveli
Kekirawa
Habarane
Puttalam
NORTH WESTERN PROVINCE
Sigiriya
Welikanda
Vendelus Bay
Kalkudah
Valaichchenai
Dambulla
Polonnaruwa
Nikaweratiya
Maho
Chenkaladi
Batticaloa
Nalanda
EASTERN PROVINCE
Maha Oya
Chilaw
Wariyapola
Kurunegala
CENTRAL PROVINCE
Matale
Polgahawela
Kalmunai
Ampara
Kandy
Senanayake Samudra
Gal Oya
Negombo
Kegalla
Peradeniya
Gampola
Bibile
Gampaha
Pidurutalagala
8281 ft
Ragalla
Badulla
COLOMBO
Talawakele
Avisawella
Nuwara Eliya
UVA PROVINCE
Mt Lavinia
Moratuwa
Panadure
WESTERN PROV.
Adams Pk
7352 ft
Totapella
7741 ft
Bandarawela
Haputale
Pottuvil
Wellawaya
Ratnapura
Balangoda
SABARAGAMUWA
Kalutara
Matugama
Opanake
Telulla
Okanda
Beruwala
Bentota
Moragalla
Rakwana
Hayes
Walawe Ganga
Little Basses
Yala
Tissamaharama
Ambalangoda
Gin Ganga
SOUTHERN PROVINCE
Kirinda
Great Basses
Gintota
Hakmana
Hambantota
Galle
Tangalla
Ahangama
Weligama
Matara (Matturai)
Dondra Hd
INDIAN OCEAN
Statute Miles
0 20 40 60
80
82
10
8
6

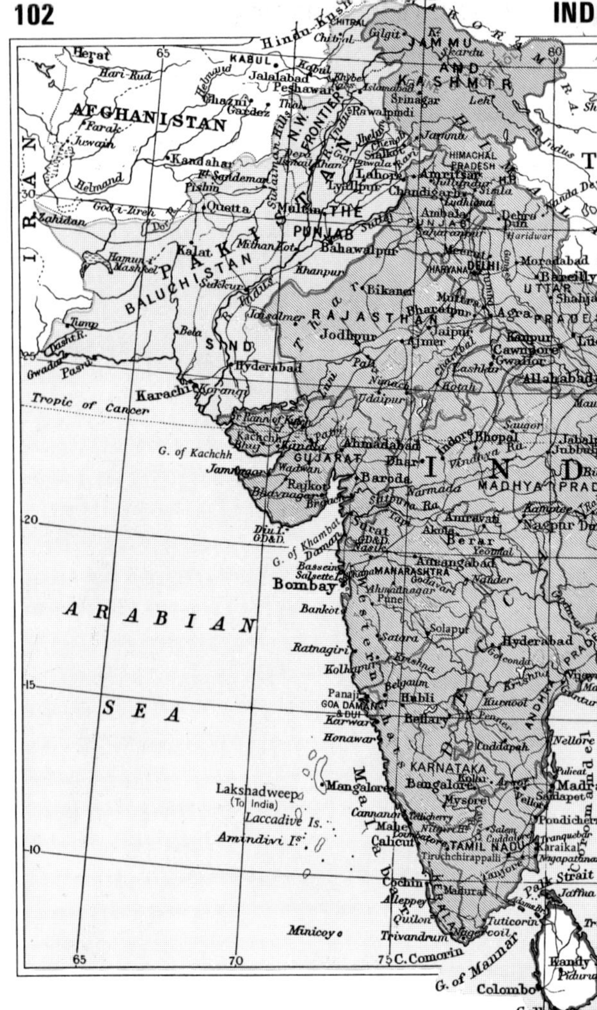
AFGHANISTAN
Herat
KABUL
Jalalabad
Peshawar
Ghazni
Gardez
Kandahar
Hari-Rud
Helmand
IRAN
Zahidan
PAKISTAN
BALUCHISTAN
Quetta
Kalat
Multan
THE PUNJAB
Lahore
Bahawalpur
SIND
Hyderabad
Karachi
Tropic of Cancer
G. of Kachchh
GUJARAT
Ahmadabad
Baroda
Rajkot
RAJASTHAN
Jodhpur
Jaipur
Ajmer
Bikaner
Udaipur
JAMMU AND KASHMIR
Srinagar
HIMACHAL PRADESH
Amritsar
Chandigarh
Ambala
HARYANA
DELHI
UTTAR PRADESH
Agra
Kanpur
Cawnpore
Gwalior
Allahabad
Meerut
Moradabad
Bareilly
INDIA
MADHYA PRADESH
Bhopal
Indore
Jabalpur
Nagpur
Surat
MAHARASHTRA
Bombay
Aurangabad
Pune
Solapur
Hyderabad
ANDHRA PRADESH
ARABIAN SEA
Goa
Panaji
Belgaum
Hubli
Bellary
Karwar
KARNATAKA
Bangalore
Mysore
Mangalore
Lakshadweep (To India)
Laccadive Is.
Amindivi Is.
Minicoy
Calicut
Cochin
KERALA
Trivandrum
C. Comorin
TAMIL NADU
Madras
Pondicherry
Madurai
Tuticorin
Palk Strait
G. of Mannar
Jaffna
Kandy
Colombo
Galle
Nellore
65
70
75
80
30
25
20
15
10

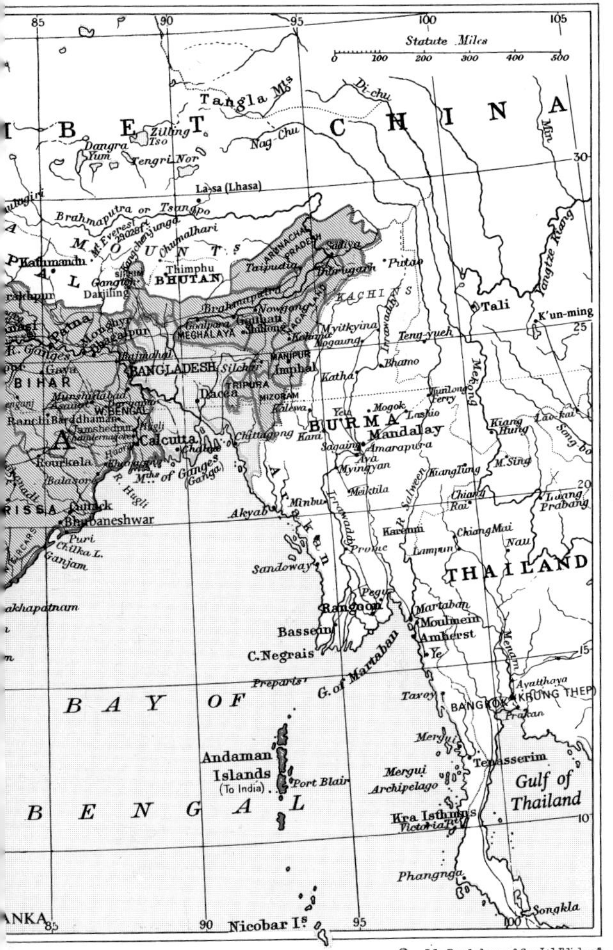

Statute Miles
TIBET
CHINA
Tangla Mts
Di-chu
Nag-Chu
Dangra Yum
Ziling Tso
Tengri Nor
La-sa (Lhasa)
Brahmaputra or Tsangpo
Mt. Everest 29028 ft.
Kangchenjunga
Chumalhari
Kathmandu
Thimphu
BHUTAN
Gangtok
Darjiling
ARUNACHAL PRADESH
Sadiya
Taipudia
Dibrugarh
Putao
KACHINS
Tali
K'un-ming
Yangtze Kiang
Min
Brahmaputra
Nowgong
Gauhati
Shillong
Goalpara
MEGHALAYA
NAGALAND
Kohima
Myitkyina
Mogaung
Irrawaddy
Teng-yueh
Patna
Monghyr
Bhagalpur
Ganges
Rajmahal
Gaya
BIHAR
BANGLADESH
Silchar
MANIPUR
Imphal
Katha
Bhamo
Mekong
TRIPURA
MIZORAM
Dacca
Murshidabad
W. BENGAL
Ranchi
Barddhaman
Jamshedpur
Hugli
Chandernagore
Calcutta
Chittagong
Kalewa
Yeu
Mogok
Lashio
Kunlong Ferry
BURMA
Mandalay
Sagaing
Amarapura
Ava
Myingyan
Kiang Hung
Lao-kai
Song-bo
Rourkela
Balasore
Mths of Ganges (Ganga)
R. Hugli
Arakan
Meiktila
R. Salween
Kiang Tung
M. Sing
Chiang Rai
Luang Prabang
ORISSA
Cuttack
Bhubaneshwar
Akyab
Minbu
Irrawaddy
Karenni
Chiang Mai
Nan
Puri
Chilka L.
Ganjam
Prome
Lampun
THAILAND
Sandoway
Pegu
Rangoon
Martaban
Moulmein
Amherst
Ye
Bassein
C. Negrais
G. of Martaban
Menam
Preparis
Tavoy
Ayatthaya
BANGKOK (KRUNG THEP)
Prakan
BAY OF BENGAL
Mergui
Andaman Islands (To India)
Port Blair
Tenasserim
Mergui Archipelago
Gulf of Thailand
Kra Isthmus
Victoria Pt.
Phangnga
Songkla
Nicobar Is
LANKA

# UTTAR PRADESH



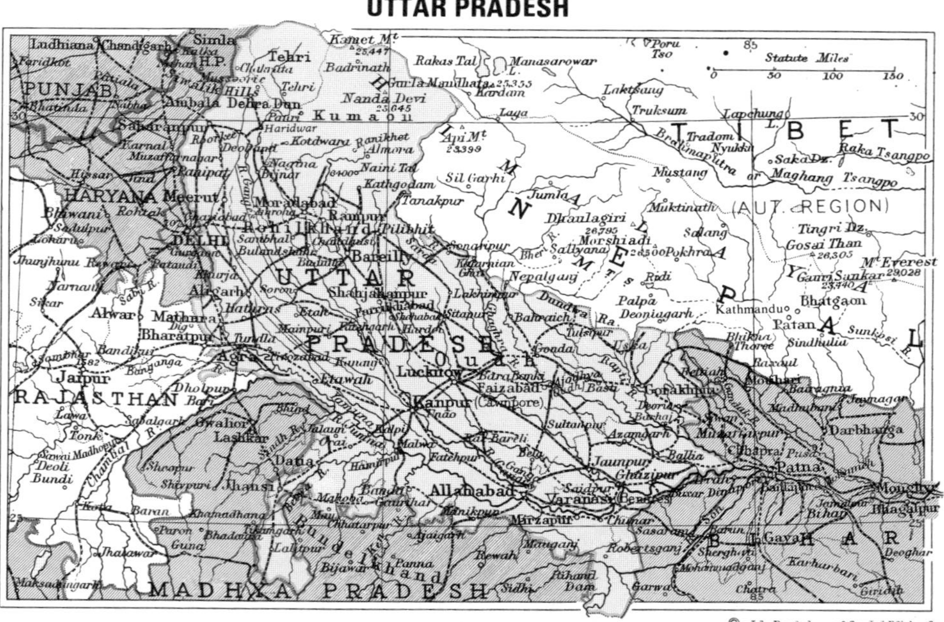

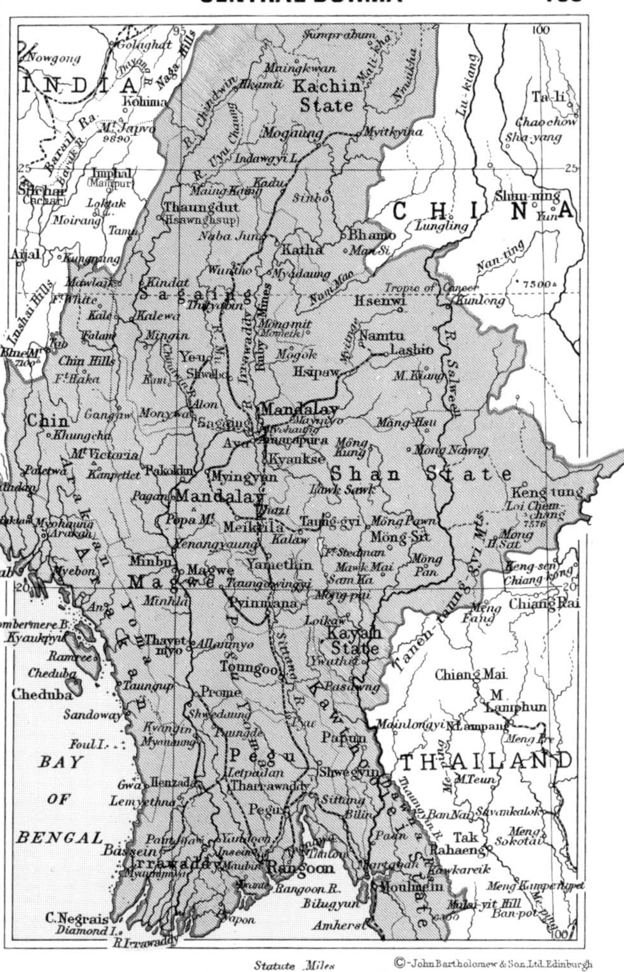
INDIA
CHINA
THAILAND
BAY OF BENGAL
Kachin State
Shan State
Kayah State
Sagaing
Mandalay
Magwe
Pegu
Irrawaddy
Chin
Arakan
Mandalay
Rangoon
Moulmein
Bhamo
Myitkyina
Lashio
Kengtung
Chiang Mai
Imphal
Kohima
Statute Miles
0 50 100 150

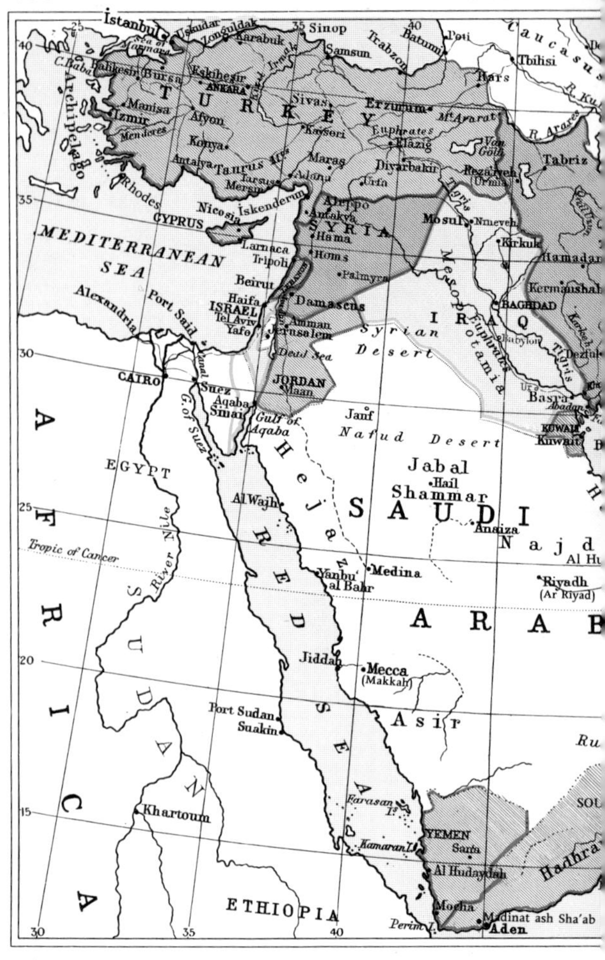
Istanbul
TURKEY
Ankara
MEDITERRANEAN SEA
CYPRUS
SYRIA
ISRAEL
JORDAN
IRAQ
BAGHDAD
Damascus
Jerusalem
Amman
Beirut
CAIRO
EGYPT
AFRICA
SUDAN
Khartoum
ETHIOPIA
RED SEA
SAUDI ARAB
Mecca (Makkah)
Medina
Jiddah
Riyadh (Ar Riyad)
KUWAIT
YEMEN
Aden
Madinat ash Sha'ab
Tropic of Cancer

U. S. S. R.
UZBEK
TURKMEN
TADZHIK
Khiva
Krasnovodsk
Kara Kum
Bukhara
Samarkand
Tashkent
Kokand
Chardzhou
Mary (Merv)
Ashkhabad
Dushanbe
Pamir Plateau
Termez
Kunduz
Hindu Kush
Andkhui
Mazar-i-Sharif
Maimana
Kushka
Herat
KABUL
Peshawar
ISLAMABAD
AFGHANISTAN
Kandahar
Quetta
Kalat
P A K I S T A N
Hyderabad
Karachi
Gwadar
Makran
I R A N
Babol
Gorgan
Bandar Shah
Mashhad
Semnan
Sabzevar
Khurasan
Kashan
Esfahan (Isfahan)
Yazd
Birjand
Gazik
Lut Desert
Hamun-i Helmand
Kerman
Zahedan
Persepolis
Shiraz
Bandar Abbas
Jask
Qeshm
Hormuz Str.
Gulf of Oman
Sharjah
Abu Dhabi
United Arab Emirates
Bahrain I.
GULF
Matrah
Muscat
Sur
Ras al Had
Oman
Masira
Kuria Muria Is
Salalah
YEMEN
Socotra (S. Yemen)
ARABIAN SEA
I N D I A
R. Indus
R. Helmand
Arghandab
Salt Desert
Great
Statute Miles
0 100 200 300 400 500 600

# TURKEY

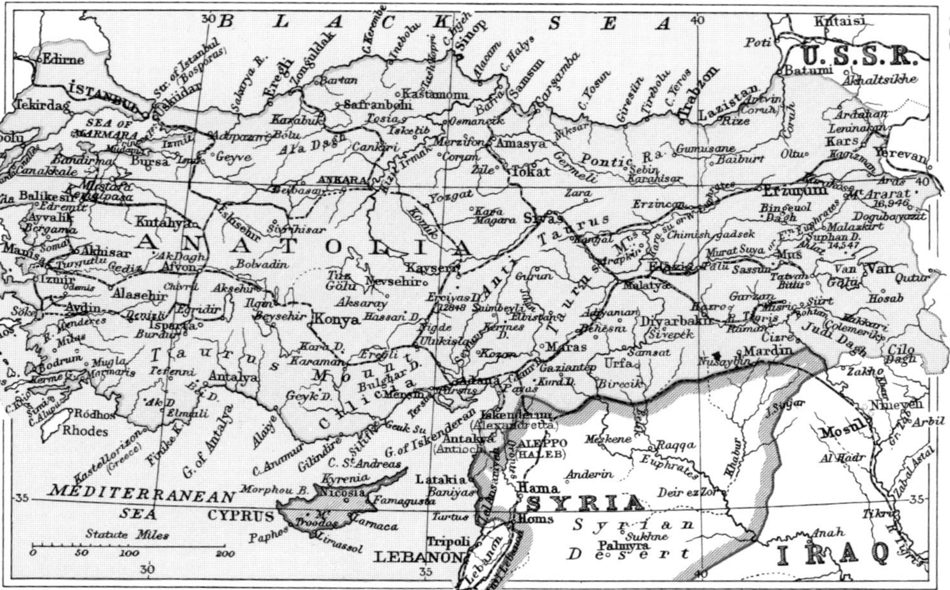

BLACK SEA
U.S.S.R.
Kutaisi
Poti
Batumi
Akhaltsikhe
Edirne
ISTANBUL
Str. of Istanbul (Bosporus)
Üsküdar
Tekirdag
SEA OF MARMARA
Gelibolu
Imroz
Canakkale
Bandirma
Bursa
Izmit
Adapazari
Geyve
Sakarya R.
Eregli
Zonguldak
Bartan
Karabuk
Bolu
Ala Dagh
C. Kerembe
Inebolu
Kastamonu
Safranbolu
Tosia
Iskelib
Cankiri
C. Injeh
Sinop
Alacam
C. Halys
Bafra
Samsun
Osmancik
Merzifon
Corum
Amasya
Zile
Tokat
Carsamba
Niksar
Germeli
C. Yosun
Giresun
Tirebolu
C. Yeros
Trabzon
Pontic Ra.
Sebin Karahisar
Gumusane
Baiburt
Lazistan
Rize
Artvin
Coruh
Oltu
Ardahan
Leninakan
Kars
Kagizman
Yerevan
Aras
Mt. Ararat 16,946
Dogubayazit
Malazkirt
Suphan D. 14,547
Ahlat
Erzurum
Bingeuol Dagh
Erzincan
Chimish gadsek
Kara su or W. Euphrates
E. Euphrates
Mus
Murat Suya
Palu
Sassun
Tatvan
Bitlis
Van
Van Golu
Qutur
Hosab
Siirt
Garzan
Hakkari
Colemerik
Cilo Dagh
Judi Dagh
Cizre
Mardin
Nusaybin
Zakho
Mosul
Nineveh
Arbil
Al Hadr
Zab al Asfal
Tikrit
R. Tigris
Anah
IRAQ
ANKARA
Beibasar
Sivrihisar
Eskisehir
Kutahya
Kizil Irmak
Yozgat
Kara Magara
Konuk
Sivas
Zara
Taurus
Anti Taurus
Kangal
Kayseri
Erciyas D. 12848
Gurun
Malatya
Elazig
Harput
Diyarbakir
R. Tigris
Raman
Siverek
Adiyaman
Behesni
Samsat
Urfa
Birecik
Belik
Maras
Gaziantep
Kurd D.
ANATOLIA
Balikesir
Edremit
Mt. Ida
Ayvalik
Bergama
Soma
Akhisar
Manisa
Izmir
Gediz
Turgutlu
Odemis
Alasehir
Afyon
Ak Dagh
Bolvadin
Chivril
Aksehir
Egridir
Denizli
Aydin
Soke
Samos
Kos
Menderes
Milas
Bodrum
Mugla
Marmaris
Rodhos
Rhodes
Isparta
Burdur
Ilgin
Beysehir
Konya
Tuz Golu
Nevsehir
Aksaray
Hassan D.
Nigde
Ulukisla
Karaman
Kara D.
Eregli
Taurus Mounts
Bulghar D.
Cilicia
Mersin
Tarsus
Adana
Kozan
Ceyhan
Payas
Iskenderun (Alexandretta)
Antakya (Antioch)
G. of Iskenderun
Geuk Su
Silifke
C. St. Andreas
Gilindire
C. Anamur
Alaiye
Antalya
G. of Antalya
Tefenni
Elmali
Ak D.
Finike K.
Kastellorizon (Greece)
MEDITERRANEAN SEA
CYPRUS
Kyrenia
Nicosia
Famagusta
Larnaca
Limassol
Troodos
Paphos
Morphou B.
Latakia
Baniyas
Tartus
Tripoli
LEBANON
Homs
Hama
Orontes
ALEPPO (HALEB)
SYRIA
Syrian Desert
Anderin
Meskene
Raqqa
Euphrates
Khabur
Deir ez Zor
J. Sinjar
Sukhne
Palmyra
Statute Miles
0 50 100 200

Statute Miles
0 20 40 60
MEDITERRANEAN SEA
Homs
Tripoli
(Tarabulus)
Batrun
BEIRUT
Juniye
el Hadeth
Sidon
(Saida)
Tyre
(Sur)
Acre
(Akko)
Haifa
Atlit
Zikhron Ya'aqov
Caesarea
Hadera
ISRAEL
Tulkarm
Herzliya
Tel-Aviv
-Yafo
Ramla
Rehovot
Ashdod
Ashqelon
Gaza
Khan Yunis
Rafah
Beersheba
Dimona
Sedom
Yeroham
Subeita
Negev
El Qussaima
Ain Kadeis
ISRAEL
MIL.
ADMIN.
Araba
LEBANON
Zahle
Baalbek
Hermil
El Kaa
Ras Baalbek
Lebye
Bsherri
Ehden
Rasheiya
Nabatiye
Qiryat Shemona
Mt Hermon
Anti Lebanon
Zebdani
Quteife
Jerud
Es Salihiye
Dumeir
Qasr Zigal
DAMASCUS
(DAMAS)
Qatana
Kiswe
SYRIA
Sadad
El Qaryatein
En Nebk
Baniyas
el Quneitra
Es Sanamein
Mesmiye
El Leja
Nawa
Sheikh Miskin
Jebel ed Nemara
Es Suweidiya
JEBEL ED DRUZ
Busra
Salkhad
Mazerib
Dera
Nasib
Irbid
Imtan
Mafraq
Oil Pipe Line
H-5
Safad
(Zefat)
Shefaram
L. of Tiberias
Tiberias
Nazareth
Afula
Beyt Shean
Jenin
Nablus
Petah Tiqva
Lydda (Lod)
Jericho
EL QUDS ESH SHERIF
JERUSALEM
Bethlehem
Hebron
(El Khalil)
Arad
Dead Sea
Bahr Lut
Jordan R.
PALESTINE
Ajlun
Jarash
Salt
Zarqa
Suweilih
Naur
AMMAN
El Mawaqqar
Qasr el Azraq
W. Rajil
Madaba
Jiza
Qal'at ed Daba
El Hazim
Dhiban
Khan ez Zabib
Karak
JORDAN
El Qatrana
Tafila
Qal'at el Hasa
W. Bayir
Bayir
Jurf ed Darawish
Shaubak
Qal'at Uneiza
PETRA
Tel Kalakh
Homs Bahret
Nahr el Kebir
El Mina
36
34
32
to Port Said 230 m.
J. to B. 120 m.
N. el-Qasimiye
Bint Jubail
Nahariyya
B. of Acre
© - John Bartholomew & Son Ltd. Edinburgh

# AFRICA

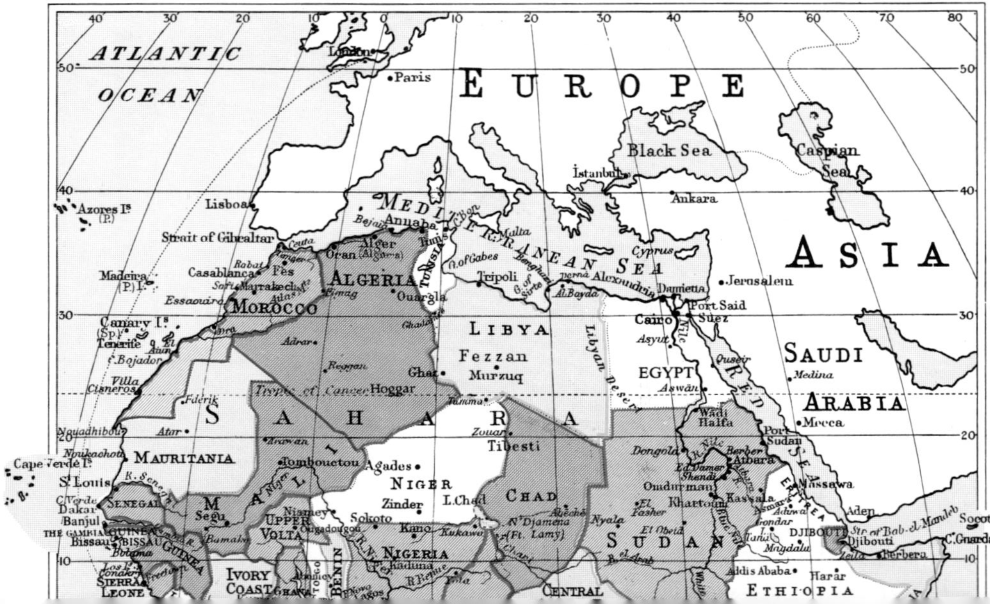
ATLANTIC
OCEAN
EUROPE
ASIA
London
Paris
Lisboa
Azores Is (P.)
Madeira (P.) I.
Canary Is (Sp.)
Tenerife
Cape Verde Is
Strait of Gibraltar
MEDITERRANEAN SEA
Black Sea
Caspian Sea
Istanbul
Ankara
Cyprus
Malta
Jerusalem
Ceuta
Tanger
Rabat
Casablanca
Fès
Safi
Marrakech
Essaouira
MOROCCO
Oran
Alger
Annaba
Bejaïa
Tunis
TUNISIA
ALGERIA
Ouargla
Adrar
Reggan
Hoggar
Ghat
Tripoli
G. of Gabes
Benghazi
Derna
Al Bayda
LIBYA
Fezzan
Murzuq
Tummo
Alexandria
Damietta
Port Said
Suez
Cairo
Asyut
Nile
EGYPT
Aswān
Libyan Desert
SAUDI
ARABIA
Medina
Mecca
RED SEA
Tropic of Cancer
SAHARA
Villa Cisneros
Fderik
Atar
Nouadhibou
Nouakchott
MAURITANIA
St Louis
C. Verde
Dakar
SENEGAL
Banjul
THE GAMBIA
Bissau
GUINEA BISSAU
GUINEA
SIERRA LEONE
MALI
Segu
Tombouctou
Agades
NIGER
Zinder
Niamey
UPPER VOLTA
Ouagadougou
IVORY COAST
GHANA
TOGO
BENIN
Sokoto
Kano
NIGERIA
Kaduna
Lagos
L. Chad
Tibesti
Zouar
CHAD
N'Djamena (Ft. Lamy)
Abéché
CENTRAL
Wadi Halfa
Dongola
Berber
Atbara
Shendi
Omdurman
Khartoum
Kassala
El Fasher
El Obeid
Nyala
SUDAN
Port Sudan
Massawa
ERITREA
Asmara
Gondar
DJIBOUTI
Djibouti
Zeila
Berbera
Aden
Str. of Bab-el-Mandeb
Socotra I.
C. Guardafui
Addis Ababa
Harar
ETHIOPIA

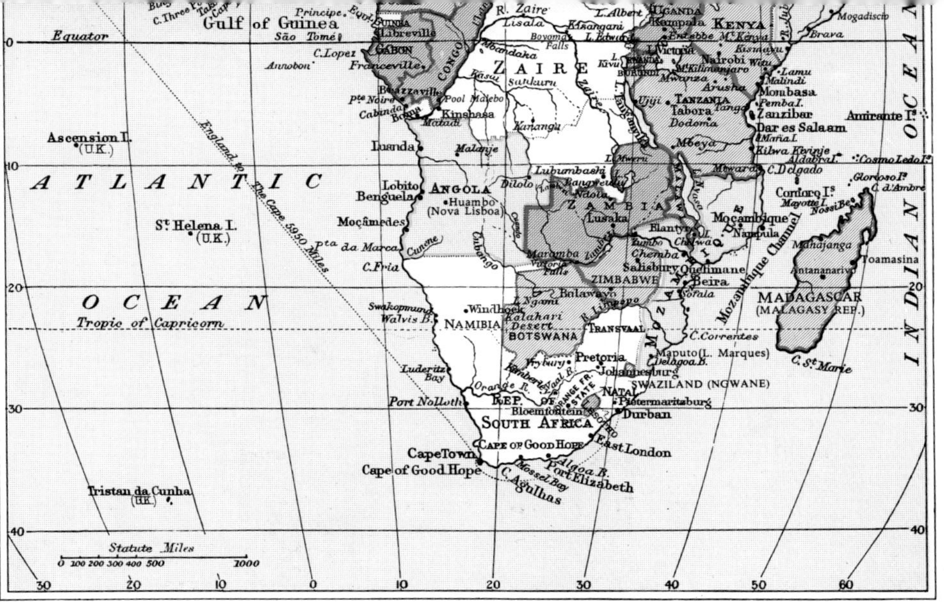

Gulf of Guinea
Principe
São Tomé
Annobon
C.Lopez
Equator
ATLANTIC
OCEAN
Tropic of Capricorn
England to The Cape 5950 Miles
Ascension I. (U.K.)
St. Helena I. (U.K.)
Tristan da Cunha (UK.)
Libreville
GABON
Franceville
CONGO
Brazzaville
Pte Noire
Cabinda
Boma
Matadi
Kinshasa
Pool Malebo
Luanda
Malanje
Lobito
Benguela
ANGOLA
Huambo (Nova Lisboa)
Moçâmedes
Pta da Marca
Cunene
C.Fria
Cubango
Cuando
Swakopmund
Walvis B.
Windhoek
NAMIBIA
Kalahari Desert
BOTSWANA
L. Ngami
Luderitz Bay
Port Nolloth
Orange R.
REP. OF SOUTH AFRICA
Kimberley
Vryburg
Vaal R.
ORANGE FR. STATE
Bloemfontein
LESOTHO
NATAL
Pietermaritzburg
Durban
East London
CAPE OF GOOD HOPE
Cape Town
Cape of Good Hope
C.Agulhas
Mossel Bay
Algoa B.
Port Elizabeth
TRANSVAAL
Pretoria
Johannesburg
SWAZILAND (NGWANE)
Maputo (L. Marques)
Delagoa B.
C.Correntes
R. Limpopo
Bulawayo
ZIMBABWE
Salisbury
Victoria Falls
Maramba
Zambezi
Chemba
Zumbo
Quelimane
Beira
Sofala
MOZAMBIQUE
Mozambique Channel
Moçambique
Nampula
Blantyre
L. Chilwa
L. Nyasa
MALAWI
ZAMBIA
Lusaka
Ndola
L. Bangweulu
Lubumbashi
Dilolo
L. Mweru
ZAIRE
R. Zaire
Lisala
Kisangani
Boyoma Falls
Mbandaka
Kasai
Sankuru
Kananga
L. Tanganyika
Ujiji
TANZANIA
Tabora
Dodoma
Mbeya
Mtwara
Kilwa Kivinje
Mafia I.
Dar es Salaam
Zanzibar
Pemba I.
Tanga
Arusha
Mwanza
Mt. Kilimanjaro
L. Kivu
RWANDA
BURUNDI
L. Victoria
L. Edward
L. Albert
UGANDA
Kampala
Entebbe
KENYA
Mt. Kenya
Nairobi
Witu
Kismayu
Lamu
Malindi
Mombasa
R. Juba
Brava
Mogadiscio
Amirante Is.
Aldabra I.
Cosmoledo Is.
Glorioso Is.
C. d'Ambre
C. Delgado
Comoro Is.
Mayotte I.
Nossi Be
Majunga
Antananarivo
Toamasina
MADAGASCAR (MALAGASY REP.)
C. Ste Marie
INDIAN OCEAN
Statute Miles
0 100 200 300 400 500 1000
30
20
10
0
10
20
30
40
50
60
© – John Bartholomew & Son Ltd. Edinburgh

# EGYPT, LIBYA

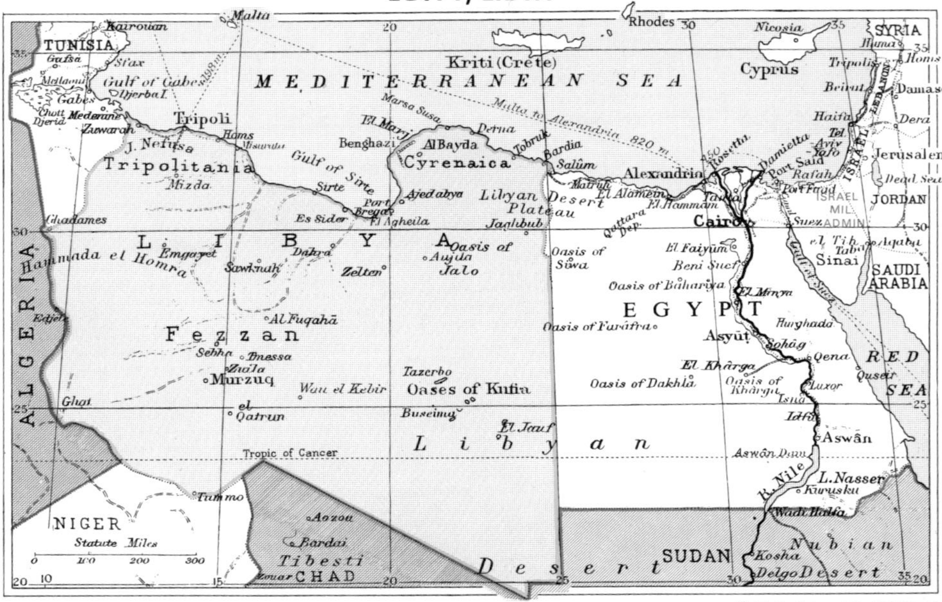

MEDITERRANEAN SEA
Kriti (Crete)
Cyprus
Nicosia
Rhodes
Malta
TUNISIA
Kairouan
Gafsa
Sfax
Gulf of Gabes
Djerba I.
Gabes
Medenine
Zuwarah
Tripoli
Hams
J. Nefusa
Tripolitania
Mizda
Ghadames
ALGERIA
Hammada el Homra
Emgayet
LIBYA
Sawknah
Dahra
Zelten
Gulf of Sirte
Sirte
Es Sider
Port Brega
El Agheila
Benghazi
El Marj
Marsa Susa
Al Bayda
Derna
Cyrenaica
Tobruk
Bardia
Salûm
Ajedabya
Oasis of Aujila
Jalo
Jaghbub
Libyan Plateau
Libyan Desert
Al Fuqahā
Fezzan
Sebha
Brak
Murzuq
Wau el Kebir
Tazerbo
Oases of Kufra
Buseima
el Qatrun
El Jauf
Ghat
Tropic of Cancer
Tummo
NIGER
Aozou
Bardai
Tibesti
CHAD
Statute Miles
0 100 200 300
Malta to Alexandria 820 m.
Alexandria
Matruh
El Alamein
El Hammam
Qattara Dep.
Oasis of Siwa
Rosetta
Damietta
Port Said
Port Fuad
Tanta
Cairo
Suez
El Faiyūm
Beni Suef
Oasis of Bahariya
El Minya
EGYPT
Oasis of Farafra
Asyūt
Sohâg
Qena
Luxor
El Khârga
Oasis of Dakhla
Oasis of Khârga
Isna
Idfu
Aswân
Aswân Dam
R. Nile
L. Nasser
Kurusku
Wadi Halfa
Nubian Desert
Kosha
Delgo
SUDAN
Hurghada
Quseir
RED SEA
Gulf of Suez
Sinai
el Tih
Taba
Aqaba
SAUDI ARABIA
ISRAEL MIL. ADMIN.
JORDAN
Dead Sea
Jerusalem
Rafah
Tel Aviv-Yafo
Haifa
ISRAEL
Beirut
LEBANON
Tripolis
Damascus
Dera
Homs
Hama
SYRIA

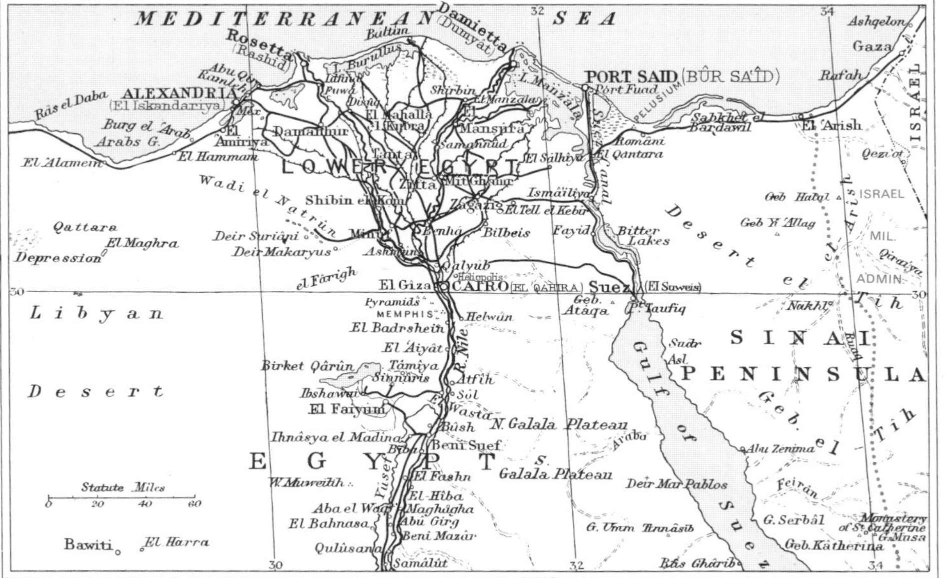
MEDITERRANEAN SEA
Rosetta (Rashid)
Damietta (Dumyat)
Baltim
L. Burullus
Abu Qir
Ras el Daba
ALEXANDRIA (El Iskandariya)
Mex
Burg el Arab
Arabs G.
El Alamein
El Hammam
El Amiriya
Damanhur
Idfina
Fuwa
Disuq
El Mahalla el Kubra
Tanta
Shirbin
El Manzala
Mansura
Samannud
L. Manzala
PORT SAID (BÛR SAÎD)
Port Fuad
PELUSIUM
Sabkhet el Bardawil
El Arish
Rafah
Gaza
Ashqelon
ISRAEL
Romani
El Qantara
Suez Canal
El Salhiya
Ismailiya
El Tell el Kebir
Fayid
Bitter Lakes
LOWER EGYPT
Zifta
Mit Ghamr
Zagazig
Shibin el Kom
Wadi el Natrun
Deir Suriani
Deir Makaryus
Benha
Bilbeis
Qalyub
Heliopolis
El Giza
CAIRO (EL QAHIRA)
Suez (El Suweis)
Pt. Taufiq
Geb. Ataqa
el Farigh
Qattara Depression
El Maghra
Pyramids
MEMPHIS
Helwan
El Badrshein
El Aiyat
Libyan Desert
Birket Qarun
Tamiya
Sinnuris
Atfih
Sol
Ibshawai
El Faiyum
El Wasta
Bush
N. Galala Plateau
Ihnasya el Madina
Beni Suef
Biba
EGYPT
S. Galala Plateau
W. Muweilih
Yusef
El Fashn
El Hiba
Maghagha
Aba el Waqf
El Bahnasa
Abu Girg
Beni Mazar
Qulusana
Samalut
Statute Miles
0
20
40
60
Bawiti
El Harra
Gulf of Suez
Sudr
Asl
SINAI PENINSULA
Desert el Tih
Geb. el Tih
Nakhl
Geb Halal
Geb Yi Allag
Qezi ot
Qiraiya
ISRAEL MIL. ADMIN.
El Arish
Araba
Abu Zenima
Feiran
Deir Mar Pablos
G. Umm Tinnasib
G. Serbal
Monastery of St. Catherine
G. Musa
Geb. Katherina
Ras Gharib
30
32
34

# NORTH-WEST AFRICA

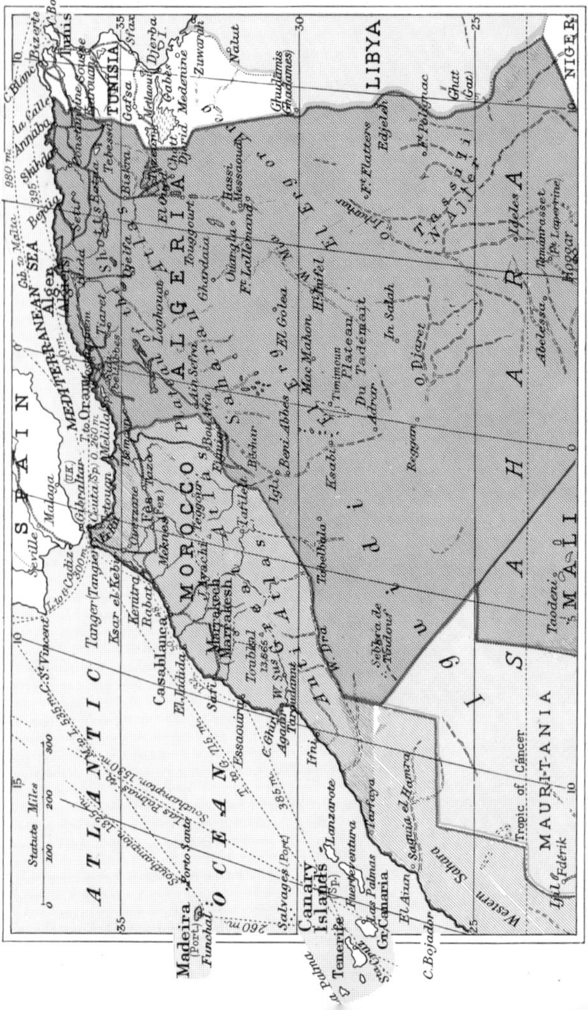

Statute Miles
0 100 200 300

ATLANTIC OCEAN
MEDITERRANEAN SEA
SPAIN
Seville
Malaga
Cadiz
Gibraltar (UK.)
Ceuta (Sp.)
Tetouan
Melilla
Tanger (Tangier)
Ksar el Kebir
Kenitra
Rabat
Casablanca
El Jadida
Safi
Essaouira
Agadir
Taroudannt
Ifni
MOROCCO
Meknes
Fès (Fez)
Taza
Ouezzane
Marrakech (Marrakesh)
Toubkal 13,665
J. Ayachi
Teggour
Tafilelt
Figuig
Great Atlas
Anti Atlas
W. Sus
W. Dra
C. Ghir
C. St. Vincent
Madeira (Port.)
Porto Santo
Funchal
Salvages (Port.)
Canary Islands (Sp.)
La Palma
Tenerife
Sta Cruz
Lanzarote
Fuerteventura
Las Palmas
Gr. Canaria
Tarfaya
El Aiun
Saguia el Hamra
C. Bojador
Western Sahara
Tropic of Cancer
MAURITANIA
Ijil
Fdérik
Sebkra de Tindouf
Igidi
Tabelbala
Taodeni
MALI
SAHARA
ALGERIA
Alger (Algiers)
Blida
Oran
Mostaganem
Tiaret
Sidi bel Abbes
Tlemcen
Setif
Bejaia
Skikda
Annaba
La Calle
Constantine
Batna
Tebessa
Biskra
Djelfa
Laghouat
Shotts
Plateau of the Shotts
Saharan Atlas
Ain Sefra
Bou Arfa
Bechar
Igli
Beni Abbes
El Erg
El Golea
Ghardaia
Touggourt
El Oued
Ouargla
Hassi Messaoud
Ft. Lallemand
Mac Mahon
Hassi Inifel
W. Mia
Ksabi
Timimoun
Plateau Du Tademait
Adrar
In Salah
Reggan
O. Djaret
O. Irharhar
Ft. Flatters
Edjeleh
Ft. Polignac
Tassili n'Ajjer
Ideles
Abelessa
Tamanrasset
Ft. Laperrine
Hoggar
Ghudamis (Ghadames)
Ghat (Gat)
LIBYA
NIGER
TUNISIA
Tunis
C. Blanc
Bizerte
C. Bon
Sousse
Kairouan
Gafsa
Metlaoui
Sfax
Gabes
Djerba I.
Medenine
Chott Djerid
Tozeur
Zuwarah
Nalut

MAURITANIA
Hodh
Nouakchott
Kiffa
Kaedi
R. Senegal
Nema
Tombouctou (Timbuktu)
Kabara
R. Niger
Bourem
Gao
Cape Verde Is.
São Antão
São Vicente
Sal
S. Nicolau
Boa Vista
Fogo
Maio
Brava
São Tiago
St. Louis
Dagana
Matam
Bakel
Rufisque
C. Verde
Thies
SENEGAL
Dakar
Diourbel
Kaolack
Kayes
Medine
Banjul
THE GAMBIA
R. Gambia
Tambacounda
Ziguinchor
GUINEA BISSAU
Bissau
Bolama
Bissagos Is. (Bijagos)
S.T. to E. 720 m.
Dakar to Rio de Oro 580 m.
Nioro
Nara
L. Debo
Hombori
Sahel
Macina
Mopti
MALI
Bafoulabe
Nyamina
Segou
San
Kita
Koulikoro
Bamako
Koutiala
Dedougou
Koudougou
Yatenga
UPPER VOLTA
Mossi
Ouagadougou
NIGER
Bobo Dioulosso
Sikasso
Siguiri
Labe
GUINEA
Mamou
R. Niger
Kankan
Ouassoulou
Boke
Conakry
Los Is. (Fr.)
Kindia
Kabala
Faranah
Daro Mt.
SIERRA LEONE
Freetown
Pendembu
Beyla
Bo
N'Zerekore
Lola
Sherbro I.
LIBERIA
Robertsport
Monrovia
Buchanan
R. Cess
Greenville
R. Kavalli
Harper
C. Palmas
Grain Coast
ATLANTIC OCEAN
IVORY COAST
Kong
Bouna
White Bandama
Sequela
Bouake
Bondoukou
Sassandra
Dimbokro
Baoule
Komoe
Abidjan
Bingerville
Tabou
Ivory Coast
Gr. Bassam
M. to S. 588 m.
Black Volta
White Volta
Gambaga
Mango
Tamale
Yendi
Salaga
GHANA
Atakpame
Sunyani
Kumasi
Koforidua
Oda
Sekondi
Takoradi
Cape Coast
Winneba
Accra
Gold Coast
C. Three Points
Ho
R. Volta
Lomé
Anécho
Palime
Sokodé
Oti
TOGO
BENIN
GULF OF GUINEA
Statute Miles
0 100 200 300 400
© – John Bartholomew & Son Ltd. Edinburgh

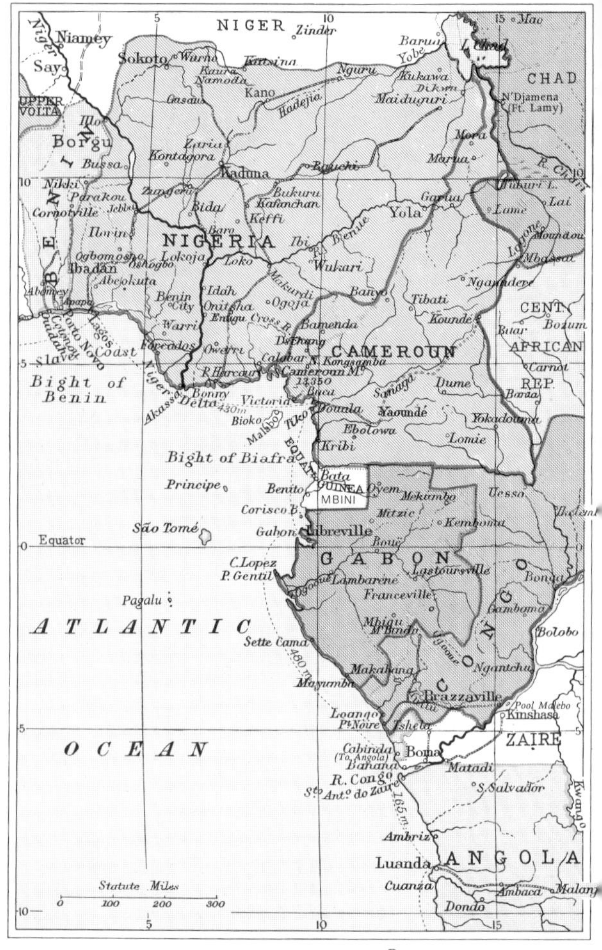
NIGER
Zinder
Niamey
Say
Sokoto
Katsina
Kano
Nguru
Kukawa
Maiduguri
L. Chad
CHAD
N'Djamena (Ft. Lamy)
UPPER VOLTA
Borgu
BENIN
Bussa
Zaria
Kontagora
Kaduna
Bauchi
Mora
Marua
Nikki
Parakou
Bida
Kafanchan
Keffi
Yola
Garua
Lame
Lai
Ilorin
NIGERIA
Lokoja
Ibi
Wukari
Moundou
Ogbomosho
Oshogbo
Ibadan
Abeokuta
Abomey
Benin City
Idah
Onitsha
Ogoja
Makurdi
Banyo
Tibati
Ngaundere
Enugu
Cross R.
Bamenda
Kounde
CENT. AFRICAN REP.
Bozum
Lagos
Porto Novo
Cotonou
Ouidah
Warri
Owerri
Calabar
CAMEROUN
Carnot
Slave Coast
Bight of Benin
P. Harcourt
Cameroun Mt.
13350
N. Kongsamba
Buea
Sanaga
Dume
Bonny
Victoria
Akassa
Niger Delta
430m
Bioko
Malabo
Tiko
Douala
Yaoundé
Yokadouma
Ebolowa
Lomie
Kribi
Bight of Biafra
EQUAT.
Bata
GUINEA
MBINI
Oyem
Mekambo
Principe
Benito
Corisco B.
Mitzic
Kemboma
Ouesso
São Tomé
Gabon
Libreville
Equator
Bouë
GABON
C. Lopez
P. Gentil
Lastoursville
Lambarene
Franceville
Bonga
Pagalu
Gamboma
CONGO
ATLANTIC
Sette Cama
Bolobo
480 m
Mbigu
M'Banda
Makabana
Ngantchu
Mayumba
Brazzaville
Pool Malebo
Kinshasa
Loango
Pt. Noire
ZAIRE
OCEAN
Cabinda (To Angola)
Boma
Banana
Matadi
R. Congo
S. Salvador
St. Antº do Zaire
165 m.
Kwango
Ambriz
Luanda
ANGOLA
Cuanza
Ambaca
Dondo
Statute Miles
0 100 200 300

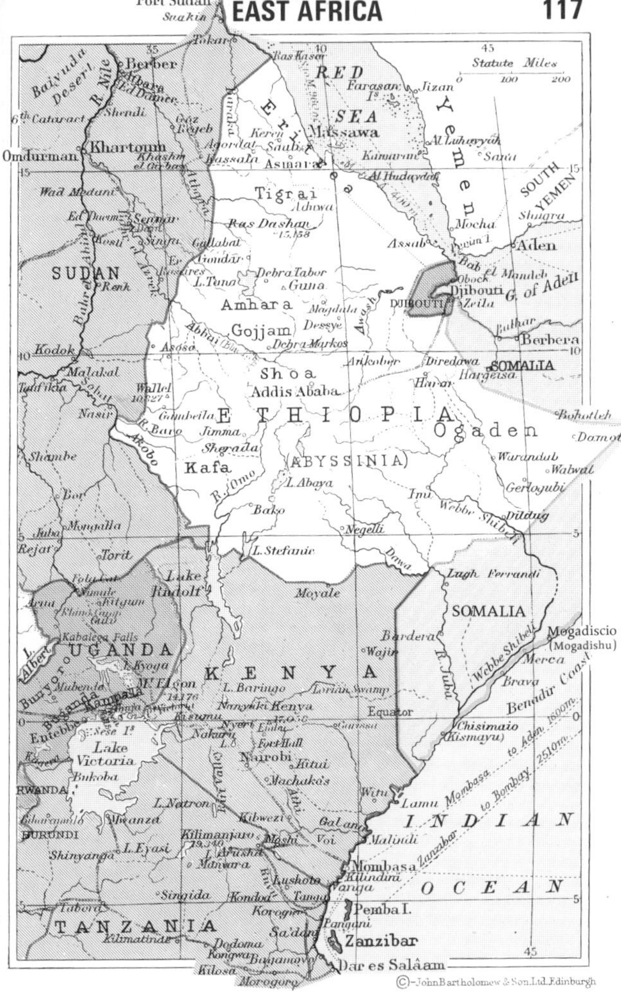
Port Sudan
Suakin
Statute Miles
0 100 200
RED SEA
Eritrea
Yemen
SOUTH YEMEN
SUDAN
ETHIOPIA
(ABYSSINIA)
DJIBOUTI
SOMALIA
UGANDA
KENYA
TANZANIA
RWANDA
BURUNDI
INDIAN OCEAN
Khartoum
Omdurman
Berber
Massawa
Asmara
Addis Ababa
Djibouti
Aden
Berbera
Mogadiscio
(Mogadishu)
Lake Rudolf
Lake Victoria
Kampala
Entebbe
Nairobi
Mombasa
Pemba I.
Zanzibar
Dar es Salâam
Benadir Coast
Equator

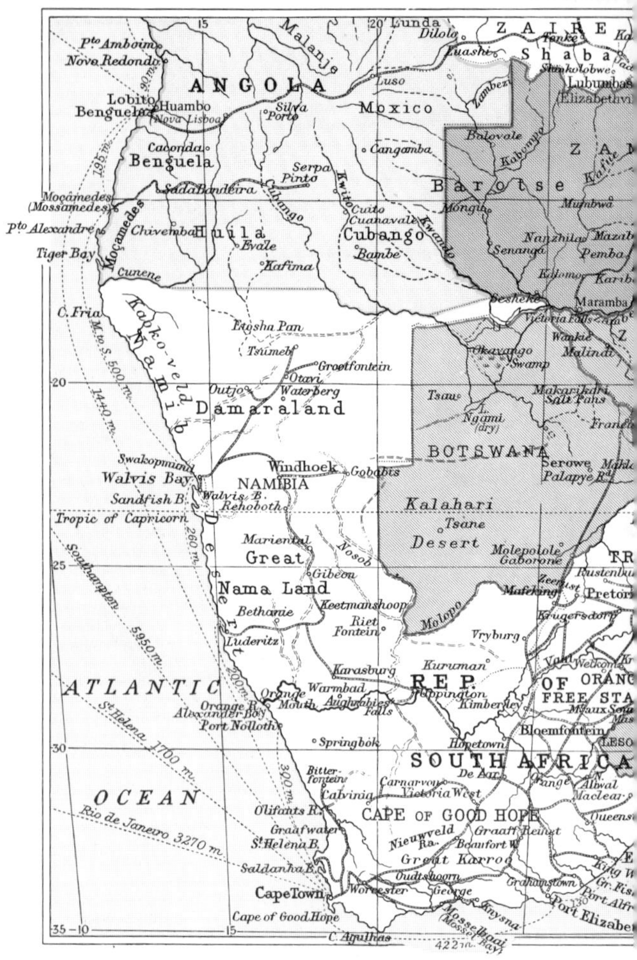
ANGOLA
ZAIRE
Shaba
Lunda
Dilolo
Malanje
Luso
Moxico
Pto Amboim
Novo Redondo
Lobito
Benguela
Huambo
(Nova Lisboa)
Silva Porto
Caconda
Benguela
Cangamba
Serpa Pinto
Sá da Bandeira
Moçâmedes
(Mossamedes)
Pto Alexandre
Tiger Bay
Mocamedes
Chivemba
Huila
Evale
Kafima
Cubango
Cuito Cuanavale
Bambe
Cunene
Kwando
Barotse
Balovale
Kabompo
Mongu
Senanga
Nanzhila
Mumbwa
Pemba
Maramba
Sesheke
Victoria Falls
Wankie
Malindi
C. Fria
Kaoko-veld
Namib
Etosha Pan
Tsumeb
Grootfontein
Otavi
Waterberg
Outjo
Damaraland
Okavango Swamp
Makarikari Salt Pans
Tsau
L. Ngami (dry)
BOTSWANA
Serowe
Palapye Rd.
Swakopmund
Walvis Bay
Windhoek
Gobabis
NAMIBIA
Walvis B.
Sandfish B.
Rehoboth
Kalahari
Tsane
Desert
Tropic of Capricorn
Mariental
Great
Nama Land
Gibeon
Nosob
Molepolole
Gaborone
Zeerust
Mafeking
Pretoria
Rustenburg
Keetmanshoop
Bethanie
Molopo
Riet Fontein
Vryburg
Kuruman
Luderitz
Karasburg
Warmbad
Upington
Kimberley
Orange Mouth
Aughrabies Falls
REP. OF ORANGE FREE STATE
Bloemfontein
Orange R.
Alexander Bay
Port Nolloth
Springbok
Hopetown
SOUTH AFRICA
De Aar
Bitterfontein
Carnarvon
Victoria West
Calvinia
Olifants R.
CAPE OF GOOD HOPE
Graafwater
St. Helena B.
Nieuwveld Ra.
Graaff Reinet
Beaufort W.
Great Karroo
Saldanha B.
Oudtshoorn
Grahamstown
Cape Town
Worcester
George
Knysna
Port Alfred
Port Elizabeth
Mossel Baai (Mossel Bay)
Cape of Good Hope
C. Agulhas
ATLANTIC
OCEAN
Southampton 5950 m.
St. Helena 1700 m.
Rio de Janeiro 3270 m.
M. to S. 500 m.
1440 m.
260 m.
200 m.
300 m.
195 m.
90 m.
422 m.
15
20
25
30
35
10

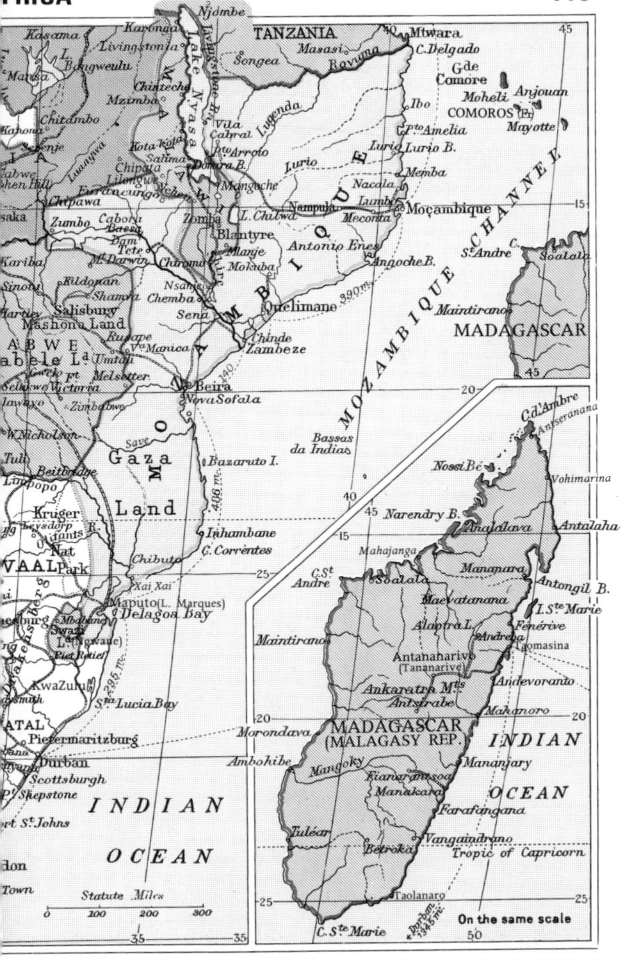
TANZANIA
MOZAMBIQUE
MALAWI
MOZAMBIQUE CHANNEL
MADAGASCAR
MADAGASCAR (MALAGASY REP.)
COMOROS (Fr)
INDIAN OCEAN
Mtwara
C. Delgado
Njombe
Karonga
Songea
Masasi
Rovuma
Livingstonia
Lake Nyasa
Lilongwe
Zomba
Blantyre
Nampula
Moçambique
Quelimane
Beira
Nova Sofala
Gaza Land
Inhambane
C. Correntes
Chibuto
Xai Xai
Maputo (L. Marques)
Delagoa Bay
Salisbury
Mashona Land
Umtali
Zambeze
Chinde
Tete
Sena
Bazaruto I.
Bassas da Indias
Kruger Nat. Park
Swazi L. (Ngwane)
KwaZulu
St. Lucia Bay
Pietermaritzburg
Durban
Scottsburgh
Pt. Shepstone
Port St. Johns
Gde Comore
Moheli
Anjouan
Mayotte
Ibo
Pto Amelia
Lurio B.
Memba
Nacala
Angoche B.
Maintirano
Nossi Bé
C. d'Ambre
Antseranana
Vohimarina
Antalaha
Narendry B.
Analalava
Mahajanga
Mananara
Antongil B.
I. Ste Marie
Fénérive
Toamasina
Antananarivo (Tananarive)
Andevoranto
Ankaratra Mts
Antsirabe
Mahanoro
Morondava
Ambohibe
Mananjary
Fianarantsoa
Manakara
Farafangana
Tuléar
Betroka
Vangaindrano
Tropic of Capricorn
Taolanaro
C. Ste Marie
Statute Miles
0 100 200 300
On the same scale

Halmahera
Manado
Ternate
MOLUCCAS
Sarawak
BORNEO
Samarinda
Kalimantan
Makassar Str.
G. of Tomini
SULAWESI
(Celebes)
Sula Is.
Seram
Buru
Ambon
Bone G.
Butung
Banda Sea
Laut
INDONESIA
Kai Is.
Aru Is.
Banjarmasin
Ujung Pandang
Tanimbar Is.
Kolepom I.
Java Sea
Flores Sea
Madura
Bali
Lombok
Flores
Solor Is.
Alor Is.
Wetar
Dili
Arafura Sea
Surabaya
JAVA
Sumbawa
Sumba
Timor
Kupang
Roti
Manokwari
Biak
Yapen
Pt. d'Urville
Irian B.
Jayapura
IRIAN JAYA
Torres
Thursday
Wessel I.
Melville B.
Cobourg Pena.
Van Diemen G.
Melville I.
Bathurst I.
Darwin
Rum Jungle
Arnhem Land
Gulf of Carpentaria
Groote Eylandt
Katherine
Timor Sea
Queens Channel
Cambridge G.
Daly R.
R. Roper
Victoria
Wellesley Is.
Birdum
Barkly Tableland
Burketown
Collier Bay
King Sd.
Wyndham
C. Leveque
Black Rocks
Derby
Newcastle Waters
Broome
Fitzroy R.
NORTHERN TERRITORY
Tennant Creek
Great Sandy Desert
Mt. Wilson
Central Mt. Stuart
Port Hedland
Roebourne
L. Mackay
Macdonnell Ra.
Onslow
Exmouth G.
N. West Cape
L. Macdonald
L. Amadeus
Alice Springs
Mt. Bruce
Ashburton
L. Disappointment
L. Hopkins
Gibson Desert
AUSTRAL
Carnarvon
Oodnadatta
L. Eyre
Shark B.
Meekatharra
Wiluna
Murchison R.
WESTERN AUSTRALIA
Great Victoria Desert
SOUTH AUSTRALIA
Steep Pt.
L. Austin
Maralinga
L. Torrens
Nullarbor Plain
L. Gairdner
Geraldton
Kalgoorlie
Boulder
Coolgardie
Eucla
Port Augusta
Whyalla
Northam
L. Lefroy
L. Cowan
Great Australian Bight
Perth
Swan R.
York
Fremantle
Geographe B.
C. Naturaliste
Bunbury
Albany
C. Leeuwin
Esperance
Recherche Archipo.
Spencer G.
St. Vincent G.
Kangaroo I.
Encounter B.
King George Sd.
INDIAN OCEAN
Statute Miles
0
500
1000
120
140
10
20
30
40
100
110
130

Equator
Gilbert Is (U.K.)
KIRIBATI
Admiralty Is
Manus
New Hanover
New Ireland
Bismarck Archipelago
Rabaul
Kokopo
Madang
New Britain
NEW GUINEA
Lae
Huon G.
Bougainville
SOLOMON ISLANDS
Choiseul
Isabel
G. of Papua
Mt Victoria
Pt Moresby
York
New Georgia
Guadalcanal
Malaita
Samarai
China Str.
Louisiade Archo
San Cristobal
Rennell
Sta Cruz Is
Ndeni
Great Barrier Reef
CORAL SEA
Willis Is
Cairns
Espiritu Santo
Banks Is
Malekula
VANUATU
Halifax B.
Townsville
Port Denison
Bowen
Chesterfield Is (Fr.)
Efate
Charters Towers
PACIFIC
FIJI
Mackay
Eromanga
Fitzroy R.
Rockhampton
New Caledonia (Fr.) Noumea
Loyalty Is
Tropic of Capricorn
Morgan
Bundaberg
Hervey B.
Maryborough
Fraser or Grt Sandy I.
Gt Dividing Ra.
Moreton Bay
Toowoomba
Brisbane
Ipswich
OCEAN
C. Byron
Barwon R.
Grafton
Darling R.
Bourke
Peel R.
Norfolk I. (Aust.)
Tamworth
New England Ra.
Port Macquarie
SOUTH WALES
Maitland
Lord Howe I. (Aust.)
Bathurst
Newcastle
Katoomba
Blue M.
Goulburn
Sydney
Wollongong
Murrumbidgee
Canberra
Albury
Mt Kosciusko 2,316
Mt Townsend
Kermadec Is (N.Z.)
Australian Alps
Cape Howe
TASMAN SEA
North C.
Melbourne
Wilsons Prom.
Auckland
Bass Strait
Hamilton
Furneaux Is
New Plymouth
Mt Egmont
North I.
East C.
Launceston
NEW ZEALAND
Cook Str.
Gisborne
Hobart
Ruapehu
Napier
Nelson
Wellington
Hokitika
South I.
Christchurch
Mt Cook 12,349
Chatham Is
West C.
Dunedin
Stewart I.
Invercargill
150
160
170
180
0
10
20
30
40

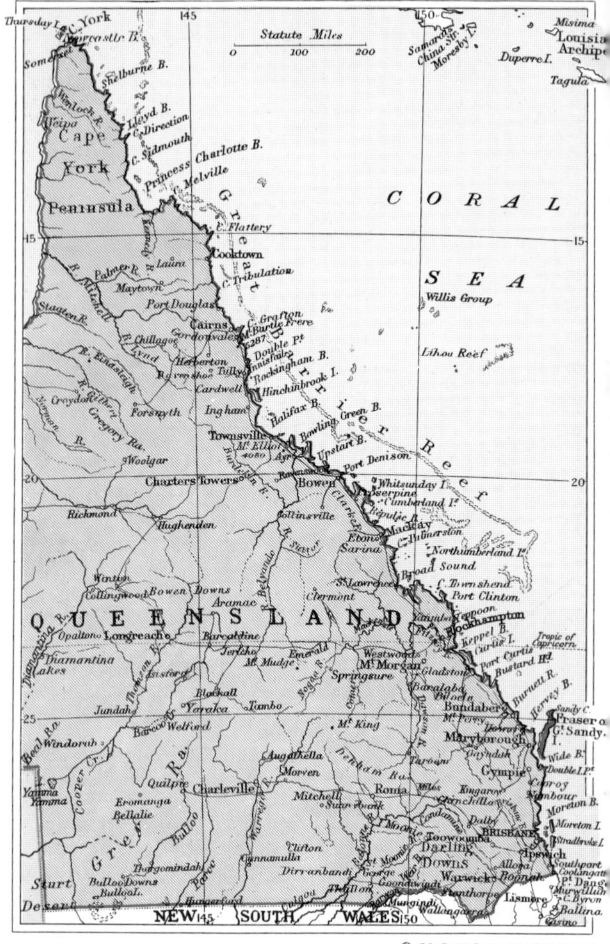
Statute Miles
0 100 200
C O R A L
S E A
Q U E E N S L A N D
Cape York Peninsula
Great Barrier Reef
Thursday I.
C. York
Newcastle B.
Shelburne B.
Lloyd B.
C. Direction
C. Sidmouth
Princess Charlotte B.
C. Melville
C. Flattery
Cooktown
C. Tribulation
Laura
Palmer R.
Maytown
Port Douglas
Cairns
C. Grafton
Mt Bartle Frere 5287
Double Pt
Innisfail
Rockingham B.
Hinchinbrook I.
Cardwell
Ingham
Halifax B.
Bowling Green B.
Townsville
Mt Elliot 4080
Ayr
Upstart B.
Port Denison
Bowen
Whitsunday I.
Proserpine
Cumberland Is
Mackay
C. Palmerston
Northumberland Is
Broad Sound
C. Townshend
Port Clinton
Yeppoon
Rockhampton
Keppel B.
Curtis I.
Port Curtis
Bustard Hd
Tropic of Capricorn
Gladstone
Burnett R.
Hervey B.
Bundaberg
Maryborough
Sandy C.
Fraser or Gt Sandy I.
Wide B.
Double I. Pt
Gympie
Cooroy
Nambour
Moreton B.
Moreton I.
Stradbroke I.
BRISBANE
Ipswich
Southport
Coolangatta
Pt Danger
Murwillumbah
C. Byron
Ballina
Casino
Lismore
Toowoomba
Darling Downs
Warwick
Stanthorpe
Wallangarra
Goondiwindi
Mungindi
Dalby
Kingaroy
Nanango
Miles
Roma
Mitchell
Surat
Condamine
Moonie R.
St George
Dirranbandi
Thallon
Cunnamulla
Clifton
Charleville
Augathella
Morven
Quilpie
Eromanga
Bellalie
Thargomindah
Bulloo Downs
Bulloo L.
Hungerford
Bulloo
Paroo
Warrego R.
Sturt Desert
Cooper Cr.
Windorah
Beal Ra.
Yamma Yamma
Grey Ra.
Jundah
Isisford
Blackall
Yaraka
Tambo
Barcoo
Welford
Longreach
Opalton
Diamantina Lakes
Diamantina R.
Barcaldine
Jericho
Emerald
Mt Mudge
Springsure
Westwood
Mt Morgan
Baralaba
Taroom
Mt King
Dawson R.
Winton
Collingwood
Bowen Downs
Aramac
Belyando
Clermont
St Lawrence
Sarina
Eton
Collinsville
R. Suttor
Hughenden
Richmond
Charters Towers
Burdekin R.
Woolgar
Forsayth
Croydon
Gregory Ra.
R. Gilbert
Norman R.
R. Einasleigh
Chillagoe
R. Lynd
Herberton
Ravenshoe
Tully
Staaten R.
R. Mitchell
Kennedy R.
Wenlock R.
Weipa
Somerset
Samarai
China Str.
Moresby I.
Misima
Louisiade Archipelago
Duperre I.
Tagula
Willis Group
Lihou Reef
NEW SOUTH WALES
145
150
15
20
25

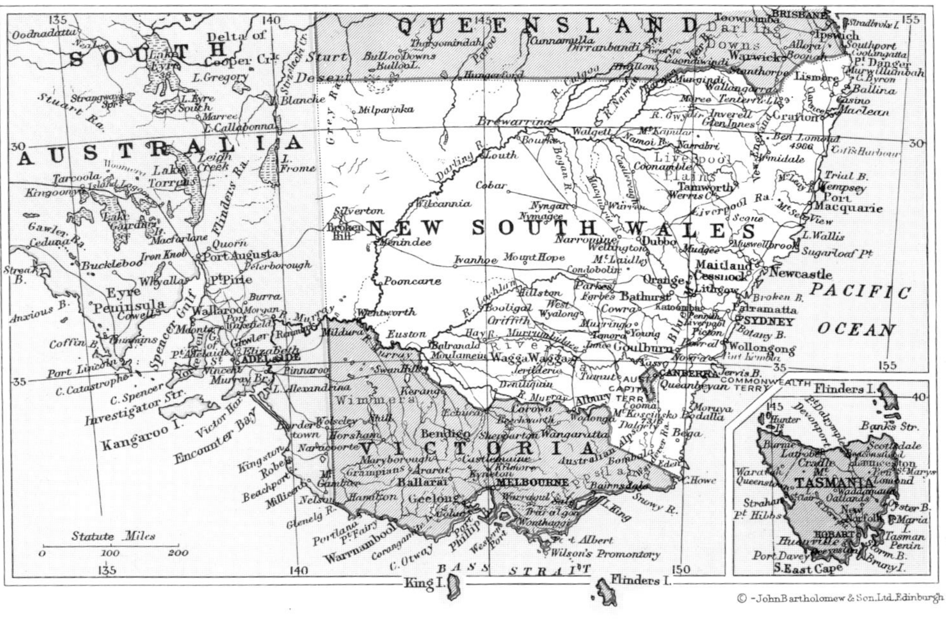
QUEENSLAND
SOUTH AUSTRALIA
NEW SOUTH WALES
VICTORIA
PACIFIC OCEAN
TASMANIA
BASS STRAIT
BRISBANE
SYDNEY
CANBERRA
MELBOURNE
ADELAIDE
HOBART
Newcastle
Wollongong
Maitland
Dubbo
Bathurst
Goulburn
Wagga Wagga
Albury
Bendigo
Ballarat
Geelong
Broken Hill
Port Augusta
Pt Pirie
Whyalla
Port Lincoln
Eyre Peninsula
Spencer Gulf
Kangaroo I.
Investigator Str.
Encounter Bay
Lake Torrens
Lake Eyre
L. Frome
Flinders Ra.
Stuart Ra.
Sturt Desert
Darling Downs
Liverpool Plains
Australian Alps
Wilson's Promontory
King I.
Flinders I.
Banks Str.
S. East Cape
Statute Miles
0
100
200
© -John Bartholomew & Son. Ltd. Edinburgh

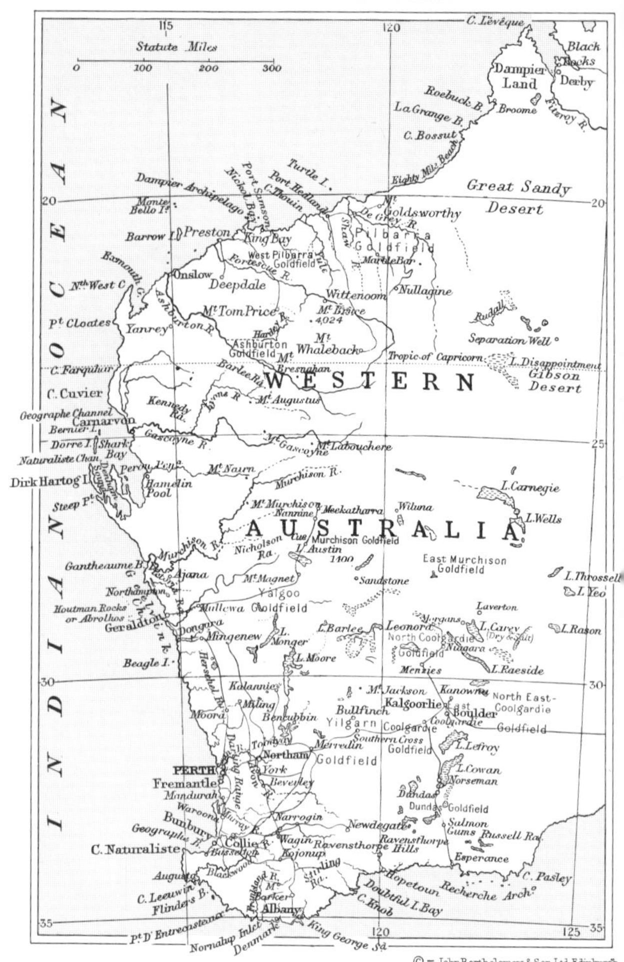
Statute Miles
0 100 200 300
WESTERN
AUSTRALIA
INDIAN OCEAN
Great Sandy Desert
Gibson Desert
Dampier Land
Derby
Broome
Roebuck B.
La Grange B.
C. Bossut
Eighty Mile Beach
Port Hedland
Pilbarra Goldfield
West Pilbarra Goldfield
Ashburton Goldfield
Murchison Goldfield
East Murchison Goldfield
Yalgoo Goldfield
North Coolgardie Goldfield
North East-Coolgardie Goldfield
Coolgardie Goldfield
Yilgarn Goldfield
Dundas Goldfield
Carnarvon
Shark Bay
Dirk Hartog I.
Geraldton
PERTH
Fremantle
Bunbury
Albany
Kalgoorlie
Boulder
Norseman
Esperance
Wiluna
Leonora
C. Naturaliste
C. Leeuwin
King George Sd.
Tropic of Capricorn
© – John Bartholomew & Son Ltd. Edinburgh

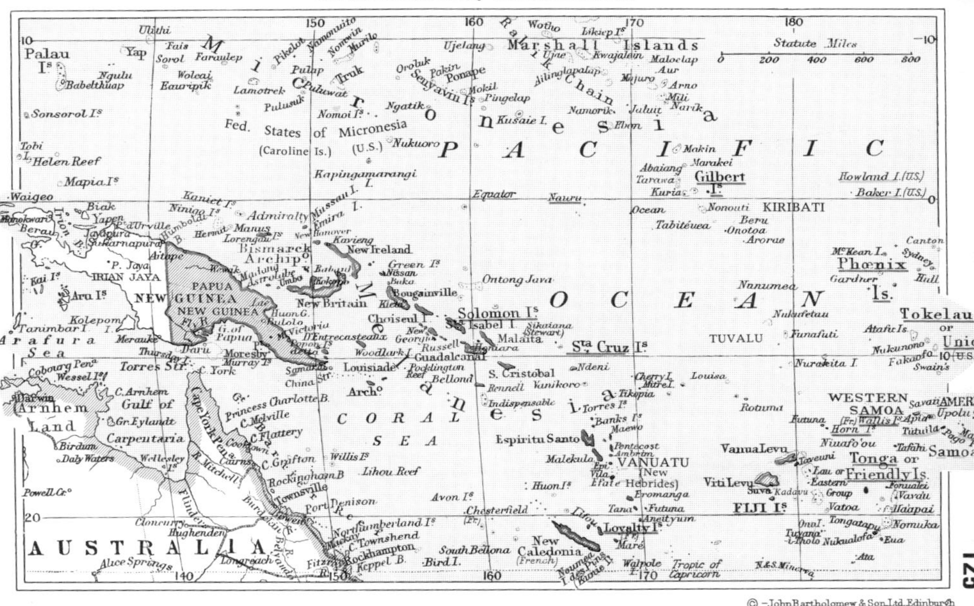
P A C I F I C
O C E A N
Statute Miles
0 200 400 600 800
180
160
170
150
140
10
20
Equator
Tropic of Capricorn
M i c r o n e s i a
M e l a n e s i a
Marshall Islands
Ralik Chain
Ratak Chain
Ujelang
Wotho
Likiep Is.
Kwajalein
Maloelap
Aur
Majuro
Arno
Mili
Jaluit
Ebon
Namorik
Kusaie I.
Pingelap
Mokil
Ponape
Pakin
Senyavin Is.
Oroluk
Ngatik
Nukuoro
Truk
Nomoi Is.
Fed. States of Micronesia
(Caroline Is.)
(U.S.)
Kapingamarangi I.
Palau Is.
Babelthuap
Ngulu
Yap
Ulithi
Fais
Sorol
Faraulep
Woleai
Eauripik
Lamotrek
Pulap
Puluwat
Pulusuk
Sonsorol Is.
Tobi I.
Helen Reef
Mapia Is.
Nauru
Ocean
KIRIBATI
Gilbert Is.
Makin
Marakei
Abaiang
Tarawa
Kuria
Nonouti
Tabiteuea
Beru
Onotoa
Arorae
Howland I. (U.S.)
Baker I. (U.S.)
Phœnix Is.
McKean I.
Gardner
Canton
Sydney
Hull
Tokelau or Union Is.
Atafu Is.
Nukunono
Fakaofo
Swain's
TUVALU
Nanumea
Nukufetau
Funafuti
Nurakita I.
Louisa
WESTERN SAMOA
Savaii
Upolu
Apia
Tutuila
Pago Pago
Manu'a
Samoa
Wallis Is. (Fr.)
Horn Is.
Futuna
Niuafo'ou
Tafahi
Tonga or Friendly Is.
Lau or Eastern Group
Taveuni
Vavau
Haapai
Vatoa
Nomuka
Tongatapu
Nukualofa
Eua
Ata
Rotuma
Vanua Levu
Viti Levu
Suva
Kadavu
FIJI Is.
N.&S. Minerva
Ono I.
Tuvana-i-Tholo
Sta. Cruz Is.
Ndeni
Vanikoro
Cherry I.
Mitre I.
Tikopia
Torres Is.
Banks Is.
Maewo
Pentecost
Ambrym
VANUATU
(New Hebrides)
Espiritu Santo
Malekula
Epi
Vila
Efate
Eromanga
Tana
Futuna
Aneityum
Loyalty Is.
Lifou
Maré
New Caledonia
(French)
Noumea
I. des Pins
Walpole
Huon Is.
Chesterfield (Fr.)
Avon Is.
South Bellona
Bird I.
Solomon Is.
Ontong Java
Sikaiana
(Stewart)
Malaita
Sta. Isabel I.
Choiseul I.
Bougainville
Kieta
Buka
Nissan
Green Is.
New Georgia
Russell
Honiara
Guadalcanal
S. Cristobal
Rennell
Bellona
Indispensable
Woodlark I.
D'Entrecasteaux
Louisiade Archo.
Coral Sea
Pocklington Reef
Willis Is.
Lihou Reef
Bismarck Archipo.
New Britain
New Ireland
New Hanover
Kavieng
Rabaul
Manus
Admiralty Is.
Lorengau
Hermit Is.
Mussau I.
Emira I.
Umboi
Lae
Huon G.
Bulolo
Madang
Wewak
Aitape
PAPUA NEW GUINEA
G. of Papua
Fly R.
Port Moresby
Daru
Murray Is.
Samarai
China Str.
C. York
Thursday I.
Torres Str.
Cape York Pena.
Gulf of Carpentaria
Gr. Eylandt
Wellesley Is.
C. Arnhem
Arnhem Land
Darwin
Coburg Pena.
Wessel Is.
Birdum
Daly Waters
Powell Cr.
Alice Springs
Cloncurry
Hughenden
Longreach
Flinders R.
Burdekin R.
Belyando R.
R. Mitchell
C. Melville
Princess Charlotte B.
C. Flattery
Cooktown
Cairns
C. Grafton
Rockingham B.
Townsville
Bowen
Port Denison
Northumberland Is.
Mackay
C. Townshend
Rockhampton
Keppel B.
Fitzroy R.
A U S T R A L I A
NEW GUINEA
IRIAN JAYA
P. Jaya
Sukarnapura
Humboldt B.
d'Urville
Biak
Yapen
Waigeo
Manokwari
Irion
Berau
Aru Is.
Kai Is.
Tanimbar I.
Kolepom I.
Merauke
Arafura Sea
Kaniet Is.
Ninigo Is.

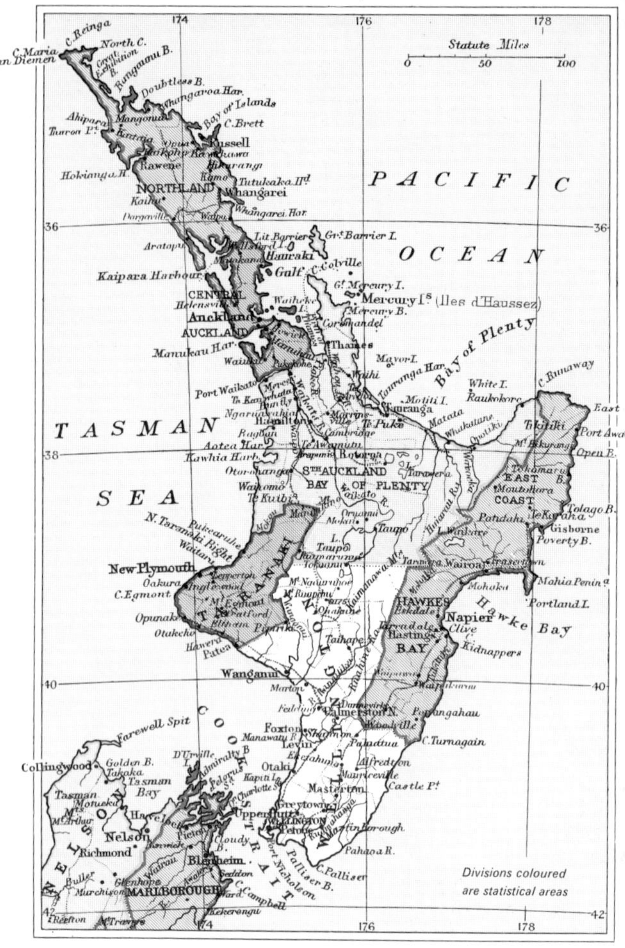
Statute Miles
0
50
100
C. Reinga
C. Maria van Diemen
North C.
Great Exhibition B.
Rangaunu B.
Doubtless B.
Whangaroa Har.
Bay of Islands
C. Brett
Ahipara
Mangonui
Kaitaia
Russell
Kawakawa
Rawene
Hokianga R.
Hikurangi
Kamo
Tutukaka Hd
NORTHLAND
Whangarei
Kaihu
Dargaville
Waipu
Whangarei Har.
Lit. Barrier
Gt. Barrier I.
Aratapu
Hauraki
Gulf
C. Colville
Kaipara Harbour
Gt. Mercury I.
Mercury Is (Iles d'Haussez)
CENTRAL
Helensville
Waiheke I.
Mercury B.
Auckland
Coromandel
AUCKLAND
Thames
Manukau Har.
Waiuku
Pukekohe
Mayor I.
Waihi
Tauranga Har.
Bay of Plenty
C. Runaway
White I.
Raukokore
Port Waikato
Motiti I.
Tauranga
Matata
Whakatane
Opotiki
Tikitiki
East
Port Awa
Ngaruawahia
Hamilton
Morrinsville
Te Puke
Raglan
Cambridge
Te Awamutu
Mt Hikurangi
Aotea Har.
Kawhia Harb.
Rotorua
Open B.
Otorohanga
STH AUCKLAND
BAY OF PLENTY
Tarawera
Tokomaru B.
EAST
COAST
Te Kuiti
Waikato R.
Tolaga B.
Te Karaka
Gisborne
Poverty B.
Taupo
L. Taupo
L. Waikare
N. Taranaki Bight
Waitara
New Plymouth
Wairoa
Frasertown
Mahia Penin.a
TARANAKI
Oakura
Inglewood
C. Egmont
Mt Egmont
Mt Ruapehu
Mohaka
Portland I.
HAWKES
Eskdale
Napier
Hawke Bay
Opunake
Stratford
Eltham
Clive
Otakeho
Hastings
C. Kidnappers
Taihape
BAY
Hawera
Patea
Wanganui
Marton
Feilding
Dannevirke
Palmerston N.
Porangahau
Farewell Spit
Foxton
Woodville
Shannon
C. Turnagain
Levin
Pahiatua
Collingwood
Golden B.
Takaka
D'Urville I.
Admiralty B.
Otaki
Alfredton
Tasman Bay
Kapiti I.
Mauriceville
Castle Pt
Tasman
Motueka
Masterton
Greytown
Havelock
Upper Hutt
WELLINGTON
Nelson
Picton
Petone
Martinborough
Richmond
Cloudy B.
Pahaoa R.
Blenheim
Palliser B.
Port Nicholson
C. Palliser
Divisions coloured are statistical areas
Buller
Glenhope
Seddon
Murchison
MARLBOROUGH
C. Campbell
Ward
Kekerengu
Reefton
Mt Travers
PACIFIC
OCEAN
TASMAN
SEA
COOK STRAIT
174
176
178
36
38
40
42

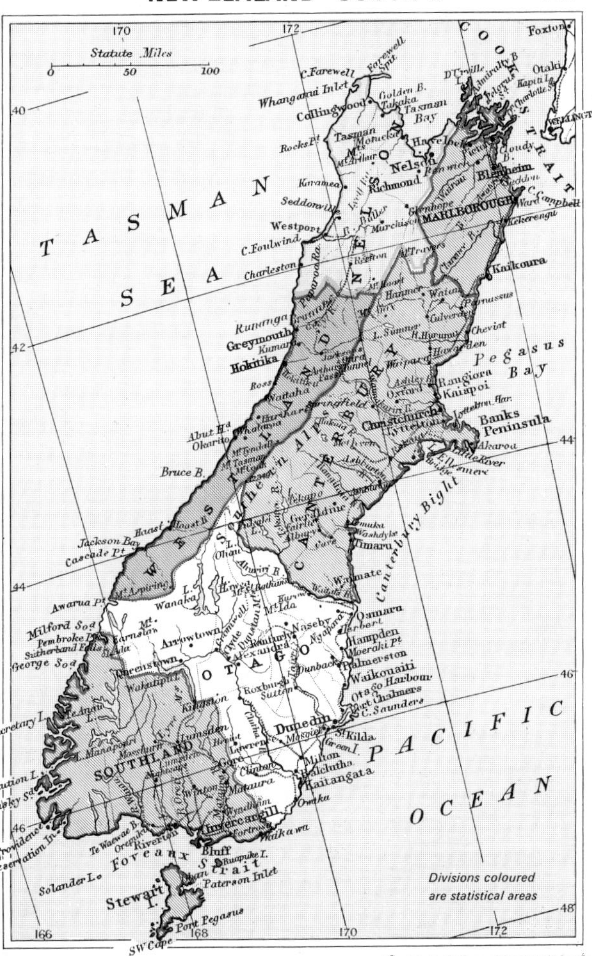
Statute Miles
TASMAN SEA
PACIFIC OCEAN
COOK STRAIT
C. Farewell
Whanganui Inlet
Collingwood
Golden B.
Tasman Bay
Nelson
Richmond
Blenheim
MARLBOROUGH
Westport
C. Foulwind
Charleston
Kaikoura
Greymouth
Hokitika
Pegasus Bay
Rangiora
Kaiapoi
Christchurch
Lyttelton
Banks Peninsula
Akaroa
Bruce B.
Canterbury Bight
Timaru
Jackson Bay
Cascade Pt.
Waimate
Oamaru
Milford Sd.
George Sd.
Arrowtown
Queenstown
OTAGO
Alexandra
Naseby
Palmerston
Waikouaiti
Otago Harbour
Port Chalmers
Dunedin
SOUTHLAND
Gore
Milton
Balclutha
Kaitangata
Invercargill
Bluff
Riverton
Foveaux Strait
Stewart I.
Paterson Inlet
Port Pegasus
SW Cape
Solander I.
WELLINGTON
Divisions coloured are statistical areas

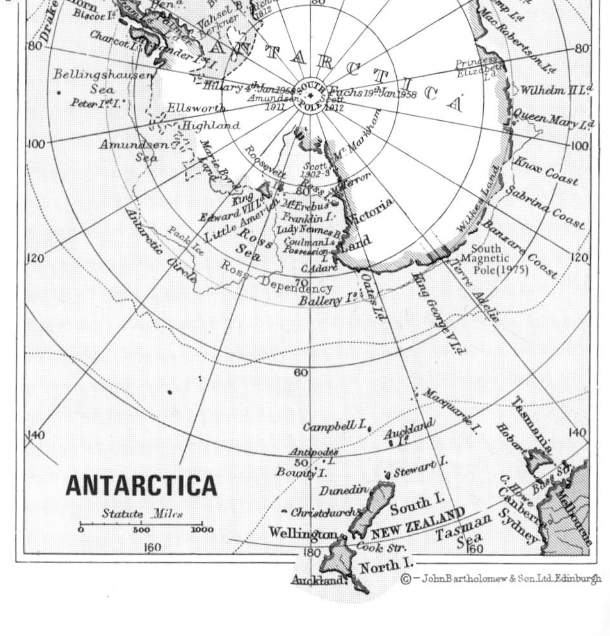
ANTARCTICA
Statute Miles
0 500 1000
Capetown
C. of Good Hope
C. Agulhas
Gough I.
Bouvet I.
Marion I.
Pr. Edward I.
S. Sandwich Is
S. Georgia
Falkland Is Dep.
Scotia Sea
S. Orkney Is
Falkland Is
Elephant I.
British Antarctic Territory
Average Limit of Drift Ice
Antarctic Circle
Kronprinsesse Martha Kyst
Prinsesse Astrid Kyst
Prinsesse Ragnhild Kyst
Princess Olav Kyst
Mainahem
C. Norvegia
Dronning Maud Land
Coats Land
Caird Ct
Weddell Sea
Bruce 1904
Vahsel B.
Berkner I.
Filchner 1912
Enderby Ld.
Kemp Ld.
Mac Robertson Ld.
Princess Elizabeth Ld.
Wilhelm II Ld.
Queen Mary Ld.
Knox Coast
Sabrina Coast
Banzare Coast
Wilkes Land
South Magnetic Pole (1975)
Terre Adelie
King George V Ld.
Oates Ld.
Victoria Land
South Shetland Is
Joinville I.
Palmer Arch.
Antarctic Pena
Drake Str.
Cape Horn
Biscoe Is
Charcot I.
Alexander Ist I.
Bellingshausen Sea
Peter Ist I.
ANTARCTICA
Hillary 4th Jan 1958
Fuchs 19th Jan 1958
SOUTH POLE
Amundsen 1911
Scott 1912
Ellsworth Highland
Amundsen Sea
Marie Byrd Land
Roosevelt I.
Scott 1902-3
Mt. Markham
Ross I.
Mt. Terror
Mt. Erebus
King Edward VII Ld.
Little America
Franklin I.
Lady Newnes B.
Coulman I.
Possession I.
C. Adare
Ross Sea
Pack Ice
Antarctic Circle
Ross Dependency
Balleny Is
Macquarie I.
Campbell I.
Auckland Is
Antipodes I.
Bounty I.
Stewart I.
Dunedin
South I.
Christchurch
Wellington
NEW ZEALAND
Cook Str.
North I.
Auckland
Tasman Sea
Tasmania
Hobart
Bass Str.
Melbourne
C. Howe
Canberra
Sydney
0
20
40
50
60
70
80
100
120
140
160
180

## Gazeteer

Entries include page number references as divided into **a**, **b**, **c**, and **d** thus:

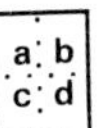


Aberdeen, city and port, N.E. Scotland 62b
Abidjan, port and cap. of Ivory Coast, Africa 115b
Accra, cap. of Ghana, West Africa 115b
Aconcagua, highest peak of Andes; 23,035 ft. 52a
Acre, state, Brazil 50a
Addis Ababa, cap. of Ethiopia 117b
Adelaide, cap. of South Australia 123d
Afghanistan, an independent state on the N.W. frontier of Pakistan; cap. Kabul 107b
Ahmadabad, town and cap. of Gujarat, India 102b
Akron, city, Ohio, S. of Cleveland 26d
Al Bayda' town, Libya 112c
Alabama, state, U.S.A.; cap. Montgomery 28d
Alagoas, state, Brazil 51b
Alaska, state of U.S.A., in N.W. America 42a
Albania, rep., on the Balkan Peninsula; cap. Tiranë 83c
Albany, city and cap. of New York 24b
Alberta, prov., Canada; cap. Edmonton 14a
Albuquerque, town, New Mexico 31c
Alexandria, city and port, Egypt 113c
Algeria, rep., on north coast of Africa 114a
Algiers (Alger), cap. of Algeria 114a
Allentown, city, Pennsylvania, N.W. of Philadelphia 25c
Alma Ata, town, Kazak, N.E. of Frunze 90b
Amapá, state, Brazil 48b
Amarillo, town, Texas 31c
Amazon, river, S. America, 4000 miles long 46b
Amazonas, state, Brazil 50a

American Samoa, prov., Pacific Ocean 125b
Amman, cap. of Jordan 106a
Amsterdam, cap, and port, Netherlands 70b
Amur, river, U.S.S.R., enters Sea of Okhotsk 91b
Andhra Pradesh, state, India 102d
Andorra, republic, Pyrenees Mts. 75b
Andros Island, Bahamas, W. Indies 44a
Angola, rep., W. Africa; cap. Luanda 111c
Anguilla, island, Leeward Is., W. Indies 45a
Anhwei, prov., China 97a
Ankara, cap. of Turkey, S.E. of Istanbul 108c
Annapurna, mt. Nepal, 26,505 ft. 104a
Antananarivo, cap. of Madagascar 119d
Antigua I., Leeward Is., W. Indies 45a
Ararat, Mount, Turkey, 16,946 ft. 108a
Argentina, rep., S. America; cap. Buenos Aires 47c
Arizona, state, W. U.S.A.; cap. Phoenix 39a
Arkansas, state, S. U.S.A.; cap. Little Rock 31a
Armenia, rep., U.S.S.R.; cap Yerevan 89b
Ascension Island, S. Atlantic Ocean 111c
Assam, state, India; cap. Shillong 103a
Asuncion, port and cap. of Paraguay 50d
Athens (Athínai), city and cap. of Greece 85d
Atlanta, cap. of Georgia, U.S.A. 28d
Auckland, prov. and city, North I., N.Z. 126a
Austin, cap. of Texas, on Colorado River 31d
Australia, state, cap. Canberra, smallest continent 121c
Austria, rep., Cent. Europe; cap. Vienna 80b
Azerbaijan, rep., U.S.S.R.; cap. Baku 89b
Badrinath, mt., India/Tibet; 23,190 ft. 104c
Baghdad, city and cap. of Iraq 106b
Bahamas, The, state, W. Indies 45c
Bahia, state, Brazil 51b

British Columbia, prov., W. Canada 14c
Brunei, state, N.W. Borneo 99c
Brussels (Bruxelles), cap. of Belgium 71c
Bucuresti (Bucharest), city, cap. of Romania 83b
Budapest, city and cap. of Hungary 81a
Buenos Aires, fed. cap. of Argentina 52b
Buffalo, city, New York, on Lake Erie 26a
Bujumbura, town, cap. of Burundi 111a
Bulawayo, town, Zimbabwe 119a
Bulgaria, rep., Balkan Pen., cap. Sofia 83a
Burma, rep., E. of India; cap Rangoon 98a
Burundi, rep., central Africa 111a
Byelorussia, rep., U.S.S.R., cap. Minsk 87c
Caicos Islands, W. Indies, N. of Hispaniola 45c
Cairo, cap. of Egypt, on the Nile 112a
Calcutta, city, port and cap. of W. Bengal 103a
Calgary, city, Alberta, S. of Edmonton 14b
California, state, W. U.S.A.; cap. Sacramento 39c
Cambodia, state, S.E. Asia, cap. Phnom-Penh 98d
Cambridge, co. town, Cambs., England 61a
Cambridge, city, Mass., suburb of Boston 24b
Camden, city, New Jersey, on Delaware River 25d
Cameroun, republic, Central Africa, cap. Yaoundé 116b
Canada, state, N. America, cap. Ottawa 12 & 13
Canary Islands, Span. group, off N.W. Africa 114d
Canberra, fed, cap. of Australia 123b
Canton, town, Ohio 26d
Cape of Good Hope (Cape Province), prov. of Republic of South Africa 118d
Cape Town, port and cap. of Cape Prov. 118c
Cape Verde Islands, group, Atlantic Oc., off N. W. Africa 115c
Caracas, cap. of Venezuela 48c
Cardiff, city and cap. of Wales 60d

Columbus, cap. of Ohio, U.S.A. 27c
Columbus, town, Georgia 28d
Comoro, isl, Mozambique Channel, cap. Moroni 119b
Conakry, port and cap. of Guinea, W. Africa 115d
Congo, river, central Africa, flows 3000 miles to Atlantic Ocean 111a
Congo, People's Rep. of, W. Africa; cap. Brazzaville 116d
Connecticut, state, N.E. U.S.A.; cap. Hartford 25a
Cook Islands, Polynesia, Pacific Ocean 53b
Cook, Mt., N.Z. 127a
Copenhagen (kobenhavn), cap. of Denmark 69d
Cork, city and co., Rep. of Ireland 65d
Corpus Christi, town, Texas 31d
Costa Rica, republic, Central America, cap. San José 44b
Cotapaxi, mt., Ecuador 19,344 ft. 49a
Coventry, city, Warwicks, England 61a
Cuba, island and rep., West Indies, cap. Havanna 45c
Cyprus, island and rep., E. Mediterranean, cap. Nicosia 108d
Czechoslovakia, rep., central Europe, cap. Prague 80b
Dacca, city, E. Bengal, cap. of Bangladesh 103a
Dahomey, see Benin
Dakar, port and cap., Senegal, West Africa 115c
Dallas, city, Texas, E. of Fort Worth 31c
Damascus, city and cap. of Syria 109b
Damavand, mt., Iran, 18,934 ft. 107a
Danube, river of Cent. Europe, length 1740 m. 80b
Dar es Salaam, port and cap., Tanzania 117d
Dayton, city, Ohio, W.S.W. of Columbus 27c
Dearborn, town, Michigan 26c
Delaware, river rises in New York and flows to Delaware B. 25c
Delaware, Atlantic state, U.S.A.; cap. Dover 25d
Delhi, city and cap. of India 102b

Denmark, kingdom, Europe; cap. Copenhagen 69d
Denver, cap. of Colorado, U.S.A. 39a
Derby, co. town, Derbyshire, England 61a
Descabezado, mt., Chile 52c
Des Moines, city and cap. of Iowa 32c
Detroit, city and port, Michigan 26c
Dykh Tau, mt., U.S.S.R. 89c
Djakarta, see Jakarta
Djibouti, rep., cap. Djibouti 117b
Dnepropetrovsk, town, Ukraine, S.W. of Kharkov 88c
Dominica, island, Leeward Is., W. Indies 45b
Dominican Rep. (Santo Domingo), Hispaniola West Indies cap. Santo Domingo 45a
Donetsk, town, Ukraine, S.E. of Kharkov 88b
Dortmund, city, W. Germany, N.E. of Cologne 77a
Dresden, city, E. Germany, E.S.E. of Leipzig 78b
Dublin, city, port, county and cap. of Rep. of Ireland 65a
Dundee, cy & pt., E. Region, Scot., on R. Tay 63a
Dunedin, city, South I., New Zealand 127d
Durban, port, Natal, on Indian Ocean 119c
Düsseldorf, city, W. Germany, on the Rhine 77a
East London, prot, Cape Province 118d
Ecuador, rep., S. America 49a
Edinburgh, cap. of Scotland, on Firth of Forth 63a
Edmonton, cap. of Alberta, Canada 14b
Egypt, cap. Cairo, N.E. Africa 112a
Elbrus, highest peak, Caucasus, U.S.S.R. 89c
Elizabeth, city, New Jersey, W. of Brooklyn 25c
Ellice Islands, see Tuvalu
El Paso, city, Texas, on Rio Grande 31c
El Salvador, rep., Cent. Amer., cap. San Salvador 44b
England, kingdom, with Wales forms the S. portion of Great Britain 58d

Grenada, island, W. Indies, Windward Is. 45b
Guadalajara, city, Mexico 44c
Guadaloupe, island, Leeward Is., W. Indies 45b
Guam,.island, Marianas Is., Pacific Ocean 53c
Guanabara, state, Brazil 51c
Guatemala, rep., central America 44b
Guatemala City, cap. of Guatemala 44b
Guinea, rep., W. Africa; cap. Conakry 115d
Gujarat, state, W. India; cap. Ahmadabad 102b
Guyana, rep., S. America; cap. Georgetown 48a
Hague, The ('s-Gravenhage), city., seat of govt., Netherlands 70d
Haiti, rep., Hispaniola, W. Indies; cap. Port-au-Prince 45c
Halifax, port and cap. of Nova Scotia 19d
Hamburg, city and port, W. Germany, on Elbe 78b
Hamilton, city, Ontario, S.W. of Toronto 16d
Hammond, town, Indiana 33c
Hannover, town, W. Germany 78b
Hanoi, cy. and cap. of Vietnam 98b
Harbin, town, N.E. China, on Sungari river 95a
Hartford, town, Connecticut 25a
Haryana, state, N. India 104c
Havana, port and cap. of Cuba, W. Indies 45c
Hawaii, largest of the Hawaiian Islands and state, U.S.A.; cap. Honolulu 43b
Heilungkiang, prov., China 95a
Helsinki, port and cap. of Finland 67a
Himachal Pradesh, state, N. India 102b
Hobart, city and cap. of Tasmania 123b
Honan, prov., Central China 97c
Honduras, Brit., see Belize
Hong Kong, British Island and col., S. China 95c
Honolulu, cap. of Hawaii, on Oahu Is., 43c

Jakarta, city and port, Java; cap. of Indonesia 99d
Jamaica, island, West Indies; cap. Kingston 45c
Jammu & Kashmir, state, India 102b
Jan Mayen, island, Arctic Ocean 55a
Jersey City, town, New Jersey, on Hudson R. 25c
Jerusalem (El Quds esh Sherif), city, Israel-Jordan 109c
Johannesburg, largest city of Transvaal, S. Africa 118d
Jordan, kingdom and river, W. Asia; cap. Amman 106a
Juncal, mt., S. America; 20,367 ft. 52a
Jungfrau, mt., Bernese Alps, Switzerland, 13,642 ft. 102b
K2, mt., Kashmir, W. Himalayas; 28,250 ft. 102b
Kabul, cap. of Afghanistan on Kabul river 107b
Kamet, mt., Uttar Pradesh; 25,447 ft. 104c
Kampala, town and cap. of Uganda, N.E. of Entebbe 117c
Kangchenjunga, mt., Himalayas; 28, 146 ft. 103a
Kanpur, city, Uttar Pradesh, India 104d
Kansas, S. central state of U.S.A.; cap. Topeka 30b
Kansas City, town, Missouri, on Missouri river 34a
Kansas City, town, Kansas, E.N.E. of Topeka 30b
Kansu, prov., China 97c
Karachi, town and port, Pakistan 102a
Karnataka, state, S. India; cap. Bangalore
Kathmandu, cap. of Nepal, E.N.E. of Lucknow 104a
Kazakhstan, republic, central U.S.S.R. 90c
Kazan, town, U.S.S.R., N.E. of Volgograd 86b
Kazbek, mt., U.S.S.R. 87b
Kentucky, an E. central state, U.S.A.; cap. Frankfort 28b
Kenya, rep., E. Africa; cap. Nairobi 117c
Kenya, Mt., Africa 117c
Kerala, state, S. India; cap. Tirvandrum 102d
Khan Tengri, mt., China; 23,620 ft. 90b
Kharkov, city, Ukraine, S. of Moscow 88c
Khartoum, cap. of Sudan 117a

Laos, kingdom, S.E. Asia; cap. Vientiane 98b
La Paz, city and dep., Bolivia, S. America 50c
La Plata, river, Argentina 52b
Latvia, rep., U.S.S.R.; cap. Riga 86d
Lebanon, state, W. Asia; cap. Beirut 109a
Leeds, city, W. Yorks, England 59b
Leeward Islands, Lesser Antilles, W. Indies 45a
Leicester, co. town of Leicestershire, England 61a
Leipzig, city, E. Germany, S.S.W. of Berlin 78b
Lena, river, U.S.S.R., flows to Arctic Ocean; 2,850 m. long 93a
Leningrad, city, U.S.S.R., near Lake Ladoga 86d
Lesotho (Basutoland), state, S. Africa 118d
Liaoning, prov., China 95a
Liberia, rep., West Africa; cap. Monrovia 115d
Libreville, tn. and cap. of Gabon, Cent. Africa 116d
Libya, rep., N. Africa; caps. Tripoli and Benghazi 112c
Liechtenstein, princ., E. Switz.; cap. Vaduz 76a
Lille, town, France, S.E. of Calais 73a
Lilongwe, town and cap. of Malawi 119a
Lima, city and cap. of Peru 49c
Lincoln, town, cap. of Nebraska 30d
Lisbon (Lisboa), city, naval base and cap. of Portugal, on River Tagus 74c
Lithuania, rep., U.S.S.R.; chief town Vilnius 86d
Little Rock, cap. of Arkansas, U.S.A. 34c
Liverpool, city and port, Merseyside, England 59d
Llullaillaco, mt., Chile; 22,057 ft. 50c
Lódz, town, Poland, S.W. of Warsaw 79b
Logan, Mount, Yukon, N.W. Canada; 19,850 ft. 12a
Lomé, cap. of Togo, W. Africa 115b
London, cap. of England and U.K., on the Thames 61c
London, port of entry, Ontario, S.W. of Toronto 16d

Nouakchott, cap. of Mauritania, W. Africa 115c
Nova Scotia, E. maritime prov., Canada; cap. Halifax 19d
Novosibirsk, town, on Ob river, U.S.S.R., E. of Omsk 90a
Nyasa, Lake, S.E. Africa 119a
Oakland, city, California, on San Francisco B. 40d
Ob, river, U.S.S.R., flows 2420 miles to Arctic Oc. 92b
Odessa, city and port, Ukraine, on Black Sea 88d
Ohio, state, U.S.A.; cap. Columbus 27c
Oklahoma, state, U.S.A. cap. Oklahoma City 31c
Oklahoma City, cap. of Oklahoma state, U.S.A. 31c
Oldham, town, Greater Manchester, England 59b
Omaha, city & riv. port, Nebraska, on Missouri 30b
Omsk, city, U.S.S.R., S.E. of Sverdlovsk 90a
Onega Lake, U.S.S.R., E. of Lake Ladoga 86d
Ontario, E. province, Canada; cap. Toronto 17c
Ontario, Lake, between Canada and U.S.A. 17c
Oporto, city, Portugal, on the Douro 74a
Orange Free State, prov., S. Africa; cap. Bloemfontein 11d
Oregon, N.W. state of U.S.A.; cap. Salem 38d
Orissa, state, India; cap. Bhubaneshwar 103c
Osaka, city and port, Honshu, Japan 96a
Oslo, city and cap. of Norway, on Oslo Fjord 67c
Ottawa, cap. of Canada, on Ottawa riv., Ontario 17b
Ouagadougou, town and cap. of Upper Volta 115a
Oxford, univ. and co. town of Oxfordshire, England 61a
Pakistan, state, S. Asia; cap. Islamabad 102b
Palermo, port and cap. of Sicily 82d
Panama City, port & cap. of the rep. of Panama 44b
Panama, republic, cent. America 44b
Papua, S.E. part of Papua, New Guinea; cap. Port Moresby 99b
Para, state, Brazil 51a
Paraguay, republic, S. America; cap. Asuncion 50d

Richmond, cap. of Virginia, U.S.A. 22b
Riga, port and cap. of Latvia, on G. of Riga 86d
Rio de Janeiro, city, Brazil 51c
Rio de Janeiro, state; Brazil 51c
Rio Grande do Norte, state, Brazil 51b
Rio Grande do Sul, state, Brazil 50d
Riyadh, Najd, cap. of Saudi Arabia 106d
Robson, Mt., Brit. Columbia 14d
Rochester, city, New York, near L. Ontario 24d
Rockford, town, Illinois 33c
Rome (Roma), city, cap. of Italy, River Tiber 82a
Romania, rep., S.E. Europe, cap. Bucharest 83b
Rondônia, state, Brazil 50a
Roraima, state, Brazil 48b
Rosa, Monte, Pennine Alps, Switzerland and Italy, height 15,216 ft. 76d
Rostov, town, U.S.S.R., at mouth of the Don 88b
Rotterdam, cy. & pt., Netherlands, on R. Maas 70d
Rudolf, Lake, N. Kenya, 170 miles long 117c
Russia = R.S.F.S.R. 92 & 93
Ruwenzori, Mt., Zaire/Uganda; 16,794 ft. 111a
Rwanda, republic, central Africa, cap. Kigali 111a
Ryukyu Archipelago, chain of Is., from Japan to Formosa 95d
Sabah (North Borneo), state of Malaysia, cap. Kota Kinabalu 99c
Sacramento, city and cap. of California 40d
St Christopher = St Kitts 45a
St Helena, island, S. Atlantic Ocean 111c
St Helens, town, Merseyside, Eng., near Liverpool 59d
St John, town and port, New Brunswick 19d
St John's, town & port, cap. of Newfoundland 19a

St Kitts, island, Leeward Is., W. Indies 45a
St Lawrence, great riv. of N. America; 2340 miles 13d
St Louis, city, Missouri, on the Mississippi 34b
St Lucia, island, Windward group, W. Indies 45b
St Paul, city, Minnesota, on Mississippi 32a
St Petersburg, town, Florida 29d
St Pierre, island, Atlantic, S. of Newfoundland 19b
St Vincent, island, Windward Is., W. Indies 45b
Salford, town, Greater Manchester, England 59b
Salisbury, cap. Zimbabwe, central Africa 119a
Salt Lake City, cap. of Utah, on River Jordan 38b
Salvador, El, rep., Cent. Amer.; cap. San Salvador 44b
San'a, cap. of Yemen, Arabia 106d
San Antonio, city, Texas, W. of Houston 31d
San Diego, city and naval base, California 39d
San Francisco, city and port, California 40d
San José, city and cap. of Costa Rica 44b
San José, town, California 39c
San Juan, cap. of Puerto Rico, W. Indies 45a
San Marino, rep., N.E. Italy 82b
San Salvador, cap. of El Salvador, Cent. America 44b
Santa Ana, town, California 41b
Santa Caterina, state, Brazil 51c
Santiago, city, cap. of Chile, S. America 52a
Santo Domingo, town and cap. of Dominican Rep., West Indies 45a
Sao Francisco, river, Brazil 51b
Sao Paulo, city, Brazil, N.W. of Santos 51c
Sao Paulo, state, Brazil 51c
Sao Tomé, island in G. of Guinea, W. Africa 116c
Saratov, town, U.S.S.R., S.E. of Moscow 87a
Sarawak, state, E. Malaysia 99d
Saskatchewan, W. prov. of Canada; cap. Regina 12d

Saskatoon, town, Saskatchewan, N.W. of Regina 14b
Saudi Arabia, kingdom, S.W. Asia; cap. Riyadh 106d
Savannah, port, Georgia, U.S.A. 29c
Scotland, northern part of Great Britain; kingdom, cap. Edinburgh 62 & 63
Scranton, city, Pensyl., N.W. of Philadelphia 25c
Seattle, port, Washington, on Puget Sound 41d
Senegal, republic and river, N.W. Africa; cap. Dakar 115c
Seoul (Kyongsong), city and cap. of S. Korea 95b
Sergipe, state, Brazil 51b
Seychelles, Is., Indian Ocean 3c
Shanghai, port, Kiangsu prov., China 97a
Shansi, prov., China 95a
Shantung, prov., China 95c
Sheffield, city, S. Yorks, England 59b
Shensi, prov., China 97c
Shen-yang (Mukden), city, N.E. China 95a
Shreveport, town, Louisiana, U.S.A. 36b
Sian (Changan), cap of Shensi prov., China 97c
Sierra Leone, rep., W. Africa; cap. Freetown 115d
Sikkim, state, N.E. India; cap Gangtok 103a
Singapore, island, rep., port and naval base, S. of Malaya 100d
Sinkiang-Uighur, aut. reg., W. China; cap. Urumchi 94a
Slave Lake, Great, N.W. Territories, Canada 12b
Sofia, city, cap. of Bulgaria 83a
Solihull, town, Warwicks., England 60b
Solomon Islands, Melanesia, Pacific Ocean 125d
Somalia, state, E. Africa; cap. Mogadiscio 117d
Southampton, port, Hampshire, England 61c
South Africa, rep., cap. Pretoria 111b
South Australia, state, Aust.; cap. Adelaide 120d
South Bend, city, Indiana, E. of Chicago 33d
South Carolina, state, U.S.A.; cap. Columbia 29a

Tacoma, town, Washington, N.E. of Olympia 38c
Tadzhikistan, rep., U.S.S.R.; cap. Dushanbe 90d
T'ai-pei, town and cap. of Taiwan 95c
Taiwan (Formosa), island and rep., to E. of China 95c
Taiyuan (Yangku), city, Shansi prov., China 95a
Ta'izz, town, Yemen 106d
Tamil Nadu, state, S.E. India, cap. Madras 102d
Tampa, town, Florida, on Tampa Bay 29d
Tanganyika, Lake, E. Africa 111a
Tanzania, rep., E. Africa, cap. Dar es Salaam 111a
Tashkent, city, cap. of Uzbekistan, N.E. of Samarkand 90d
Tasman, Mt., N.Z. 127a
Tasmania, island state, Commonwealth of Aust. 123b
Tbilisi, cap. of Georgian rep., U.S.S.R. 89b
Tegucigalpa, cap. of Honduras, Cent. America 44b
Tehran, cap. of Iran, S. of Caspian Sea 107a
Tennessee, state, U.S.A.; cap. of Nashville 28b
Texas, a southern state of U.S.A.; cap. Austin 31d
Thailand, kingdom, S.E. Asia; cap. Bangkok (Krung Thep) 98c
Thimphu, town and cap. of Bhutan 103a
Tibet, aut. reg.., W. China; cap. La-sa (Lhasa) 94c
Tientsin, port, Hopeh, China, S.E. of Peking 95a
Timor, prov., Indonesia, S.E. of Sulawesi 99b
Tinguiririca, Mt., Chile 52a
Tiranë, cap. of Albania, Europe 83c
Titicaca, Lake, Peru and Bolivia, in the Andes 50a
Tobago, island, Trinidad and Tobago 48a
Togo, rep. W. Africa, cap. Lomé 115b
Tokelau Is., group, Pacific Ocean 125b

Tokyo, city and cap. of Japan, Honshu I. 96a
Toledo, town, Ohio, W. of Cleveland 26d
Tolima, mt., Colombia 48c
Tonga Islands, Polynesia, Pacific Ocean 53d
Topeka, city, cap. of Kansas, U.S.A. 30b
Torbay, town, Devon, England 60d
Toronto, city, cap. of Ontario, Canada 17c
Torrance, town, California 41b
Transvaal, prov., S. Africa; cap. Pretoria 118d
Trenton, city and cap. of New Jersey 25c
Trinidad, island, W. Indies, part of the rep. of Trinidad and Tobago; cap. Port of Spain 48a
Tripoli, port and naval base, Libya 112c
Tristan da Cunha, volcanic island, S. Atlantic Oc. 111d
Tsingtao (Ch'ing-tao), port, Shantung, on Kiaochow Bay 95c
Tucson, town, Arizona, S.E. of Phoenix 39b
Tulsa, town, Oklahoma 31a
Tunis, town and cap. of Tunisia 114a
Tunisia, rep., North Africa; cap. Tunis 114a
Tupungato, mt., S. America 52a
Turin, town, Piedmont, N. Italy 84d
Turkey, rep., Europe and Asia; cap. Ankara 108c
Turkmenistan, rep., U.S.S.R.; cap. Ashkhabad 90d
Turks Islands, group of islands, S. of the Bahamas 45a
Tuvalu, in Pacific, N. of Fiji, cap. Funafuti 125b
U.K. = United Kingdom of Great Britain and Northern Ireland 58
U.S.A. = United States of America 20 & 21
U.S.S.R. = Union of Soviet Socialist Republics 92 & 93
Ufa, town, U.S.S.R., S.W. of Sverdlovsk 87a
Uganda, state, Africa; cap. Kampala 117c
Ukraine, rep., U.S.S.R. cap. Kiev (Kiyev) 88c
Ulaanbaatar, town and cap. of Mongolia 94b

Union of Soviet Socialist Republics, state, Europe and Asia; cap. Moscow 92 & 93
United Arab Emirates, fed., on the Gulf 107c
United Kingdom of Great Britain and Northern Ireland, state, W. Europe; cap. London 58
United States of America, state, N. America; cap. Washington 20 & 21
Upper Volta, rep., W. Africa; cap. Ouagadougou 115a
Uruguay, rep. and river, S. America; length 950 miles cap. Montevideo 47a
Utah, inland state, U.S.A.; cap. Salt Lake City 38b
Uttar Pradesh, state, India; chief tn. Lucknow 104d
Utica, town, New York, N.W. of Albany 24d
Uzbekistan, rep., U.S.S.R.; cap. Tashkent 90d
Vaduz, cap. of principality of Liechtenstein 76a
Valencia, port, Spain, on east coast 75c
Valletta, port and cap. of Malta 82d
Vancouver, city & port, Brit. Columbia, W. Canada, N. of Victoria 14d
Vänern, lake, S.W. Sweden; length 95 miles 67c
Vanuatu, island group, W. Pacific 125b
Venezuela, rep., S. America; cap. Caracas 48c
Vesuvius, Mount, vol., Italy, on B. of Naples 82d
Victoria, state, S.E. Aust., cap. Melbourne 123b
Victoria, cap. of Br. Columbia on Vancouver I. 14d
Victoria, cap. and chief port, Hong Kong 95c
Victoria, Lake, Africa, between Uganda, Tanzania and Kenya 117c
Vienna (Wien), city, cap. of Austria, on Danube 80b
Vientiane, town and cap. of Laos, on Mekong R. 98b
Vietnam, rep. cap. Hanoi, S.E. Asia 98b
Virgin Islands group in West Indies 45a
Virginia, a S. Atlantic state, U.S.A.; cap. Richmond 22b

Wu-han (Hankow), river port, China, on Yangtze Kiang, in Hupeh prov. 97a
Wyoming, N.W. state, U.S.A.; cap. Cheyenne 38b
Yangtze Kiang, river, China, rises in Tibet; length 3000 miles 94 & 95
Yaoundé, cap. of Cameroun, Africa 116b
Yemen, rep., S.W. Arabia; cap. San'a 106d
Yemen, South, Rep. of S. Arabia, cap. Madinat ash Sha'ab 106d
Yenisey, river, U.S.S.R., flows to Arctic Sea 93a
Yerevan, town and cap. of Armenia 89b
Yokohama, port, Japan, Honshu Island 96a
Yonkers, town, New York 25a
York, city and co. town of N. Yorkshire, England 59b
Youngstown, town, Ohio 26b
Yugoslavia, republic, S.E. Europe, in Balkans; cap. Belgrade 83a
Yukon, river, Yukon and Alaska, flows S.W. to the Bering Sea 10c
Yukon, territory, N.W. Canada; cap. Whitehorse 12a
Yunnan, prov., China 94d
Zagreb, city, Croatia, Yugoslavia, on R. Sava 82b
Zaire, W. Africa, cap. Kinshasa 116d
Zaire, river, central Africa, flows 1600 miles into the Atlantic Ocean 111a
Zambezi, river, S. Africa, flows 1600 miles into the Indian Ocean 111a
Zambia, republic, central Africa; cap. Lusaka 119a
Zanzibar, island & town, Tanzania 117d
Zaporozh'ye, town, Ukraine, W.S.W. of Donetsk 88d
Zimbabwe, state, central Africa, cap. Salisbury 119a